Praise for *Apache Hudi: The Definitive Guide*

As a core contributor to Apache Hudi's architecture, it's gratifying to see the elegant design principles and internals demystified so effectively. This book is the definitive resource for understanding not just how to use Hudi but how to tune for scale, throughput, and performance and build truly correct incremental pipelines.

—Balaji Varadarajan, engineering, Applied Intuition,
Apache Hudi PMC

Modern data platforms are moving toward LLM-ready architectures—fresh context assembled at query time for AI. Hudi pushes the lakehouse there: incremental upserts, indexing, and partial updates keep that data continuously correctable, low-latency, and affordable for AI workloads.

—Ananth Packkildurai, principal engineer, Zeta Global,
and author, Data Engineering Weekly

If you're looking to build enterprise AI systems on lakehouse tables, look no further than Apache Hudi and this book. If you need incremental pipelines, primary keys for correct training data, time travel for data versioning, and upserts for GDPR compliance, look no further than the OG OTF.

—Dr. Jim Dowling, CEO, Hopsworks

In our batch data organization at Uber, Apache Hudi has been an important part of enabling incremental ingestion and upserts at scale, supporting the reliability and efficiency of our modern data platform.

—Jack Song, director of engineering, Uber

At Kuaishou.com, we have successfully modernized our traditional data warehouse into a lakehouse architecture using Apache Hudi. This unified platform supports both streaming and batch data ingestion, accommodates both BI data warehouse and AI sample storage, and delivers integrated SQL analytics and machine learning training capabilities. Authored by core members of the Apache Hudi project, *Apache Hudi: The Definitive Guide* not only provides deep insight into its design philosophy and best practices but also stands as the essential reference for building a modern lakehouse.

—*Wang Jing, head of data platform department, Kuaishou.com*

Authored by Hudi's core team, *Apache Hudi: The Definitive Guide* demonstrates unparalleled depth and authority. It offers a comprehensive statement of how Hudi reshapes best practices in data processing and management. Its value has been proven in practice at JD.com. As a core user and contributor, JD.com has leveraged Hudi to build near-real-time efficient data pipelines, accelerating the transition from traditional data warehouses to the lakehouse paradigm.

—*Zhang Ke, head of AI and data infrastructure, JD.com*

As an ecosystem community partner, we are delighted to see the remarkable achievements Hudi has made in building real-time data lakes. StarRocks + Hudi has already enabled many users to achieve outstanding performance in real-time data lake analytics. I'm glad that this book can share these experiences with a wider audience!

—*Andy Ye, cofounder and COO, CelerData*

Apache Hudi: The Definitive Guide
Building Robust, Open, and
High-Performing Data Lakehouses

Shiyan Xu, Prashant Wason,
Bhavani Sudha Saktheeswaran, Rebecca Bilbro
Foreword by Vinoth Chandar

O'REILLY®

Apache Hudi: The Definitive Guide

by Shiyan Xu, Prashant Wason, Bhavani Sudha Saktheeswaran, and Rebecca Bilbro

Acquisitions Editor: Andy Kwan	**Indexer:** Judith McConville
Development Editor Gary O'Brien	**Cover Designer:** Susan Brown
Production Editor: Jonathon Owen	**Cover Illustrator:** José Marzan Jr.
Copyeditor: Audrey Doyle	**Interior Designer:** David Futato
Proofreader: Rachel Rossi	**Interior Illustrator:** Kate Dullea

October 2025:   First Edition

Revision History for the First Edition
2025-10-24:   First Release

See *http://oreilly.com/catalog/errata.csp?isbn=9781098173838* for release details.

978-1-098-17383-8

[LSI]

Table of Contents

Foreword

When we began building Apache Hudi in 2016, our goal was clear but ambitious: bring transactional database capabilities to the data lake. At the time, this idea sounded counterintuitive—even controversial. Data lakes were, by design, append-only file stores optimized for high throughput and scale, not fine-grained updates or consistent reads. At Uber, where Hudi was first conceived, our data volumes doubled every few months, and the traditional data warehouse could no longer keep up. Streaming systems were too expensive and lacked the capabilities we needed.

We needed a new kind of data platform—one that could scale like a data lake, provide transactional capabilities like a data warehouse, and deliver data incrementally like streaming systems.

That idea became Apache Hudi, and the first data lakehouse was born, even before the term was coined.

Hudi introduced several foundational concepts that have since become synonymous with the modern lakehouse architecture: incremental change capture, write-optimized storage formats like Merge-on-Read, record-level upserts, and background table services for compaction, clustering, and cleaning. These ideas were novel at the time but have since become core pillars across the ecosystem. Systems like Delta Lake and Apache Iceberg, which followed Hudi, adopted many of these principles and extended the conversation around openness and interoperability.

At the time, these ideas were radical. Today, they're foundational.

In many ways, Hudi sparked one of the most significant shifts in database technology over the past decade. The vibrant Hudi community has been instrumental in this journey. What began as an internal project has grown into a thriving open source ecosystem with contributors from across the world—engineers, architects, researchers—each helping to evolve the system to meet new use cases and challenges. This vision, powered by Hudi and its successors, has redefined what it means to build data platforms at scale.

But Hudi has always charted its own course. It was the first to enable incremental pipelines natively, allowing downstream systems to consume only what changed. It was the first to unify streaming and batch ingestion within the same table abstraction. Today, it continues to lead with innovations like secondary indexing, non-blocking concurrency control, and metadata-driven optimizations, and to evolve toward AI-ready storage formats that support vector searches, feature engineering, and model training at scale.

This book arrives at an important moment—when more organizations than ever are embracing lakehouse architectures but often struggle to piece together the underlying concepts, trade-offs, and best practices. Hudi is a powerful system, but like any foundational technology, its real strength is unlocked when engineers understand both its design philosophy and practical applications. That's what makes this book so valuable. The authors—longtime Hudi contributors and practitioners—have distilled years of collective experience into clear explanations, hands-on examples, and actionable design patterns. Whether you're building your first transactional data lake or tuning an existing Hudi deployment, this book will help you grasp the advanced ideas behind Hudi's architecture and apply them with confidence—turning Hudi into a power tool in your lakehouse toolkit.

I'm thrilled to see how far Hudi has come—and even more excited about where it's going.

— *Vinoth Chandar*
Original creator of Apache Hudi
Founder & CEO, Onehouse

Preface

Why This Book, and Why Now

Modern data platforms are being asked to do more than ever before. They must serve fresh data to dashboards, power machine learning features in real time, and support operational applications alongside traditional analytics. At the same time, volumes of data are growing rapidly, pipelines are increasingly complex, and organizations cannot afford downtime or inconsistency. The gap between what businesses expect and what legacy systems can deliver has only widened.

Apache Hudi emerged to address exactly this gap. By bringing transactions, incremental ingestion, and advanced table services to the data lake, Hudi redefined what was possible. It pioneered the data lakehouse architecture, which unifies the openness and scalability of lakes with the reliability and performance of warehouses. In recent years, Hudi has matured into one of the most widely adopted open table formats, supported by a vibrant community and deployed at scale in industries ranging from technology and finance to retail and research.

The world of data architecture is at an inflection point. Lakehouses have transitioned from a cutting-edge idea to an industry standard. Hudi has kept pace, introducing powerful features such as multiwriter concurrency control, metadata-driven optimizations, and integrated streaming ingestion. Yet with this power comes the responsibility to make the right choices—there are design trade-offs, operational considerations, and architectural choices that can be difficult to navigate. This book exists to make those choices clearer, drawing on both the lessons of early adopters and the latest best practices.

Who This Book Is For

This book is written for practitioners: the engineers, architects, and technical leaders who design, build, and operate large-scale data platforms. You'll find it useful if you are one of the following:

- A data engineer or platform engineer responsible for building ingestion pipelines or managing high-velocity data streams

- A data architect evaluating ways to unify data lakes and warehouses

- A developer or analyst who needs consistent, incremental access to large and evolving datasets

- A technical manager or leader making strategic decisions about adopting lakehouse technologies

This is not a beginner's introduction to databases or distributed systems. Readers should already be comfortable writing SQL, familiar with distributed processing engines such as Apache Spark or Apache Flink, and have a basic understanding of data pipelines. While deep expertise is not required, the book moves quickly from foundational principles to advanced operational guidance.

The Technology and Its Moment

At its heart, Hudi transforms the data lake into something more like a database—a transactional data lake—one that can ingest incrementally, perform upserts and deletes efficiently, and serve consistent snapshots of data at any point in time. It automates tedious table maintenance such as compaction, clustering, and cleaning to ensure performance as datasets grow. Most importantly, it unifies batch and streaming on the same storage, eliminating the need to manage parallel data systems.

The broader data ecosystem has been moving in this direction as well. The lakehouse architecture has become the centerpiece of modern platforms, combining openness, reliability, and performance. Since it became open source in 2017, Hudi has advanced rapidly and is now one of the leading open table formats, alongside other open source lakehouse projects. Its adoption reflects a broader industry trend toward open, interoperable systems that can serve both analytical and operational workloads in real time.

What's in This Book

The chapters in this book are designed to guide you from basic principles to advanced practices while also serving as a reference you can revisit as your Hudi deployment progresses. Each chapter introduces core concepts, explains their design rationale, and demonstrates how to apply them in practice. While the initial chapters lay the groundwork for understanding the system, later chapters delve into specific components of the architecture, and the final chapters explore end-to-end applications and equip readers with operational tools to run Hudi in production:

Chapter 1, "What Is Apache Hudi?"

This chapter sets the stage by exploring the rise of the data lakehouse as a unifying architecture for modern data needs. It explains the limitations of traditional warehouses and data lakes, and how Hudi emerged to close the gap between streaming and batch workloads. You'll learn the core ideas behind incremental ingestion, transactional tables, and real-time access. By the end, you'll see why Hudi is foundational to the lakehouse paradigm.

Chapter 2, "Getting Started with Hudi"

Here, we take a hands-on approach: creating your first Hudi table, inserting data, and issuing queries. The chapter introduces Hudi's two main table types—Copy-on-Write and Merge-on-Read—while showing you how these affect updates and queries. You'll also get familiar with table metadata, commits, and the overall lifecycle of a Hudi dataset. This practical starting point lays the essential foundations and ensures that you can move confidently into deeper topics.

Chapter 3, "Writing to Hudi"

This chapter covers writing data to Hudi, a key process for reliable, efficient lakehouses. It begins by explaining the full write flow, from record preparation to transaction finalization, ensuring correctness at scale. It then links these concepts to real-world tasks like insert, upsert, delete, and bulk insert, using an Internet of Things (IoT) data provider as an example. Lastly, it discusses advanced features like key generators, schema evolution, and bootstrapping, equipping readers to build high-performance, adaptable pipelines on Hudi.

Chapter 4, "Reading from Hudi"

A system is only as valuable as its ability to serve data. This chapter covers how Hudi tables can be read in multiple modes: snapshot queries for current views, incremental queries for change data capture, and time travel for debugging or compliance. It demonstrates how Hudi integrates with engines like Spark, Presto, and Apache Hive, while maintaining strong guarantees. Readers walk away knowing how to expose reliable, consistent data to downstream consumers.

Chapter 5, "Achieving Efficiency with Indexing"

This chapter describes how Hudi achieves efficiency and scalability via its indexing system. It covers basic indexing in a lakehouse, showing how indexes assist writers in quickly locating records for updates and deletes, and readers by pruning files and partitions to accelerate queries. The chapter then discusses different index types, from general-purpose record indexes to specialized ones like Bloom, bucket, and expression indexes, catering to various workloads. By the end, readers will learn to choose and implement the right index strategy to optimize performance, cost, and complexity for near-real-time lakehouse performance at scale.

Chapter 6, "Maintaining and Optimizing Hudi Tables"

Hudi's background services are what keep tables healthy over time. This chapter explores primary table services like cleaning, compaction, indexing, and clustering, showing how they reclaim storage, optimize file layout, and boost query performance. It explains when to run these services synchronously versus asynchronously, and how to tailor them for your workloads. With this foundation, you'll be prepared to operate tables that scale smoothly without manual firefighting.

Chapter 7, "Concurrency Control in Hudi"

This chapter examines concurrency control in Hudi, emphasizing how to keep data consistent and accurate in data lakes with many readers and writers. It addresses challenges in distributed setups and explains how Hudi combines techniques like optimistic, multiversion, and non-blocking concurrency control to enhance scalability and accuracy. The chapter discusses multiwriter scenarios, conflict resolution, and locking strategies, providing practical tips for efficient parallel operations without sacrificing data quality. Ultimately, it guides readers in creating reliable, scalable data pipelines while managing the complexities of modern data lakes.

Chapter 8, "Building a Lakehouse Using Hudi Streamer"

Streaming ingestion is where Hudi truly shines. This chapter introduces Hudi Streamer, a ready-to-use tool for bringing data from Apache Kafka, Amazon S3, or other event sources directly into Hudi tables. You'll see how to configure incremental pipelines with schema evolution, transformations, and checkpoints built in. By the end, you'll understand how to unify streaming and batch data in a single, coherent platform.

Chapter 9, "Running Hudi in Production"

Moving from development to production introduces a whole new set of challenges. This chapter equips you with operational tools like the Hudi CLI, savepoints and restores for disaster recovery, post-commit callbacks, and catalog syncing across engines. It also covers monitoring strategies and performance tuning for Spark and Flink, ensuring that your pipelines remain robust. Readers gain the confidence to run Hudi at scale while minimizing risk and overhead.

Chapter 10, "Building an End-to-End Lakehouse Solution"

The final chapter brings everything together in a real-world scenario. Using the example of RetailMax Corp., you'll follow data from ingestion through Bronze, Silver, and Gold layers into downstream analytics and AI applications. The chapter demonstrates how to combine Flink, Kafka, Debezium, and Hudi into a unified lakehouse architecture that supports both operational and analytical needs. It serves as both a blueprint and inspiration for building your own end-to-end data platform.

How to Use This Book

This book is designed to be flexible. Newcomers to Hudi or the lakehouse paradigm will benefit from reading sequentially, as the concepts build naturally from one chapter to the next. More experienced practitioners may want to jump directly to the sections most relevant to their needs—for example, indexing and table services for performance tuning, or concurrency control for managing multiwriter workloads.

The concluding end-to-end application in Chapter 10 can be read at any stage. It can serve as early inspiration to see what's possible, or as a practical integration guide once you're ready to design your own lakehouse platform.

Above all, our hope is that this book becomes a trusted reference: a resource you can return to as your data platform evolves, whether you are just starting to explore Hudi or scaling a production system to its limits.

Conventions Used in This Book

The following typographical conventions are used in this book:

Italic
: Indicates new terms, URLs, email addresses, filenames, and file extensions.

`Constant width`
: Used for program listings, as well as within paragraphs to refer to program elements such as variable or function names, databases, data types, environment variables, statements, and keywords.

`Constant width bold`
: Shows commands or other text that should be typed literally by the user.

`Constant width italic`
: Shows text that should be replaced with user-supplied values or by values determined by context.

> This element signifies a tip or suggestion.

> This element signifies a general note.

This element indicates a warning or caution.

O'Reilly Online Learning

For more than 40 years, *O'Reilly Media* has provided technology and business training, knowledge, and insight to help companies succeed.

Our unique network of experts and innovators share their knowledge and expertise through books, articles, and our online learning platform. O'Reilly's online learning platform gives you on-demand access to live training courses, in-depth learning paths, interactive coding environments, and a vast collection of text and video from O'Reilly and 200+ other publishers. For more information, visit *https://oreilly.com*.

How to Contact Us

Please address comments and questions concerning this book to the publisher:

O'Reilly Media, Inc.
141 Stony Circle, Suite 195
Santa Rosa, CA 95401
800-889-8969 (in the United States or Canada)
707-827-7019 (international or local)
707-829-0104 (fax)
support@oreilly.com
https://oreilly.com/about/contact.html

We have a web page for this book, where we list errata and any additional information. You can access this page at *https://oreil.ly/apache-hudi-definitive-guide*.

For news and information about our books and courses, visit *https://oreilly.com*.

Find us on LinkedIn: *https://linkedin.com/company/oreilly-media*.

Watch us on YouTube: *https://youtube.com/oreillymedia*.

Acknowledgments

This book would not exist without the work of the Apache Hudi community. From Hudi's earliest days at Uber to the vibrant, global project it is today, countless contributors have shaped Hudi's design, implementation, and documentation. Their code, ideas, and feedback are the foundation on which this book is built.

We are especially grateful to the members of the Project Management Committee (PMC) and active committers, who have not only written core functionality but also guided the project's direction and nurtured its community. Many of the insights in these pages come directly from lessons they shared in design discussions, user support threads, and production battle stories.

Thanks also go to the Apache Software Foundation (ASF) for providing the governance and infrastructure that make collaborative open source innovation possible.

Special thanks go to our technical reviewers—Benjamin Bengfort, Vikram Singh Chandel, and Michal Gancarski. Their thoughtful feedback sharpened the explanations, caught gaps, and ensured that the examples reflect real-world usage. Their careful attention and practical insights have made this book stronger and more reliable for its readers.

Finally, we'd like to acknowledge the users of Hudi—the engineers, analysts, and architects across industries who pushed the system to new limits and, in doing so, helped it evolve. Your real-world challenges, successes, and feedback are reflected throughout this book.

To all of you: thank you.

## CHAPTER 1

What Is Apache Hudi?

No one opens a book on data platforms because they're having an easy week at work.

That's because building data platforms is not for the faint of heart; it's often a matter of custom development and experimentation, requiring constant research into the rapidly evolving open source landscape and painstaking architectural tuning over periods of months or even years. We don't embark on such journeys casually.

Interestingly, most people are blissfully unaware of the data platform at their organization. They only start discussing it when something has gone very wrong.

Our assumption is that you are reading this book because you are looking to improve how your organization works with data. Perhaps customers have begun complaining about seeing stale or inconsistent data. Or the legacy database that served you for a decade is buckling under the analytical query load or new machine learning features. Maybe your data warehouse has simply become too expensive to scale as data-driven workloads keep spiking.

If any of these scenarios sound familiar, this book may be just what you need. In fact, if the preceding description resonates, it is probably because your organization needs a data lakehouse—a modern data platform that not only addresses these challenges but also unlocks new opportunities for faster insights, advanced analytics, and data-driven innovation at scale.

The lakehouse architecture is the current state of the art for orchestrating the efficient storage, processing, and analysis of large volumes of data. Apache Hudi stands out as an open source technology that empowers data platform teams to implement and maintain this architectural paradigm with ease.

In this opening chapter, we'll prepare you for your lakehouse odyssey by reviewing the evolution of data management architectures, including Hudi's own origins at

Uber. We'll outline Hudi's key features, dive into the architectural stack, and explore its real-world applications, giving you a solid mooring for the concepts covered in the rest of this book.

The Evolution of Data Management Architectures

From humble beginnings with spreadsheets and rudimentary file formats to massively distributed systems, the journey to the lakehouse is a tale of technological evolution in an age of explosive growth in data volume, variety, and velocity.

Traditional relational databases offered the first solution, providing strong consistency and structured storage optimized for transactions. However, their row-oriented architecture ultimately proved inadequate for large-scale analytical queries, failing to deliver the necessary performance at scale. To address this, *data warehouses* were introduced, providing structured query and reporting features ideal for business intelligence and analytics but offering limited support for unstructured and semi-structured data and becoming costly at scale.

The *data lake* architecture emerged to handle those problems, allowing organizations to leverage cost-effective distributed file systems like the Hadoop Distributed File System (HDFS) to store large volumes of raw, heterogeneous data without immediate structuring or processing. This flexibility lays the groundwork for advanced analytics (e.g., real-time models) and machine learning applications (e.g., generative AI) that thrive on large, diverse datasets. Data lakes allow you to capture all the data for your organization, not just what you already know you need today.

But even if you incorporate a data lake into your platform, you may still have problems such as the following:

Lack of mutability
  Synchronizing data between a lake and its upstream sources is a pain, especially if the synchronization needs to support real-time analysis. Data lakes conceive data as fundamentally immutable (i.e., not subject to transactions or upserts), and as such are designed to be updated in batches, not in real time. That lack of mutability introduces latency, often resulting in stale analytics.

Lack of schema and structure
  Unlike your data warehouse, where users can easily inspect table schema to get hints at how to construct their analytical queries, the unstructured nature of data lakes often results in "data swamps" that downstream users perceive as inconvenient or inscrutable.

Insufficient transactional support
  Without transactional capabilities and ACID guarantees (Atomicity, Consistency, Isolation, Durability), data is harder to trust. It's difficult to manage concurrent

operations (e.g., a bursty ETL job could clobber a complex analytical process). You may fail to restore the correct state of the data in the case of system failures.

Data governance

Data lakes are not designed to provide data governance and provenance measures out of the box, which means it's your problem to implement policies and granular access controls to prevent data breaches and so that you do not jeopardize regulatory compliance.

The Rise of Data Lakehouses

The lakehouse architecture emerged to address the limitations of data lakes and traditional data warehouses by combining the core features of each into a unified platform, as illustrated in Figure 1-1.[1] By utilizing the scalability and flexibility of data lakes while integrating the performance, reliability, and governance capabilities of data warehouses, the lakehouse offers a more comprehensive approach to data management.

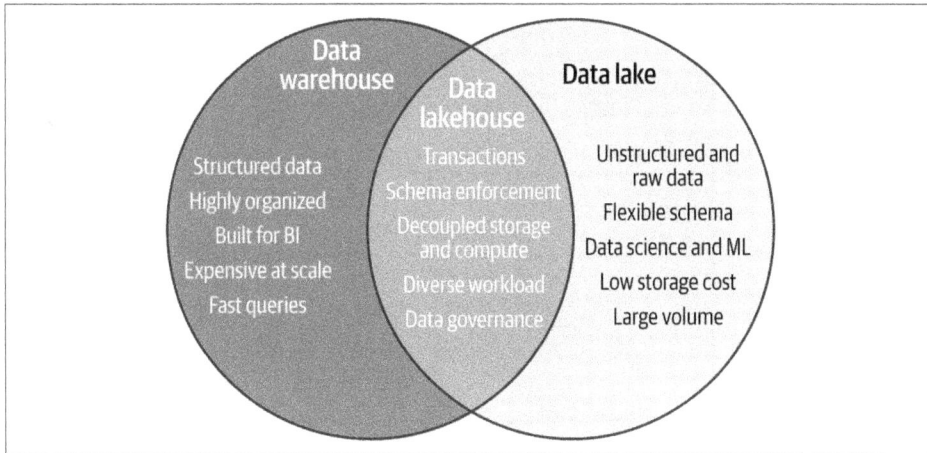

Figure 1-1. Lakehouses combine the best of data warehouses and data lakes

The lakehouse architecture (shown in Figure 1-2) is built upon a distributed file system (e.g., HDFS) or a cloud storage system (e.g., Amazon S3). This foundation serves as the primary storage layer, accommodating large volumes of data in its raw form, whether structured, semi-structured, or unstructured.

Atop this storage layer, the lakehouse implements a transaction layer, which is crucial for enhancing data management capabilities. This layer typically defines the file

---

1 The term *lakehouse* was first coined by Michael Armbrust et al. in "Lakehouse: A New Generation of Open Platforms That Unify Data Warehousing and Advanced Analytics" (*https://oreil.ly/tibZu*) (CIDR 2021).

format (which defines how data is structured and encoded on disk within a single file) and table format (which defines how a collection of data files is managed and presented as a single table), facilitates running table services, supports transactions, and so on. This transaction layer is key to transforming a traditional data lake into a lakehouse. It enables advanced features such as ACID transactions, time travel queries, change data capture (CDC), and data versioning.

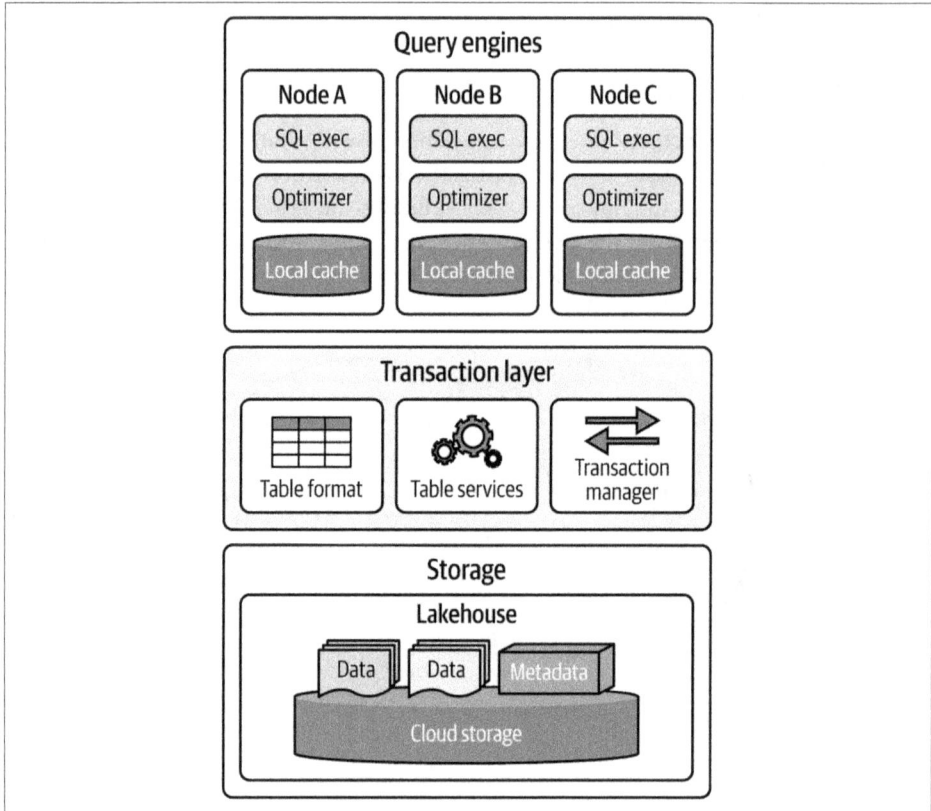

Figure 1-2. Lakehouse architecture

These capabilities are fundamental for ensuring data reliability and consistency within the system, while also enabling query engines to access and process data correctly and efficiently.

Although this architecture offered early adopters significant gains, it also introduced more complexity. The story of Hudi's incubation at Uber, told in the next section, is a story about managing this complexity in real time and harnessing the power of a highly tailored distributed data system built from the ground up.

Uber's "Transactional Data Lake" Problem

In early 2016, amid a period of hypergrowth, Uber embarked on a transition from a warehouse architecture to a data lake–based architecture. This shift, necessitated by the growing scale and complexity of Uber's operations, presented challenges that demanded innovation, particularly in ensuring transactional guarantees atop immutable storage. At that time, the idea of a lakehouse was not yet in the industry's vocabulary. Uber's engineers described their approach as a "transactional data lake"— a data lake augmented with database-like functionality. With no production-ready solutions available, Uber had to invent its own.

Central to Uber's operations is the "trips" data (Figure 1-3), which, while captured live in online databases, required extensive offline analytical processing for any meaningful analysis—analysis that underpins much of Uber's decision making. The limitations of the initial data lake of "trips" became evident quickly in the face of its sheer magnitude—about 120 TB per day!

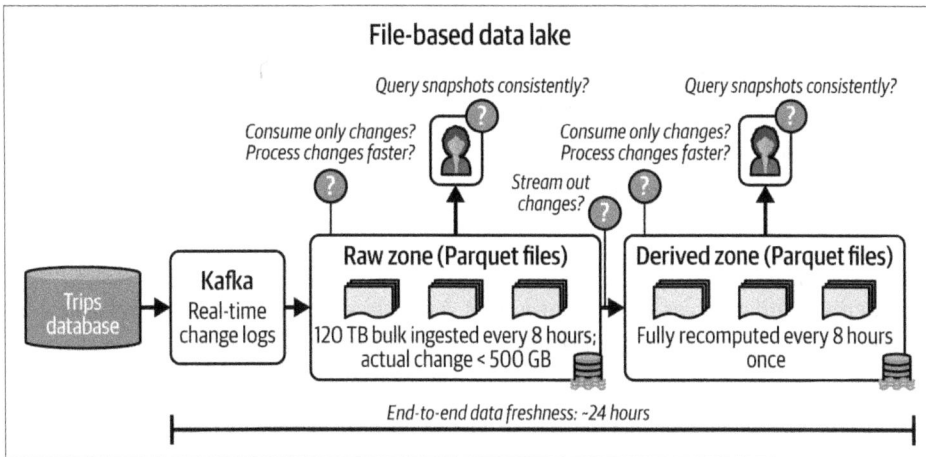

Figure 1-3. Uber's old, file-based data lake architecture and its challenges

As shown in Figure 1-3, it was starting to get quite complex to manage and process data at that scale. Changelogs from upstream databases were ingested into raw tables formatted in Apache Parquet files. Every 8 hours, the lake reingested the entire 120 TB, though the actual changes constituted less than 500 GB. This inefficiency extended downstream, where pipelines built on the raw layer also recomputed the entire dataset every 8 hours, resulting in end-to-end data freshness of around 24 hours. This lag was particularly problematic given that the average ride is over in just 20 minutes.

Not only was the platform throttling analysis and decision making, but there was no effective control over failure recovery scenarios. A single ingestion job failure could cascade into widespread pipeline disruptions, necessitating extensive cleanup and retries.

The engineering team came together to discuss how to approach the problem.

They wondered:

- Can we consume only the changes instead of performing a full recompute? If so, it would drastically reduce the amount of data and compute resources required for each ingestion. And can downstream tables do the same?
- Can we also devise a method to absorb these changes more quickly into the tables? The complexity doesn't end with the initial raw table; downstream derived tables face similar challenges.
- Throughout this process, can readers consistently query snapshots of the table without being exposed to partial or corrupted data?

These considerations became the guiding principles and laid the foundation for Hudi's core primitives and capabilities:

Database abstraction
Provide snapshot isolation between readers and writers. Never expose inflight or corrupt data.

Incremental processing
Identify and process only records that have changed since the last refresh. Full recompute is no longer the norm.

Efficient upserts
Apply change records into the table using indexes with specialized concurrency controls.

With these capabilities in place, along with background table services to maintain and optimize the tables, Hudi evolved into a serverless transaction layer with database-like abstractions for DFS-compatible storage. This new architecture (shown in Figure 1-4) led to significant operational gains, with upserts capturing only 500 GB of data in less than 10 minutes and reducing end-to-end latency from 24 hours to just 1 hour. These improvements fueled a growing number of internal use cases at Uber, driving rapid evolution of the Hudi project. By the end of 2016, Hudi was in production at Uber, with the initial version already encompassing essential features such as upserts, indexing, and change streams.

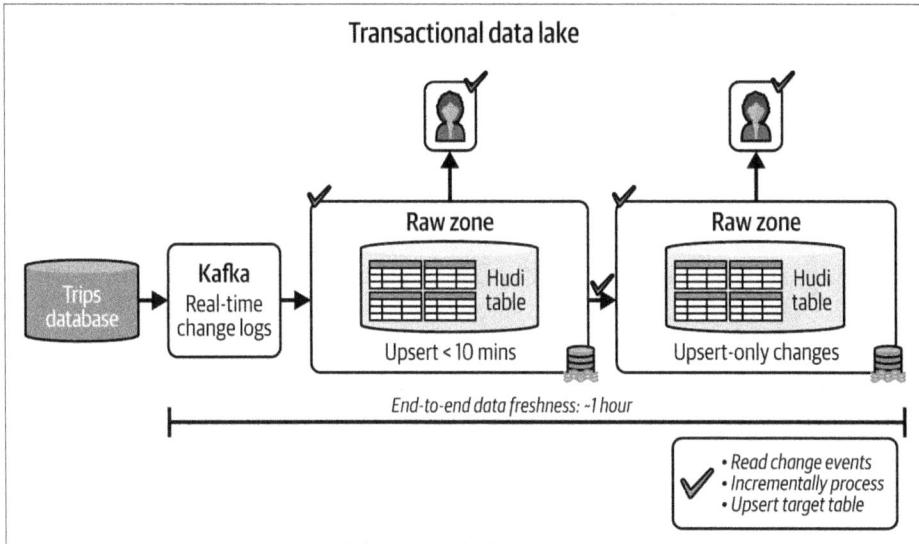

Figure 1-4. Uber's new Hudi-based transactional data lake

Recognizing Hudi's broader potential beyond Uber, the company decided to make the project open source in 2017. This move allowed Hudi to gain wider adoption, garner support from various query engines, and expand its cloud compatibility. In 2019, Uber donated Hudi to the Apache Software Foundation (ASF), making it freely available under the Apache License 2.0. This decision aimed to foster innovation and collaboration and to establish Hudi as a standard framework for managing data in large-scale distributed environments. The project graduated to a top-level Apache project in 2020.

Since its inclusion in the ASF, Hudi has experienced rapid adoption and development. The open source community has embraced the project, with contributions from engineers and data scientists across a variety of industries. The first official release of Hudi under the ASF occurred in January 2019, and since then, the project has maintained a consistent release cadence, introducing new features, enhancements, and bug fixes. Hudi has added multiwriter concurrency, metadata-driven query acceleration, and deep integrations with Apache Spark, Apache Flink, Apache Hive, Presto, and cloud native storage. Its evolution illustrates how the original concept of a transactional data lake anticipated what the industry later came to call a *lakehouse*: a unified architecture that combines the reliability and performance of warehouses with the scale and openness of lakes.

Today, Hudi continues to thrive as a leading open source lakehouse platform. It is widely adopted by organizations such as Uber, Walmart, Kuaishou, and JD.com, supporting diverse workloads that demand both real-time freshness and large-scale analytics. With its 1.0 release (*https://oreil.ly/ByY39*), Hudi has solidified its role as a comprehensive data lakehouse management system (DLMS), staying true to its original vision while shaping the future of data platforms.

What Is Hudi?

Hudi is an open data lakehouse platform designed to address a wide range of data management challenges across various industries. Real-world lessons from some of the largest data lakehouses in the world about processing high-throughput heterogenous data efficiently are encoded into Hudi's multilayered architecture, which includes a mix of data lake, database, and data warehouse functionalities.

With its native high-performance table format, Hudi offers a robust solution for workloads involving frequent changes, such as updates or deletions. Its indexing and file layout optimization strategies streamline data operations, making it particularly beneficial for dealing with CDC scenarios and streaming data with minute-level data freshness. This capability effectively unifies both batch and streaming use cases on the same data, providing an efficient alternative to real-time data marts for a wide range of data applications.

Hudi is also designed to be highly compatible with other open source and commercial data libraries, tools, and systems. As shown in Figure 1-5, Hudi can incorporate data files across various data storage systems, including HDFS and cloud stores like Amazon S3, Google Cloud Storage (GCS), and Azure Blob Storage. Hudi supports various file formats, including Parquet, Apache ORC, and Apache Avro, ensuring compatibility with event-streaming tools like Apache Kafka, as well as popular OLAP engines and data warehouses.

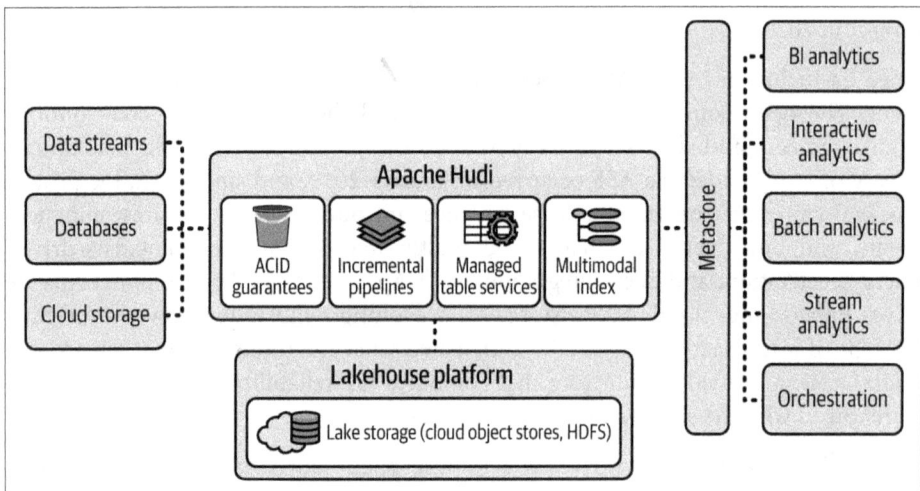

Figure 1-5. Hudi in the big data ecosystem

Hudi enables data platform engineers to conveniently implement critical features and application semantics into their lakehouse architectures, such as ACID transactions, efficient indexing, and advanced table maintenance services. Its key features include:

ACID transactions

Hudi ensures data consistency and integrity through ACID transactions, preventing issues like partial writes or data corruption, which are common in traditional data lakes. Developers can rely on the correctness of their data, simplifying application development, debugging, and compliance in production systems.

Mutable workloads

Unlike most table formats that are optimized for append-only use cases, Hudi natively supports fast upserts and deletes. With its extensible indexing and efficient storage layout, Hudi can handle workloads involving streaming data, bursty traffic, out-of-order events, and deduplication. This makes your lakehouse behave more like a database system, not just a static archive.

Flexible and powerful indexing

Hudi maintains rich, extendable indexes about the data it manages, enabling faster writes and optimized queries, especially for large and wide tables, and it can be customized to suit specific workloads. This makes large-scale analytical queries far more efficient than relying only on partition pruning.

Streaming-first design

Hudi was created to bridge the gap between batch and stream processing, and as a result, it offers unique capabilities for managing streaming data. It handles event-time ordering natively, ensuring that tables stay consistent and accurate even when data arrives out of order—an everyday reality in real-world pipelines.

Scalable metadata for large-scale datasets

Hudi's metadata table is designed to manage petabytes of data efficiently by storing the metadata in an indexed storage format. It also maintains additional metadata, such as column statistics, so that query planning scales with the number of queried columns rather than the total size of the table or file count. This ensures reliable performance even for very large or wide datasets where traditional flat-file approaches struggle.

Incremental processing

By capturing and processing only data changes, Hudi significantly reduces processing time and resource consumption while also enabling near-real-time freshness. Downstream systems benefit from CDC feeds, supporting both streaming and microbatch workloads.

Concurrency control

Hudi offers advanced concurrency control mechanisms with multiversion concurrency control (MVCC) and optimistic concurrency control (OCC), ensuring that multiple jobs can write safely to the same table. It also supports innovative non-blocking concurrency control (NBCC) to avoid bottlenecks in high-throughput pipelines such as streaming workloads, ensuring reliable updates without sacrificing ingestion speed.

Automated table services

Hudi automates table services, including clustering, compaction, cleaning, and indexing, to ensure that your tables are highly optimized for both read and write operations and that they are well maintained for efficient storage. Different deployment modes are supported for flexible needs in the production environment, including automatic scheduling and execution.

Multicloud support and wide integration

Hudi is built for broad ecosystem adoption, preinstalled on major cloud platforms and integrated with leading engines like Spark, Flink, Hive, Presto, and Trino. It also offers native tools for auto-ingestion from Kafka or Debezium and automatic catalog sync for discoverability. With support across languages like Python and Rust, Hudi fits naturally into diverse data ecosystems.

The Hudi Stack

Hudi achieves the data lakehouse architecture by adding core warehouse and database functionality directly to a data lake, transforming it from a simple collection of files into a system of well-managed tables. The Hudi stack consists of five component groups that work in tandem, as illustrated in Figure 1-6:

- High-performance table format
- Storage engine
- Programming API
- User access
- Shared platform components

We will briefly go through these groups in the remainder of this section.

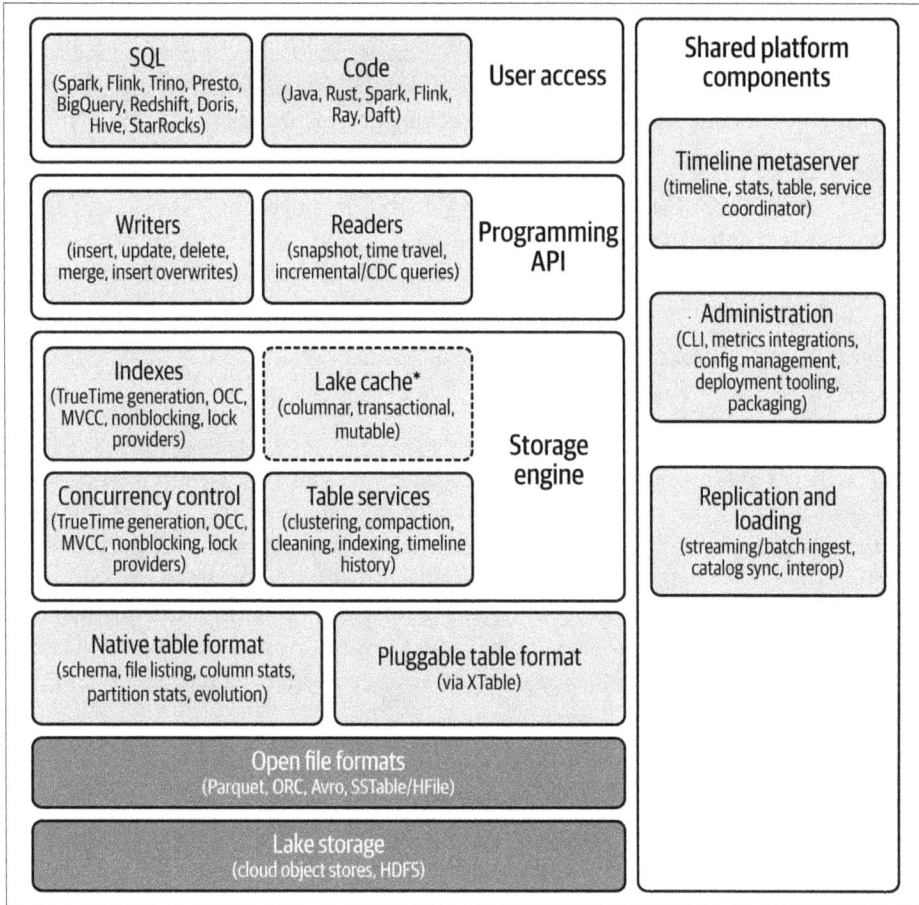

Figure 1-6. Hudi stack

Native Table Format

The Hudi table format refers to the way data is stored and organized in Hudi tables (i.e., the file storage mechanism and layout). Hudi's table format is responsible for tracking table schema, partitions, files, and table-level statistics. It has three main components:

File groups and file slices

Hudi organizes data files into logical units called *file groups*, each identified by a unique file ID. File groups are further divided into file slices, which can be thought of as versions. Each file slice may contain a base file and a list of log files, representing the state of all records in that file group at a specific point in time.

Timeline
> The timeline serves as an event log, providing an ordered list of actions performed on the table over time. Stored under the *.hoodie* folder in the table base path, the timeline allows for efficient tracking and management of table changes.

Metadata table
> Located at *.hoodie/metadata*, this internal table enhances write and read performance by centralizing metadata operations. It supports various metadata types, including partition and file lists, column statistics, record-level indexing, and expression indexes.

Chapters 2 and 5 will explore these concepts in greater detail.

Pluggable Table Format

Hudi achieves interoperability with a pluggable table format layer, enabling it to both read and write in formats like Apache Iceberg and Delta Lake. Unlike solutions limited to reader compatibility, Hudi preserves its transactional and performance benefits while supporting multiple table formats. This flexibility allows organizations to conform to diverse ecosystem standards and integrate seamlessly with downstream systems. By decoupling its storage engine from the table format, Hudi positions itself as a future-proof, multiformat lakehouse platform for an evolving data ecosystem.

Storage Engine

The *storage engine* components bring the "database experience" (i.e., ACID transactions, efficient upserts and deletes, query optimizations) to your data lake, with highly optimized and advanced implementations of core database functionality.

Indexes

Hudi implements an extensible indexing layer that makes data lakes truly efficient for both writes (updates and deletes) and queries. Indexes allow Hudi to quickly locate records during upserts and deletes, avoiding costly full-table scans. At the same time, they enable queries to skip over irrelevant files, reducing latency and improving performance even at massive scale. Various indexes are available:

- Record index
- Bucket index
- Simple index

- Bloom index
- Secondary index
- Expression index

These index types cater to diverse data patterns and traffic scenarios. By choosing the right indexing strategy, organizations can optimize their lakehouse for diverse workloads. Chapter 5 will dive deeper into how indexing works in Hudi for both writes and reads, and how to select suitable index types.

Lake cache (currently in development)

The lake cache component provides a multitenant caching tier that optimizes the trade-off between write speed and query performance in data lakes. It stores pre-merged file slices and leverages Hudi's timeline for cache policy management. Unlike traditional query engine caches, this integrated caching layer is shared across engines and supports transactional operations like updates and deletions, effectively serving as a unified buffer pool for data lakes.

Concurrency control

Hudi ensures atomic writes and provides snapshot isolation across writer processes, table services, and readers. It employs three main concurrency control mechanisms:

MVCC
Implemented in a lock-free, nonblocking manner between writers and table services, and between different table services.

OCC
Used between writers with a locking mechanism to resolve conflicts during commits.

NBCC
Enables multiple writers to operate on the table simultaneously without blocking, eliminating wasted retries and keeping streaming pipelines fast and consistent—ideal for high-throughput use cases like multistream writes into the same table.

Chapter 7 will unpack Hudi's concurrency model in more detail.

Table services

Hudi includes built-in table services that perform maintenance and administrative tasks to ensure smooth and efficient operation. These services can run in inline, asynchronous, or offline mode. Key table services include:

Compaction
Merges base files with changelogs to create updated base files, allowing concurrent writes to the same file group.

Clustering
Groups and colocates similar data in lake storage, improving query performance through data locality and larger file sizes.

Cleaning
Removes file slices older than the desired retention period for incremental queries.

Indexing
    Builds and maintains different types of indexes to speed up queries and updates by reducing the amount of data scanned from storage.

Chapter 6 will provide an in-depth look into maintaining and optimizing Hudi tables using these table services.

Working together, indexes, lake cache, concurrency control, and table services serve as a robust, efficient, and flexible storage engine in the Hudi stack, enabling advanced data management capabilities in a lakehouse environment.

Programming API

The *programming API* components provide developers with direct access to Hudi's core functionalities through well-defined interfaces. This lower-level integration point offers the flexibility to handle complex data scenarios, implement custom logic, and fine-tune both write and read operations. This will enable advanced users to extend Hudi's capabilities beyond the standard offerings, supporting diverse use cases from batch processing to real-time analytics.

Writers

Hudi tables extend beyond simple Parquet/Avro sinks, supporting both incremental operations (`insert`, `upsert`, `delete`) and batch operations (`insert_overwrite`, `delete_partition`, `bulk_insert`) through Spark, Flink, and Java applications. Key features include:

Operation-based optimizations
    Hudi optimizes each operation type: upserts and deletes merge by key with index lookups, inserts skip unnecessary steps and retain efficiency, and bulk inserts provide several sort modes for controlling initial file sizes and file counts. These capabilities make data pipelines faster, more consistent, and highly scalable.

MVCC-based batch writes
    Hudi uses MVCC to bring transactional safety to typical batch overwrite semantics. With this foundation, teams can confidently switch between incremental ingestion for regular runs and batch jobs for backfilling or dropping older partitions, while preserving consistency and reliability.

Record keys at the core
    Record keys are first-class citizens in Hudi, guaranteeing the uniqueness of records across partitions or within partitions of Hudi tables. Record keys are used everywhere, from indexing, merging, clustering, and compaction to consistently tracking/controlling the movement of records within a table and across files. In addition to record keys, Hudi preserves record-level metadata, enabling record-level change streams and incremental queries.

Extensible key generators

Hudi provides built-in and customizable key generators for defining unique record identifiers. Keys are materialized in metadata, allowing better consistency and fine-grained control over how updates are applied.

Merge modes

Users can configure merge mode for common merging semantics or define a custom merging strategy for complex conflict resolution. This ensures data consistency and efficiency for even complex business use cases.

Chapter 3 will walk through Hudi's writing capabilities in depth.

Readers

Hudi ensures consistent, reliable views of data through snapshot isolation, even as writes occur in the background. By tracking record-level event and commit time-stamps, it supports powerful capabilities like time travel query and incremental query, including CDC, enabling analysts, data scientists, and business users to work with the most relevant and up-to-date information—crucial for real-time analytics and continuously evolving lakehouses.

The primary reader-oriented features of the programming API include:

Broad query engine compatibility

Hudi integrates seamlessly with popular query engines such as Spark, Flink, Hive, Presto, and Trino, allowing organizations to analyze their data using the tools they already know and trust.

Optimized read performance with vectorized operations

Hudi supports vectorized reading of Parquet files and scan pruning through column statistics, enabling faster, more efficient reads—especially beneficial for large-scale, high-performance analytics workloads.

Time travel

With record-level metadata on event and commit timestamps, Hudi enables time travel queries, facilitating auditing and debugging across historical snapshots.

Incremental queries

Readers can pull only the records changed for a given time window, cutting down on latency and overhead for dashboards, machine learning pipelines, and real-time applications. With CDC mode, incremental queries can serve much richer insights about the record changes.

Snapshot isolation

Hudi guarantees consistent query results with snapshot isolation, even under concurrent writes—ensuring reliability in both batch and streaming lakehouse environments.

Chapter 4 will explore Hudi's reading capabilities in detail.

User Access

The *user access* components in the Hudi stack serve as the bridge between Hudi's sophisticated data management capabilities and its end users' varied needs, enabling them to harness Hudi's data lakehouse features while working with their preferred tools and languages.

SQL

Hudi's versatility extends to its support for a wide range of SQL engines, enabling flexible data processing for both batch and streaming workloads.

Most teams use Spark for batch processing with Hudi, leveraging its distributed ETL capabilities, and Hudi also integrates seamlessly with Flink and Spark Structured Streaming for real-time, incremental data processing. In fact, one of Hudi's key features is its ability to handle incremental queries, allowing users to efficiently process only the changes since the last run.

Hudi's query interface abstracts the complexities of underlying data storage formats (e.g., Parquet) and provides a unified access layer. This allows users to query Hudi datasets seamlessly without needing to understand the low-level data layout.

As such, Hudi is designed to meet your queries where they already are; all the modern query engines, such as Trino and Presto, are supported, enabling fast, interactive, SQL-like querying of Hudi datasets. This means there's no need to learn a whole new query language.

Finally, Hudi's support for high-performance analytical databases like ClickHouse and StarRocks enables fast querying of large-scale data. With built-in support for ACID transactions, schema evolution, and optimized query performance through indexing and partitioning, Hudi provides both consistency and scalability, making it an ideal choice for analytical workloads in dynamic environments.

Code

Hudi's code level integration complements its SQL capabilities, recognizing that while SQL remains the dominant tool for data engineering, developers and data scientists often need to analyze data using sophisticated algorithms with full expressiveness of programming languages like Java, Scala, and Python. Hudi addresses this need by supporting several widely used data processing frameworks that give users the flexibility to work in their preferred languages. Beyond its core support for distributed frameworks like Spark and Flink, Hudi extends its reach to Python-based distributed systems including Daft and Ray, while also offering native Rust bindings for seamless integration with C/C++-based engines.

Shared Platform Components

Hudi is more than a table format. It comes with a rich suite of built-in utilities that make managing data pipelines and production operations seamless. These shared components reduce integration effort, simplify streaming, and provide the guardrails needed to run Hudi tables at scale:

Effortless streaming and ingestion
Hudi includes Hudi Streamer, a popular ingestion tool that can continuously consume from Kafka, DFS, or other streaming sources; apply transformations; and write to Hudi tables. It also integrates tightly with Kafka Connect and Debezium, making it simple to perform CDC from upstream databases and land it in Hudi with minimal setup. This eliminates the need to build complex, custom CDC pipelines.

Seamless catalog and metadata management
Hudi supports automatic synchronization with Hive Metastore, AWS Glue Data Catalog, DataHub, and other catalogs, ensuring that tables are immediately queryable by popular engines without extra steps.

Comprehensive administration and monitoring
The Hudi CLI provides users with control over table states, running table services, and more. Metrics integration with Prometheus, Datadog, and Amazon CloudWatch enables robust monitoring, giving engineers visibility into ingestion pipelines and table services.

Hudi in the Real World

As more and more businesses find themselves drowning in data and driven to develop more robust, scalable, and versatile solutions, many are turning to Hudi to solve their data management challenges. Following are a few use cases across industry verticals:

Large-scale data analytics and data lake modernization
Telecom providers use Hudi to manage billions of call detail records daily, optimizing storage through data clustering and cleaning while improving query performance. Ad-tech companies process large volumes of user interaction data for targeted advertising, using Hudi's deduplication features to reduce storage costs and enhance analytics.

Incremental processing and CDC
In supply chain management, global retailers use Hudi to maintain real-time inventory views across stores during high-volume sales events. Hudi's incremental processing capabilities significantly reduce processing time and resource

consumption, enabling efficient propagation of changes from source systems to the lakehouse platform.

Compliance, auditing, and data governance
Banks use Hudi to maintain auditable transaction trails, allowing state views at any point in time for investigations and regulatory compliance. For GDPR compliance, organizations leverage Hudi's indexing capabilities to efficiently locate and delete specific user data across large datasets. Hudi's ACID transactions and time travel features further support comprehensive data governance practices.

Near-real-time analytics and stream processing
Ecommerce platforms use Hudi to process clickstream data, updating product recommendations instantly. Energy companies analyze smart meter data with Hudi, enabling low-latency monitoring of energy consumption and quick anomaly detection. Hudi's lakehouse mutability feature handles bursty traffic and out-of-order events efficiently in these dynamic environments.

Data-driven personalization and fraud detection
Content platforms use Hudi to aggregate and analyze user behavior dynamically, facilitating near-real-time personalization. Financial services companies use Hudi for fraud detection, quickly identifying suspicious activities through near-real-time processing of large transaction volumes.

Machine learning, AI, and data-intensive research
Autonomous vehicle companies use Hudi to manage massive datasets for AI model training, enabling faster iterations and more accurate near-real-time decision making. In genomics and climate science, researchers use Hudi to process petabyte-scale datasets efficiently, reducing analysis time and enabling more frequent model updates.

The key to supporting this broad spectrum of use cases lies in Hudi's sophisticated architecture, composed of several essential component groups. In Chapters 8, 9, and 10, we'll explore more real-world examples that illustrate how Hudi's novel features translate directly into platform capabilities.

Summary

In this chapter, we rehashed the journey to the lakehouse, including Uber's own complex adventure from data warehouse to data lake, and eventually to lakehouse (and namely, to Hudi).

We learned about what we mean when we say that Hudi is a lakehouse (it extends a data lake with database and data warehouse capabilities). We took a short tour through Hudi's key features, including large-scale data processing capabilities, ACID transaction support, and efficient upsert and delete operations, and learned about use cases for Hudi across several different industries including ecommerce, supply chain, financial services, and of course, rideshare apps.

We introduced Hudi's software stack, including its storage engine components, programming API components, user access components, and shared platform components, and learned that Hudi is designed to be highly compatible with all of our favorite data platform services and query engines.

With this foundation, let's dive deeper into Hudi's capabilities and implementation strategies.

## CHAPTER 2

Getting Started with Hudi

In Chapter 1, we explored the foundational concepts that make Apache Hudi a compelling choice for modern data architectures. We explored how data lakes have evolved into lakehouses, discussed Hudi's position in this ecosystem, and reviewed its high-level architecture, the Hudi stack, and key feature highlights. While these concepts provide essential context, the best way to truly understand Hudi's capabilities is through hands-on experience.

This chapter shifts from theory to practice. Rather than simply listing features, we'll demonstrate how Hudi tables behave under different configurations and operations, allowing you to observe firsthand how the underlying table layout evolves as you perform common lakehouse operations.

We'll start with a simple purchase tracking table and use Apache Spark to perform typical Create, Read, Update, and Delete (CRUD) operations. As we execute these commands, we'll examine the resulting changes to the table's physical structure, helping you develop an intuitive understanding of how Hudi organizes and manages your data behind the scenes.

The chapter is organized into three progressive sections that build upon each other. "Basic Operations" creates a Hudi table using the default Copy-on-Write (COW) table type and explores fundamental CRUD operations. As we execute SQL examples, we'll examine how each operation affects the table layout and learn core concepts like record keys, partitioning, and the timeline internals.

"Choose a Table Type" introduces Hudi's Merge-on-Read (MOR) table type by re-creating our purchase table with this alternative configuration. Comparing both table layouts side by side reveals the performance trade-offs and practical scenarios where each approach excels, helping you choose the right table type for your use cases.

Finally, "Advanced Usage" demonstrates additional SQL patterns for working with lakehouse tables. These examples showcase operations like CTAS, merge into, updates using nonrecord key fields, time travel queries, and incremental queries—addressing complex requirements beyond simple CRUD operations.

By the end of this chapter, you'll have a solid understanding of how Hudi tables work in practice and a strong foundation for the more advanced topics covered in subsequent chapters.

Basic Operations

In this section, we'll build a simple purchase table that serves as a source of truth for tracking customer transactions in our lakehouse. This table stores information about individual purchases, with each record representing a single transaction containing essential details such as customer identifier, purchase date, purchase amount, and status. Each purchase is uniquely identified by purchase_id. The complete schema is shown in Table 2-1.

Table 2-1. The purchase table schema

Column name	Data type	Description
purchase_id	STRING	Unique identifier for the purchase.
customer_id	BIGINT	Identifies the customer who made the purchase. This would be the unique identifier in a customer table.
amount	FLOAT	The amount paid for the purchase.
status	STRING	Purchase status (e.g., COMPLETED, PENDING).
purchase_date	STRING	The date string when the purchase was made (e.g., 2026-12-01).

We will use Hudi as the storage format for our purchase table. By implementing the table as a Hudi table, execution and query engines can natively understand the format and leverage Hudi's advanced capabilities such as time travel and incremental processing. You can work with Hudi tables using different engines such as Spark, Apache Flink, Apache Hive, Presto, Trino, and more. In the following sections, we will use Spark SQL for all examples to showcase some common operations you can do on this table.

Create the Table

Before creating our purchase table, we need to initialize a Spark SQL session with Hudi support and then execute the CREATE TABLE statement. This process will establish the table structure and generate the initial directory layout for examining the Hudi table's organization.

Assuming you have Spark 3.5 installed properly in your environment, you can start the session with:

```
export HUDI_VERSION=1.1.0
spark-sql \
--packages <dependency identifier for a Hudi Spark bundle jar> \ ❶
--conf \
spark.sql.extensions=org.apache.spark.sql.hudi.HoodieSparkSessionExtension\
--conf \
spark.sql.catalog.spark_catalog=org.apache.spark.sql.hudi.catalog.HoodieCatalog\
--conf spark.serializer=org.apache.spark.serializer.KryoSerializer\
--conf spark.kryo.registrator=org.apache.spark.HoodieSparkKryoRegistrar
```

❶ Instructs Spark to download a Hudi-Spark bundle jar as a dependency library according to the specified versions.

An example value of a Hudi-Spark bundle jar could be `org.apache.hudi:hudi-spark3.5-bundle_2.13:$HUDI_VERSION`. Hudi also offers bundle jars for other engines, such as Flink and Trino. A bundle jar for your engine is the main artifact that you will need to install in your application stack to work with Hudi tables.

> Several Spark configurations are included with the command; these are required for working with Hudi tables. For development convenience, you can set them in Spark configuration files like *spark-defaults.conf* to avoid repeating them each time.
>
> Similarly, Hudi supports passing configurations via a central configuration file, *hudi-defaults.conf*, located in the */etc/hudi/conf* directory by default. You can use this to define commonly used configs across all Hudi tables in your environment, reducing config repetition and simplifying table setup across your lakehouse.

Now create the `purchase` table using our schema from Table 2-1:

```
CREATE TABLE purchase (
    purchase_id STRING,
    customer_id BIGINT,
    amount FLOAT,
    status STRING,
    purchase_date STRING
) USING HUDI ❶
TBLPROPERTIES (
    primaryKey = 'purchase_id' ❷
)
PARTITIONED BY (purchase_date) ❸
LOCATION '<base path to the Hudi table>'
```

❶ Indicates that the table will follow the Hudi table format specification.

❷ Represents the fields that ensure record uniqueness; also known as *record key fields*.

❸ Represents the fields used for organizing data into directories; also known as *partition fields*.

We will discuss these settings and their related concepts in "Insert, Update, Delete, and Fetch Records" on page 26. First, let's execute the SQL and see the initial Hudi table layout.

Initial table layout

After executing the SQL command, you'll see a *.hoodie/* directory with files and subdirectories being created under the table's base path:

```
<base path of the purchase table>
└── .hoodie/ ❶
    ├── .aux/
    ├── .schema/
    ├── .temp/
    ├── hoodie.properties ❷
    └── timeline/ ❸
        └── history/ ❹
```

❶ The *.hoodie/* directory stores all sorts of metadata about the table. Created when you specify USING HUDI, this directory implements the Hudi format specification and instructs execution engines to treat the table according to the specification rather than as plain data files.

❷ The *hoodie.properties* file stores table-level properties used by both writers and readers, including configurations for record key fields and partition fields.

❸ The *timeline/* directory contains transaction logs that track all table changes. These logs help enforce ACID properties for the Hudi table and serve as the entry point for the Hudi reader and writer to interact with the table. We refer to the timeline stored here as the *active timeline*.

❹ The *history/* directory stores compacted timeline entries. Hudi implements an LSM-Tree (*https://oreil.ly/gR4d3*) structure to store the transaction log for the table in the timeline—when entries in *timeline/* exceed some configurable threshold, older entries will be compacted and archived to *timeline/history/*. This design provides performant timeline operations while achieving storage efficiency. We refer to the timeline stored here as the *archived timeline*.

You should not manually modify *hoodie.properties* to update the table configurations—this would corrupt the file as a checksum was computed by Hudi for validation. Only Hudi writers or migration tools are allowed to update it with proper handling logic implemented in the Hudi artifact like a Spark-Hudi bundle jar.

Record key fields

Records in a Hudi table can be uniquely identified by one or multiple fields. In the absence of a user-configured key, Hudi will auto-generate highly compressible record keys, which will be discussed further in Chapter 3. In the `CREATE TABLE` statement described earlier, you used `primaryKey` as shorthand for setting the record key fields; the corresponding entry stored in `hoodie.properties` is `hoodie.table.recordkey.fields`, which takes a comma-delimited list for the case of multiple fields jointly defining the record uniqueness.

Record key fields are required for update and delete operations, which need to act on matching records. You may omit this configuration when creating the table—this effectively makes the table append-only, allowing only insert operations. Chapter 3 discusses writer capability in detail.

Partition fields

Partitioning improves read and write efficiency for lakehouse tables. The SQL clause `PARTITIONED BY` indicates fields used for partitioning; the corresponding entry stored in `hoodie.properties` is `hoodie.table.partition.fields`.

When multiple partition fields exist, the partition path becomes nested based on field order. For example, `PARTITIONED BY (a, b)` creates partition paths like `a=foo/ b=bar/`. Partition fields aren't required for Hudi tables—without them, all data files are stored under the table's base path.

By default, partitioned tables created via Spark SQL use Hive-style partitioning with paths formatted as *<partition_field_ name>=<partition_field_value>*. This ensures compatibility with Spark tables, which usually remove partition fields from data files and use partition paths to show those fields. Because Hudi retains partition fields in data files, you can disable this format by setting this in the `TBLPROPERTIES` clause:

```
'hoodie.datasource.write.hive_style_partitioning'='false'
```

By organizing the data into directories based on partition field values, query engines can skip unmatching partitions when relevant predicates are present. For example:

```
SELECT * FROM purchase WHERE purchase_date = '2026-12-01';
```

With `purchase_date` as the partition field, query engines scan only the *purchase_date=2026-12-01/* directory, saving time and compute cost. This process is usually referred to as *partition pruning*.

However, partitioning isn't always beneficial. Overpartitioning can lead to creating many small files that hurt query performance. Partitioning also reduces flexibility for predicates unrelated to partition fields. Hudi favors powerful indexing techniques to augment partitioning—we'll explore this in Chapter 5.

Insert, Update, Delete, and Fetch Records

Let's perform write operations by first inserting five records into the `purchase` table using Spark SQL:

```
INSERT INTO purchase
VALUES
('purchase-1', 101, 21.9, 'COMPLETED', '2026-11-30'),
('purchase-2', 101, 123.09, 'PENDING', '2026-11-30'),
('purchase-3', 102, 390.15, 'PENDING', '2026-12-01'),
('purchase-4', 103, 41.5, 'COMPLETED', '2026-12-01'),
('purchase-5', 101, 98.3, 'COMPLETED', '2026-12-01');
```

Now we'll update one of the purchase records based on the record key:

```
UPDATE purchase
SET status = 'COMPLETED'
WHERE purchase_id = 'purchase-2';
```

Next, we'll delete another purchase record based on the record key:

```
DELETE FROM purchase
WHERE purchase_id = 'purchase-3';
```

Lastly, let's query the table and verify the records:

```
SELECT purchase_id, customer_id, amount, status, purchase_date
FROM purchase ORDER BY purchase_id;
```

After running the SQL, we can see the output:

```
purchase_id    customer_id    amount  status     purchase_date
purchase-1     101            21.9    COMPLETED  2026-11-30
purchase-2     101            123.09  COMPLETED  2026-11-30
purchase-4     103            41.5    COMPLETED  2026-12-01
purchase-5     101            98.3    COMPLETED  2026-12-01
```

The results are as expected: the status of `purchase-2` was updated to `COMPLETED` from the initial `PENDING`, and `purchase-3` was deleted.

COW table layout after writes

With write operations on the table, we can explore more of the table layout with new files being written to *.hoodie/* and the partition paths based on `purchase_date`:

```
<base path of the purchase table>
├── .hoodie/
│   ├── hoodie.properties
│   ├── metadata/ ❶
│   └── timeline/
│       ├── 20261201022554235_20261201022556713.commit ❷
│       ├── 20261201022554235.commit.requested
│       ├── 20261201022554235.inflight
│       ├── 20261201022558299_20261201022558980.commit ❸
│       ├── 20261201022558299.commit.requested
│       ├── 20261201022558299.inflight
│       ├── 20261201022600486_20261201022600958.commit ❹
│       ├── 20261201022600486.commit.requested
│       ├── 20261201022600486.inflight
│       └── history/
├── purchase_date=2026-11-30/ ❺
│   ├── .hoodie_partition_metadata ❻
│   ├── ffa5854b-9104-402b-8099-0482d0844554-0_0-2-4_20261201022554235.parquet
│   └── ffa5854b-9104-402b-8099-0482d0844554-0_0-4-8_20261201022558299.parquet
└── purchase_date=2026-12-01/
    ├── .hoodie_partition_metadata
    ├── ba5a740b-0db6-4a21-902a-0eb397e4ab4f-0_0-7-1_20261201022600486.parquet
    └── ba5a740b-0db6-4a21-902a-0eb397e4ab4f-0_1-2-5_20261201022554235.parquet
```

❶ The home to the metadata table, an indexing subsystem within the Hudi table; we will discuss this in more detail in Chapter 5.

❷ Represents the first `commit` action in the timeline corresponding to the insert operation. It contains starting and ending timestamps of the change, indicating that the transactional action is complete.

❸ Represents the second `commit` action in the timeline corresponding to the update operation.

❹ Represents the third `commit` action in the timeline corresponding to the delete operation.

❺ Partition path that stores all records in which `purchase_date` is 2026-11-30.

❻ A file that contains metadata for the enclosing partition, useful for partition discovery.

You may also notice that there are Apache Parquet files stored under each partition path, with *UUID* as the prefix and timestamps matching the timeline entries. We will explore these in "Base files and log files" on page 31. Let's first understand the files that form the Hudi timeline.

Timeline, actions, and instants

In Hudi, all changes performed on a table are recorded in a chronological list of transaction logs called the *timeline*, located in the *.hoodie/timeline/* directory. An *action* represents the actual change made to the table—the transaction itself. Each file stored in the *.hoodie/timeline/* directory represents an *instant* of the timeline. One or more instants with the same timestamp prefix constitute an action started at that timestamp.

The instant files follow a specific naming convention:

```
<action start timestamp>[_<action end timestamp>].<action type>[.<action state>]
```

Action timestamps. The *action start timestamp* is a monotonically increasing value that represents when the action starts. Similarly, the *action end timestamp* marks the completion of the action, and it'll only be there for completed actions. The timestamps follow the format yyyyMMddHHmmssSSS. All action timestamps used on the timeline follow TrueTime semantics and are monotonically increasing globally across various processes involved.

About TrueTime Semantics

Google Spanner's TrueTime API (introduced in this paper (*https://oreil.ly/2mh1V*)) overcomes the challenges of time management in distributed systems by providing a globally synchronized clock with a well-defined, bounded uncertainty. Unlike traditional systems that suffer from clock drift and inconsistent timelines, TrueTime provides every node with a consistent view of time, guaranteed to be accurate within a small, known interval. This capability is crucial for Spanner to achieve external consistency in distributed transactions. It allows the system to assign timestamps with confidence, ensuring that no past or future operations will have conflicting timestamps, thereby solving long-standing problems of clock synchronization and causality.

Action types. The *action type* represents what type of change was made to the table. In the previous example, we see the action is a commit, representing a write operation. There are other actions, such as deltacommit, replacecommit, clean, and rollback. We will discuss deltacommit in "Choose a Table Type" on page 29, where we talk about setting the Hudi table type. We will introduce other actions as we encounter them in subsequent chapters of the book.

Action states. The *action state* indicates whether the action is *requested*, *inflight*, or *completed*. Here is an example of a completed `commit` action that starts at 20261201022554235 and ends at 20261201022556713:

```
├── 20261201022554235_20261201022556713.commit
├── 20261201022554235.commit.requested
├── 20261201022554235.inflight
```

> Following are two naming conventions for the action instant files:
>
> - Completed actions do not include a state suffix like requested or inflight—they simply end with the action type.
> - The `commit` action is unique in that its inflight instant omits the action type after the timestamp.

An action always starts with the requested state, and then moves to inflight, before reaching completion. Three instants under each of the three states form a completed action. Without the completed instant—that is, with only the requested instant or both requested and inflight instants—the action is considered *pending*.

The timeline tracks the complete history of table changes and enables features like time travel query and incremental query (introduced in "Advanced Usage" on page 39 and discussed further in Chapter 4). Understanding how to read the timeline will help you debug data issues, understand the impact of changes, and perform data audits.

Choose a Table Type

In the previous section, we created our `purchase` table using Hudi's default table type, Copy-on-Write, and explored fundamental CRUD operations while observing the table's physical structure. However, Hudi offers two distinct table types, each optimized for different use cases and performance characteristics. To fully understand your options and make informed decisions about table configuration, we need to examine how the alternative table type, Merge-on-Read, handles the same operations.

Create a Merge-on-Read Table

Let's re-create the `purchase` table using the MOR table type. The table creation SQL is nearly identical to our previous example, with only one configuration change required:

```
CREATE TABLE purchase (
    purchase_id STRING,
    customer_id BIGINT,
    amount FLOAT,
    status STRING,
    purchase_date STRING
) USING HUDI
TBLPROPERTIES (
    type = 'mor', ❶
    primaryKey = 'purchase_id'
)
PARTITIONED BY (purchase_date)
LOCATION '<base path to the Hudi table>'
```

❶ The only difference for creating an MOR table is specifying the `type` property. Note that for COW tables, you can explicitly set `type = 'cow'`, though it's optional because COW is the default.

After creating the MOR table, run the identical SQL commands from the previous section to perform insert, update, delete, and select operations on the new table. You'll see the same query results as before, demonstrating that both table types provide consistent data access despite their different underlying storage strategies.

MOR Table's Layout After Writes

Now let's examine how the table's physical structure differs when using the MOR table type:

```
<base path of the purchase table>
├── .hoodie/
│   ├── hoodie.properties
│   ├── metadata/
│   └── timeline/
│       ├── 20261201040547825_20261201040549713.deltacommit ❶
│       ├── 20261201040547825.deltacommit.inflight
│       ├── 20261201040547825.deltacommit.requested
│       ├── 20261201040551271_20261201040551832.deltacommit ❷
│       ├── 20261201040551271.deltacommit.inflight
│       ├── 20261201040551271.deltacommit.requested
│       ├── 20261201040553967_20261201040554439.deltacommit ❸
│       ├── 20261201040553967.deltacommit.inflight
│       ├── 20261201040553967.deltacommit.requested
│       └── history/
├── purchase_date=2026-11-30/ ❹
│   ├── .d4bd5df5-f5dd-411c-bb77-a1dbf02ef0fd-0_20261201040551271.log.1_0-55-97
│   ├── .hoodie_partition_metadata
│   └── d4bd5df5-f5dd-411c-bb77-a1dbf02ef0fd-0_0-31-46_20261201040547825.parquet
└── purchase_date=2026-12-01/
    ├── .06be74aa-6d0e-4406-bc38-981ed3e0d7e4-0_20261201040553967.log.1_0-79-139
    ├── .hoodie_partition_metadata
    └── 06be74aa-6d0e-4406-bc38-981ed3e0d7e4-0_1-31-47_20261201040547825.parquet
```

❶ This represents the first `deltacommit` action in the timeline, corresponding to the insert operation.

❷ This represents the second `deltacommit` action in the timeline, corresponding to the update operation.

❸ This represents the third `deltacommit` action in the timeline, corresponding to the delete operation.

❹ Under this partition path, notice the presence of both a Parquet file and a Hudi log file (with a *.log* in the extension) sharing the same UUID prefix after a leading dot.

The timeline instants in an MOR table follow the same naming conventions introduced in the previous section, but they use `deltacommit` actions instead of `commit` actions to represent write operations. This distinction signifies that the corresponding data written to the table can be stored in either Parquet files (as configured) or Hudi log files—a key difference that we'll explore next to understand the design rationale behind using these file formats.

Base files and log files

A *base file* in Hudi stores the primary data of the table optimized for analytical queries. Base files are in columnar format (e.g., Parquet or Apache ORC) or indexed formatted files (e.g., HFile), which can be configured when creating the table (default is Parquet). We saw base files in the table layout from the previous section. Now let's explore their naming convention in detail:

```
<file ID>_<write token>_<action start timestamp>.<base file extension>
```

The naming components serve specific purposes:

File ID
Identifies and groups files sharing the same ID within a Hudi table

Write token
A unique string for every attempt to write the file, enabling proper handling of failures and retries

Action start timestamp
Associates the file with an action in the timeline via its start timestamp

Base file extension
Denotes the file format (*.parquet*, *.orc*, *.hfile*, etc.)

A *log file* is a native Hudi-formatted file encoded as a series of data blocks. The actual data bytes are serialized into Apache Avro, Parquet, or HFile format depending on your configuration, with Avro as the default. Log files follow this naming convention:

```
.<file ID>_<action start timestamp>.log.<sequence number>_<write token>
```

Each component in the log file name has a specific role:

File ID
> Identifies and groups files sharing the same ID within a Hudi table

Action start timestamp
> Associates the file with an action in the timeline via its start timestamp

Sequence number
> Indicates the order of a log file among other log files written during the same action

Write token
> A unique string for every attempt to write the file, enabling proper handling of failures and retries

Action start timestamps serve as the key mechanism for associating transactional actions in the timeline with their corresponding physical files. This coordination enables Hudi writers and readers to understand which actions are currently in progress and determine the correct files to write to or read from.

File IDs provide the essential linkage between different base files and log files, allowing writers and readers to locate and process the appropriate files for relevant records. We'll discuss the design and concepts around file ID next.

File groups and file slices

Now that we understand the individual file types in Hudi, we need to examine how these files are organized into logical structures that enable efficient data management and querying. Hudi employs a hierarchical organization system that groups related files together and tracks their evolution over time (Figure 2-1).

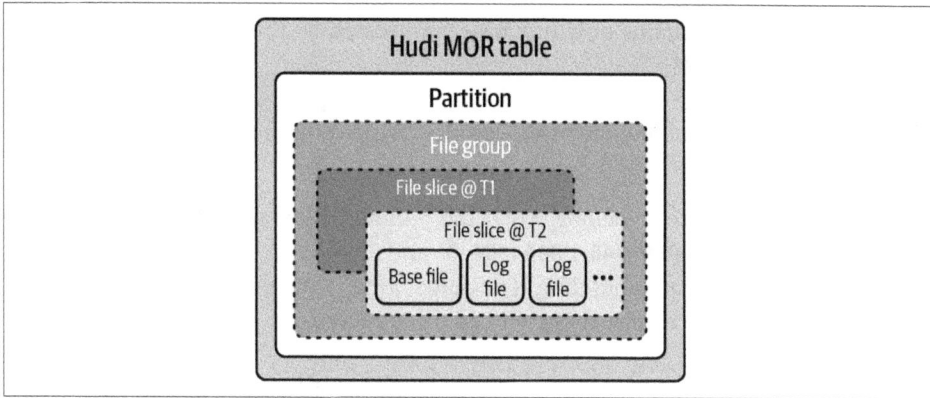

Figure 2-1. File group and file slices in an MOR table

Data files—whether base files or log files—are organized into logical concepts called *file groups*, each uniquely identified by a file ID. This file ID serves as the common identifier that links related base files and log files together, forming a cohesive unit for data storage and retrieval.

The relationship between records and file groups is fundamental to Hudi's design: each record in the table is identified by a unique key and mapped to a single file group at any given time. This one-to-one mapping allows the Hudi reader and writer to efficiently locate records by determining which file group contains them, reducing the file scanning space.

Within each file group, data files are further organized into *file slices*. A file slice represents the state of all records in the file group at a specific point in time and contains, at most, one base file and optionally a list of log files. Let's revisit the purchase tables created in earlier sections to better understand these concepts.

File slices in COW tables. In the COW purchase table, we only see base files created under each partition. In this example, there is a file group containing multiple file slices, each consisting of one base file:

```
.hoodie/timeline/
├── 20261201022554235_20261201022556713.commit ❶
├── 20261201022558299_20261201022558980.commit ❷
purchase_date=2026-11-30/
├── ffa5854b-9104-402b-8099-0482d0844554-0_0-2-3_20261201022554235.parquet ❸
└── ffa5854b-9104-402b-8099-0482d0844554-0_0-4-8_20261201022558299.parquet ❹
```

❶ The commit action that performed the insert operation

❷ The commit action that performed the update operation

❸ A file slice that contains only one base file created by the commit action at time 20261201022554235

❹ A file slice that contains only one base file created by the commit action at time 20261201022558299

These two file slices belong to the same file group with file ID ffa5854b-9104-402b-8099-0482d0844554-0, and they each represent a version of the file group at the corresponding associated time, with the more recent version containing the updated record along with all other records.

> Note that there is no physical structure to place data files into file slices and file slices into file groups—they are all logical groupings. The physical files are simply stored on the same path—either a partition path or the table's base path.

File slices in MOR tables. In the MOR purchase table, we see base files and log files created under each partition. In this example, there is a file group containing one file slice, consisting of one base file and one log file:

```
.hoodie/timeline/
├── 20261201040547825_20261201040549713.deltacommit ❶
├── 20261201040551271_20261201040551832.deltacommit ❷
purchase_date=2026-11-30/
├── .d4bd5df5-f5dd-411c-bb77-a1dbf02ef0fd-0_20261201040551271.log.1_0-5-9 ❸
└── d4bd5df5-f5dd-411c-bb77-a1dbf02ef0fd-0_0-3-4_20261201040547825.parquet ❹
```

❶ The deltacommit action that performed the insert operation

❷ The deltacommit action that performed the update operation

❸ A log file that belongs to the file slice created at time 20261201040547825, while the log file itself was created during the deltacommit started at 20261201040551271

❹ A base file that belongs to the file slice created at time 20261201040547825

The file slice belongs to a file group with file ID d4bd5df5-f5dd-411c-bb77-a1dbf02ef0fd-0. The log file contains only the updated record encoded in Hudi log format, while the base file contains all the records created by the insert operation.

File slicing. *File slicing* is the process of determining which files belong to which file slice within a file group. In MOR tables, this is more complex than in COW tables.

Because COW tables contain no log files, each base file stores all the records mapped to the file group and forms a file slice associated with the `commit` action start time.

In MOR tables, however, log files may only contain a subset of the records mapped to the file group, requiring us to identify the relevant base file to form a complete file slice. The logic involves finding the most recent base file (based on its action start timestamp) that is earlier than the log file's action end time.

In our `purchase` table example, the log file `.d4bd5df5-f5dd-411c-bb77-a1dbf02ef0fd-0_20261201040551271.log.1_0-55-97` is associated with the `deltacommit` action that started at `20261201040551271` and ended at `20261201040551832`. The target base file to associate with is `d4bd5df5-f5dd-411c-bb77-a1dbf02ef0fd-0_0-31-46_20261201040547825.parquet`, as its action start time is earlier than the log file's `deltacommit` end time `20261201040551832` and it is the most recent base file (no other base file exists) in that file group.

You might wonder why we introduce all these complexities when COW offers apparent simplicity. In the next section, we'll discuss the different characteristics between these two table types and understand the design rationale behind these concepts and grouping logic.

Copy-on-Write Versus Merge-on-Read

Both COW and MOR table types address the fundamental challenge of balancing write performance against read performance in lakehouse environments. While they share the same logical organization concepts of file groups and file slices, their approaches to handling updates differ significantly, leading to distinct performance characteristics and optimal use cases.

Understanding how each table type processes updates helps clarify when to choose one approach over the other. The key lies in recognizing that COW optimizes for consistent read performance by absorbing update costs during writes, while MOR optimizes for fast writes by deferring merge costs to read time or compaction processes.

COW table's update process

In COW tables, record updates or deletes trigger the creation of new base files in a file group, with no log files written. When an update operation occurs, Hudi identifies all base files containing records that need modification and completely rewrites these files with the updated data.

Here's how the COW update process works (Figure 2-2):

1. *Identify the target file groups:* For each record to be updated, Hudi uses the metadata table to locate the specific file group containing that record.

2. *Merge the records:* After locating the file group, the existing records will be extracted from the latest base file and merged with the incoming updates; all unchanged records will be preserved.

3. *Write the data:* A completely new base file is written as a new file slice in the file group, containing both updated and unchanged records.

4. *Write the metadata:* Metadata about all the newly written files is written to the metadata table.

5. *Publish to the metadata table's timeline:* A new `deltacommit` action is recorded in the metadata table's timeline.

6. *Publish to the data table's timeline:* A new `commit` action is recorded in the data table's timeline, indicating the transaction is complete.

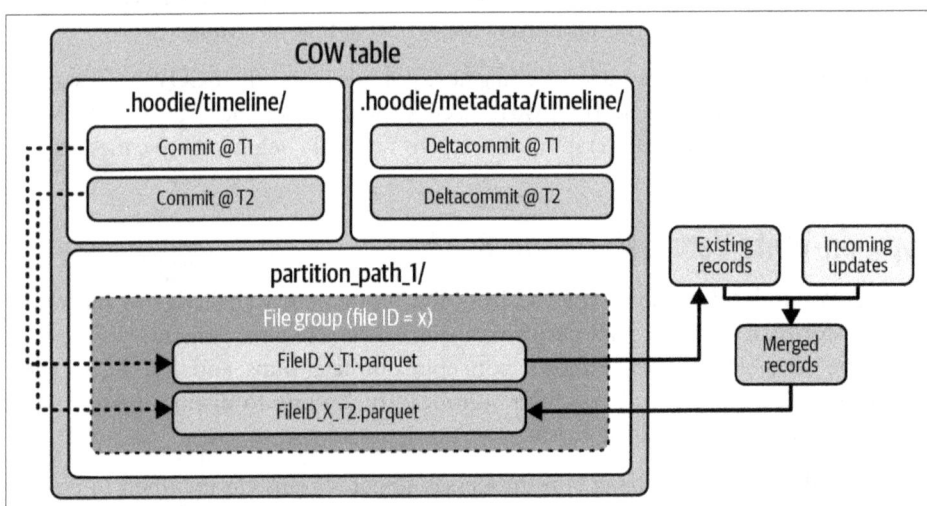

Figure 2-2. COW table's update process

This approach ensures that every query reads only base files, providing excellent and predictable read performance. However, the write amplification can be significant—updating a single record in a 1 GB Parquet file requires rewriting the entire file.

MOR table's update process

MOR tables balance write and read performance by using lightweight log files along with base files and running periodic compaction. Updates and deletes are initially written to log files, avoiding the immediate cost of rewriting base files.

The MOR update process follows these steps (Figure 2-3):

1. *Identify the target file group:* Similar to COW, for each record to be updated, Hudi uses the metadata table to locate the specific file group containing that record.

2. *Write the data:* Instead of rewriting the base file, updates are appended to log files within the file group.

3. *Write the metadata:* Metadata about all the newly written files is written to the metadata table.

4. *Publish to the metadata table's timeline:* A new `deltacommit` action is recorded in the metadata table's timeline.

5. *Publish to the data table's timeline:* A new `deltacommit` action is recorded in the data table's timeline, indicating the transaction is complete.

6. *Accumulate the changes:* Subsequent update operations continue writing to log files, building up a series of changes over time.

7. *Compact the files:* Periodically, a compaction process merges the accumulated log files with the base file to create a new base file as a new file slice.

> Compaction is one of the Hudi table services that manages the merging of log files with base files to maintain optimal query performance in MOR tables. Compaction strategies, scheduling, and configuration options will be covered in detail in Chapter 6.

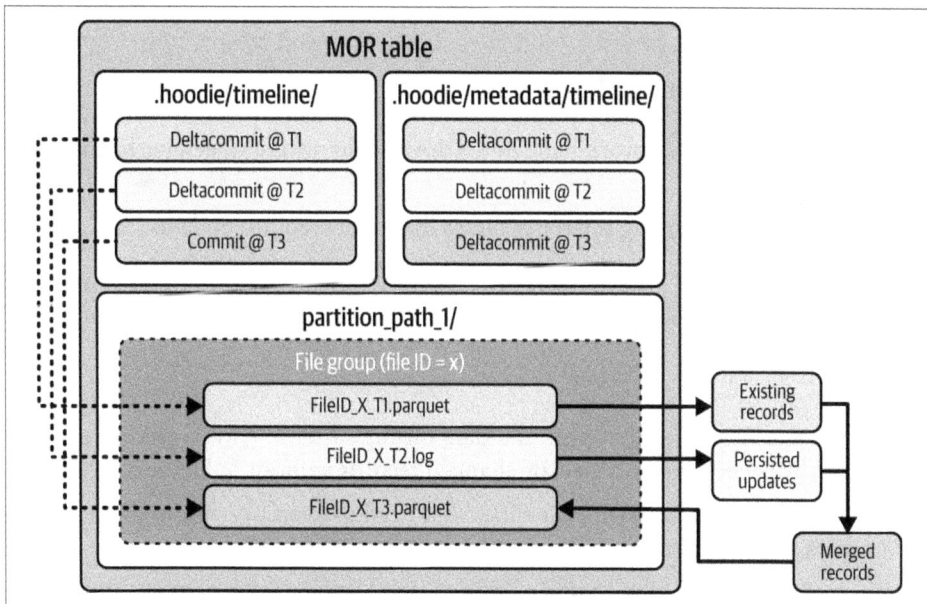

Figure 2-3. MOR table's update process

Data updates and deletes are written to log files in the row-based Hudi log format, and these changes are merged dynamically with base files during query execution or compaction. This approach dramatically reduces write amplification because only the changed records need to be written, but it introduces overhead during reads because the query engine must merge base files and log files to produce the most up-to-date results.

The trade-offs

The choice between COW and MOR involves fundamental trade-offs that affect both operational characteristics and use case suitability. Table 2-2 summarizes the high-level trade-offs between these two table types.

Table 2-2. Trade-offs between COW and MOR

Trade-off	COW	MOR
Write latency	Higher	Lower
Query latency	Lower	Higher
Update cost	Higher (rewrite entire base files)	Lower (append to log files)
Read amplification	None (reads only base files)	O(records_changed) for target file groups
Write amplification	O(records_of_target_file_groups) for given update pattern	O(records_changed) for target file groups
Base file size	Needs to be smaller to avoid high update (I/O) cost	Can be larger because update cost is low and amortized
Operational complexity	Lower (simpler file structure and behavior)	Higher (requires compaction management)

We can further infer that COW excels for:

- Read-heavy analytical workloads and OLAP scans where query performance is paramount
- Static or slowly changing reference tables that rarely require updates
- Batch ETL pipelines that process data in large, infrequent batches
- Scenarios where operational simplicity is preferred over write optimization

And MOR is ideal for:

- Incremental pipelines that promote data through bronze–silver–gold layers efficiently, by processing only new or changed records without full table rewrites
- Change data capture (CDC) pipelines that need to keep up with high-frequency updates from upstream systems
- Streaming data ingestion requiring minute-level latency for data availability

- Tables with frequent updates and deletes, such as user activity tracking or inventory management

- Hybrid batch and streaming workloads that serve both low-latency operational queries and batch analytics

The evolution of data processing requirements—from pure batch analytics toward real-time streaming—has made MOR tables increasingly popular. As the Hudi project evolves and merging costs for MOR tables continue to be optimized, MOR is becoming the preferred table type for most workload scenarios.

Advanced Usage

While the previous sections demonstrated fundamental operations such as basic CRUD, real-world lakehouse environments often require handling more complex logic. This section showcases advanced SQL usage that addresses complex requirements beyond basic insert, update, and delete scenarios.

Create Table As Select

The CREATE TABLE AS SELECT (CTAS) statement allows you to create a new Hudi table from the results of a query in a single operation. This is particularly useful for migrating data from other formats or creating derived tables efficiently:

```
-- Create a summary Hudi table from the existing purchase table
CREATE TABLE purchase_summary
USING HUDI ❶
TBLPROPERTIES (
    primaryKey = 'customer_id,purchase_date' ❷
)
AS SELECT
    customer_id,
    purchase_date,
    ROUND(SUM(amount), 2) as total_amount, ❸
    COUNT(*) as purchase_count ❹
FROM purchase
GROUP BY customer_id, purchase_date;
```

❶ Specifies the table format as Hudi for the purchase_summary table

❷ Uses composite record key fields

❸ Sums the amount to get the total amount for each customer and purchase date

❹ Counts the purchases for each customer and purchase date

Run a SELECT statement to check the results:

```
SELECT customer_id, purchase_date, total_amount, purchase_count
FROM purchase_summary
ORDER BY customer_id, purchase_date;
```

Output:

customer_id	purchase_date	total_amount	purchase_count
101	2026-11-30	144.99	2
101	2026-12-01	98.3	1
103	2026-12-01	41.5	1

Merge Source Data into the Table

The MERGE INTO statement enables flexible upsert operations by joining source data with the target table and performing different actions based on matching conditions:

```
-- Create a staging table with updates
CREATE TABLE purchase_updates ( ❶
    purchase_id STRING,
    customer_id BIGINT,
    amount FLOAT,
    status STRING,
    purchase_date STRING
) USING PARQUET;

-- Merge updates into the purchase table
MERGE INTO purchase t
USING (
    SELECT purchase_id, customer_id, amount, status, purchase_date
    FROM purchase_updates
) s
ON t.purchase_id = s.purchase_id ❷
WHEN MATCHED THEN
    UPDATE SET t.amount = s.amount, t.status = s.status ❸
WHEN NOT MATCHED THEN
    INSERT (purchase_id, customer_id, amount, status, purchase_date) ❹
    VALUES (s.purchase_id, s.customer_id, s.amount, s.status, s.purchase_date);
```

❶ Creates a staging table containing new and updated purchase records to be merged into the main table

❷ Defines the join condition based on purchase_id to match records between source and target tables

❸ Updates existing records when a match is found, modifying only the amount and status fields while preserving other data

❹ Inserts new records when no match is found, creating completely new entries in the target table

Update and Delete Using Nonrecord Key Fields

Hudi supports update and delete operations using fields other than the primary key, enabling flexible data management based on business logic.

Run the following SQL to perform an update with predicates on `customer_id` and `amount` on the `purchase` table we've worked on in previous sections:

```
-- Update the purchases based on customer_id and amount
UPDATE purchase
SET status = 'PENDING'
WHERE customer_id = 101 AND amount > 100.0; ❶
```

❶ Predicates are not on any record key field.

Run a SELECT statement to check the results:

```
SELECT purchase_id, customer_id, amount, status, purchase_date
FROM purchase
ORDER BY purchase_id;
```

Output:

```
purchase_id    customer_id    amount  status     purchase_date
purchase-1     101            21.9    COMPLETED  2026-11-30
purchase-2     101            123.09  PENDING    2026-11-30 ❶
purchase-4     103            41.5    COMPLETED  2026-12-01
purchase-5     101            98.3    COMPLETED  2026-12-01
```

❶ The status of `purchase-2` was updated to `PENDING`.

Run the following SQL to perform a delete with predicates on `status` and `purchase_date` on the `purchase` table:

```
-- Delete purchases based on status and date criteria
DELETE FROM purchase
WHERE status = 'PENDING'
AND purchase_date BETWEEN '2026-11-01' AND '2026-11-30'; ❶
```

❶ Predicates are not on any record key field.

Run a SELECT statement to check the results:

```
SELECT purchase_id, customer_id, amount, status, purchase_date
FROM purchase
ORDER BY purchase_id;
```

Output:

```
purchase_id    customer_id    amount  status     purchase_date
purchase-1     101            21.9    COMPLETED  2026-11-30
purchase-4     103            41.5    COMPLETED  2026-12-01
purchase-5     101            98.3    COMPLETED  2026-12-01
```

From the output, we can see that the `purchase-2` that matches the predicates was deleted.

Time Travel Query

Time travel queries allow you to access historical versions of your data, enabling auditing, debugging, and analysis of how data has evolved over time. This capability leverages Hudi's timeline design and file slice versioning to retain and retrieve record versions that match the given timestamp. Chapter 4 will explore time travel queries and other query types in greater detail.

Following is an example of a time travel query:

```
-- Query the table as it existed at a specific commit time
SELECT purchase_id, customer_id, amount, status
FROM purchase TIMESTAMP AS OF '202612010040547825' ❶
WHERE customer_id = 101;

-- Query using a readable timestamp format
SELECT customer_id, COUNT(*) as purchase_count
FROM purchase TIMESTAMP AS OF '2026-12-01 10:30:00' ❷
GROUP BY customer_id;
```

❶ The syntax `TIMESTAMP AS OF` is for setting the past time of querying. The format can be the same as the timeline timestamp format.

❷ The syntax `TIMESTAMP AS OF` also accepts a more commonly used timestamp format.

Incremental Query

Incremental queries retrieve only the data that has changed since a specific point in time, enabling efficient incremental processing pipelines that dramatically reduce compute costs. This capability leverages Hudi's timeline and file group organization to efficiently locate changed records. Chapter 4 will cover incremental queries and the benefits in detail.

Following is an example of incremental queries:

```
-- Retrieve only the changed records since a specific timestamp
SELECT *
FROM hudi_table_changes('purchase', 'latest_state', '202612010040547825'); ❶

-- Retrieve only the changed records since a specific timestamp, using CDC mode
SELECT *
FROM hudi_table_changes('purchase', 'cdc', 'earliest', '20260516000000'); ❷
```

❶ The table-valued function `hudi_table_changes` takes in parameters for running incremental queries.

❷ The table-valued function `hudi_table_changes` takes in parameters for running incremental queries in CDC mode that return before and/or after images of the changed records.

These advanced SQL usages demonstrate Hudi's power in handling complex lakehouse scenarios. From efficient data migration using CTAS to building CDC pipelines with incremental queries, these operations provide the foundation for sophisticated data processing workflows that combine the best of traditional database capabilities with the scale and flexibility of data lakes.

Summary

This chapter transformed theoretical knowledge into practical understanding through hands-on exploration of Hudi tables. By working with a purchase tracking table, we observed how table layouts evolve during common lakehouse operations. The key concepts covered include:

Table layouts and properties
  We explored the structure of the *.hoodie/* directory and introduced key table properties like record key fields and partition fields.

Timeline, actions, and instants
  We examined the entries stored under *.hoodie/timeline/* and explained how time-stamped actions like the `commit` and `deltacommit` transition instant states enable ACID guarantees and advanced query capabilities.

Base files, log files, file groups, and file slices
  We explained how base files are optimized for reads while log files contain incremental changes, and how these files are logically organized into file groups and file slices for efficient data management.

Table type comparison
  We compared COW and MOR table types, revealing how COW optimizes for read performance through file rewriting while MOR prioritizes write performance using log files to absorb frequent updates.

We also demonstrated advanced SQL usage including CTAS, `MERGE INTO` statements, and updates using nonrecord key fields. Time travel queries and incremental queries showcase Hudi's unique value proposition for auditing and efficient data processing.

The concepts introduced here form essential foundations for upcoming chapters: timeline management and file organization underpin the write operations detailed in Chapter 3, while our SQL examples serve as a warm-up for the comprehensive query capabilities explored in Chapter 4. The *metadata/* directory glimpsed in our table layouts will be thoroughly examined in Chapter 5, and the MOR compaction process briefly mentioned here will receive detailed coverage in Chapter 6.

## CHAPTER 3

Writing to Hudi

The write operation is a critical function in any data lakehouse, directly shaping its reliability and performance. A deep understanding of the Hudi writer's internal behavior—and which of its many features to leverage for your specific use case—is therefore essential. Building upon the foundational concepts of table layouts, timeline structures, and table type trade-offs from Chapter 2, this chapter combines deep dives on internals and usage examples, serving as your go-to guide to understanding write operations in Apache Hudi.

This chapter is organized into three sections to provide a comprehensive exploration of Hudi's write capabilities. "Breaking Down the Write Flow" dissects the end-to-end Hudi write process. We will trace each step of the journey, from data preparation to the final transactional commit, revealing the internal mechanics that ensure data correctness and efficiency.

To ground our discussion in practical application, "Exploring Write Operations" introduces a real-world use case for a data provider, DataCentral, Inc., which specializes in analyzing sensor data from millions of Internet of Things (IoT) devices. We will demonstrate all of Hudi's write operations—including upsert, delete, insert, and bulk_insert—showing you how to solve common data manipulation challenges in a real-world context.

The power and efficiency of Hudi's core write operations stem from several important features designed to handle complex lakehouse data patterns. To avoid distracting from the main write flow, we explore these more involved features in "Highlighting Noteworthy Features."

By completing this chapter, you will be able to effectively write data to Hudi. You will gain a clear understanding of the write flow, learn how to apply various write operations for different scenarios, and know how to use advanced features to build efficient and reliable data lakehouse pipelines.

Breaking Down the Write Flow

To effectively use Hudi for building data lakehouses, a clear understanding of its internal write flow is essential. This section explains the Hudi write flow step by step, guiding you through each stage from commit initiation, through record preparation and data writing, to commit finalization.

Figure 3-1 provides an overview of the Hudi write flow, which consists of both main and optional steps.

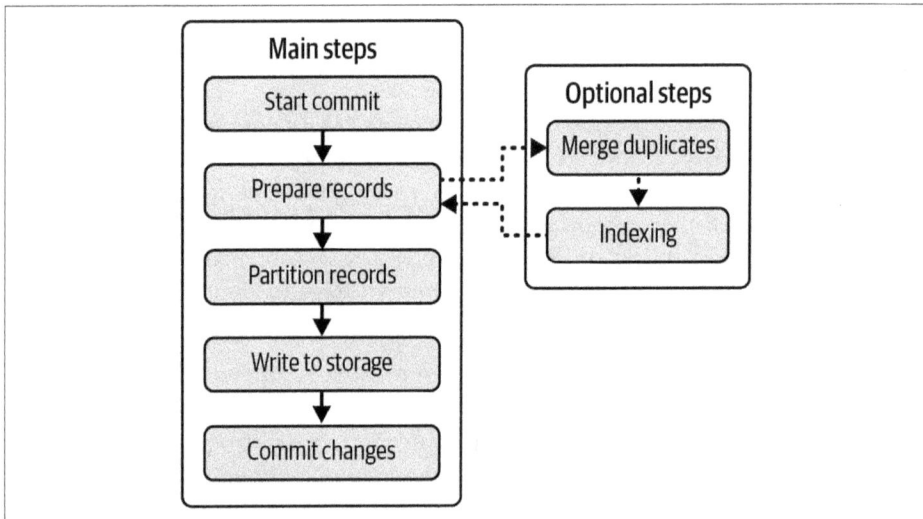

Figure 3-1. Hudi write flow overview

The main steps encompass processes common to most write operation types, while the optional steps are applicable only to specific types. In the following sections, we will use `upsert`, the default write operation, as an example to walk through all these steps.

> When we refer to "commit" in this context, we are referencing the transactional commit concept commonly used in databases. This concept also applies to Hudi tables, where each transactional action is sometimes referred to as a *commit*. It is important not to confuse this broader transactional "commit" with the specific `commit` action recorded on the Hudi timeline (as introduced in Chapter 2).

Start Commit

The *start commit* step marks the beginning of any Hudi write operation, with the Hudi write client serving as the primary entry point. This client, which is engine compatible (e.g., `SparkRDDWriteClient` for Apache Spark, `HoodieFlinkWriteClient` for Apache Flink, or `HoodieJavaWriteClient` for Apache Kafka Connect), first ensures a clean slate for the upcoming write. It does this by checking the table's timeline for any previously failed actions and performing a necessary rollback. Once these preliminary checks are complete, the client initiates the write by creating a "requested" `commit` (or `deltacommit`, if it's Merge-on-Read [MOR]) action on the timeline. This stage also typically involves reconciling user-provided configurations with existing Hudi table properties, passing the finalized configuration set to the client for subsequent operations.

Prepare Records

This step involves making necessary transformations to the incoming data. Before delving into these transformations, it's important to understand `HoodieRecord`, an internal Hudi data structure. As illustrated in Figure 3-2, `HoodieRecord` is designed to encapsulate incoming records with additional metadata, including the record key, partition path, ordering value, and both its current and new locations.

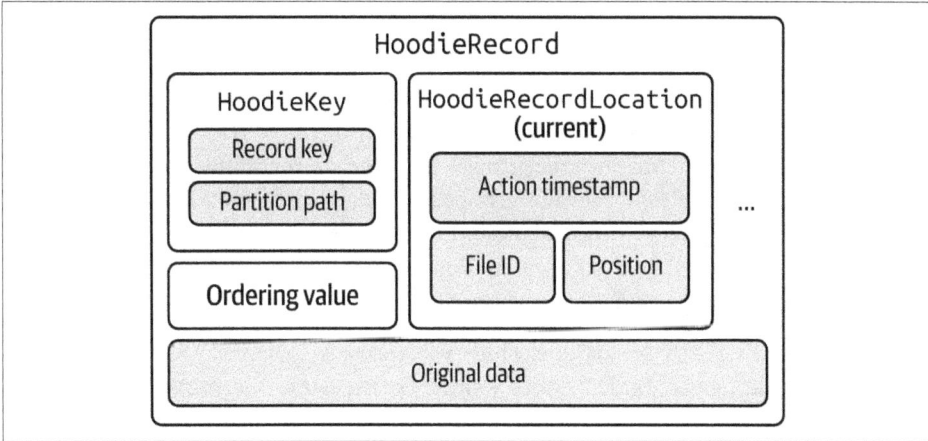

Figure 3-2. `HoodieRecord` wraps the original data with additional metadata

The `HoodieKey` field contains the record key and partition path, which together uniquely identify a record within a Hudi table. The ordering value field determines the order of records with the same `HoodieKey`. Storing this information along with the record data is critical for many use cases that rely on ordering. For example, when replicating database tables using change data capture (CDC), records may share the same primary key. An ordering value from the source is therefore required to identify the most recent record and ensure correct replication.

Merging duplicate records

The records with the same `HoodieKey` are considered duplicates. In the case of processing CDC records, which usually contain duplicates, we need to merge them properly based on the ordering values such that the latest record version is captured. Merging at this step before writing to storage reduces the workload for the subsequent write steps.

For `upsert` and `delete` operations, the step of merging duplicate records is performed by default during the preparation step. In operations like `insert` or `bulk_insert`, merging is not performed by default, as their write semantic is designed for append-only writes.

To handle various use cases that require merging, Hudi supports merge modes to define the merging behavior. This topic will be discussed in "Merge Modes" on page 66.

Indexing

The next optional step during record preparation is indexing, which is about locating incoming records in the table for any matching existing records such that they can be identified as updating records or new records.

The `HoodieRecordLocation` information is vital for pinpointing record locations. Within a Hudi table, a record's location can be determined by first using the partition path and file ID to identify its file group, then the action timestamp to pinpoint the specific file slice within that file group, and finally the position information to quickly locate the record within the containing base file. During indexing, the current `HoodieRecordLocation` field (shown in Figure 3-2) will be populated to indicate where the record exists at the time of this write.

For `upsert` and `delete` operations, Hudi writers must perform indexing, because we need to have new record changes written to the same file groups where those existing records reside, adhering to Hudi's file group and file slice design. This design ensures that different versions of the same records live in distinct file slices, with action timestamps associating versioning with write time. For write operations like `insert` or `bulk_insert` that have append-only semantics, indexing is not necessary and will be skipped. In both databases and data lakehouses, indexing is a very broad and yet critical technique for improving write and read performance. In Chapter 5, we will delve into this topic in detail.

Partition Records

After records are prepared, the next step is to partition them. This involves splitting the incoming records into reasonably sized in-memory partitions for distributed processing. For `upsert` and `insert` operations, the partitioning process allows a bin-packing algorithm to distribute the records such that it can address small-file issues and maintain a performant table layout. We will discuss the small-file handling feature in more detail in "Small-file handling for insert and upsert operations" on page 55.

Write to Storage

At this step, records are ready to be written to file slices on storage. Hudi uses different "write handle" operations to process updates and inserts distinctively. For example, in the case of a Copy-on-Write (COW) table, the "write handle" operation for inserts may create a new file group to host the new records. For updates, the "write handle" operation needs to read the located file slices and merge the existing records with the incoming updates, and then it writes the merged records to new file slices in their corresponding file group. The "write handle" operations also report back the write-related metadata and statistics for finalizing the transaction.

Commit Changes

In this final step, the Hudi writer undertakes multiple tasks to correctly conclude the transactional action.

The metadata table, as the indexing subsystem of the data table (covered in Chapter 5), will be updated as part of the same write transaction. Metadata about the write operation will be saved, which synchronizes the index data with the latest records to ensure data consistency and correctness.

The Hudi writer checks for data conflicts if concurrent writers are configured for the table (covered in Chapter 7). The metadata and statistics reported by "write handle" operations will be aggregated and used to generate an overall "write report," which is subsequently persisted in the completed action instant on the Hudi timeline.

Hudi creates *marker files* before writing data to storage. Marker files are empty files used to track the base files and log files being written during the operation. If a write fails halfway, the marker files will be left in a directory under *.hoodie/.temp/*, which facilitates cleaning up the residual files. When the write is successful (the action appears as complete on the timeline), the marker files will be deleted as a post-commit task. The marker files are also useful for implementing early conflict detection in multiwriter scenarios, which will be discussed in Chapter 7.

As we briefly mentioned in Chapter 2, the Hudi timeline implements an LSM-tree (*https://oreil.ly/gR4d3*) structure to store the action instants. When the number of action instants exceeds a configurable threshold, older instants will be archived to the *timeline/history/* directory. As a post-commit task, the archiving service will be triggered when the threshold is reached. This will bound the number of action instants in the active timeline, maintaining efficiency for writes and reads.

If you're using Spark as the execution engine, you can run pre-commit validation in this step. You can add `hoodie.precommit.validators` in your writer configuration with a value such as `org.apache.hudi.client.validator.SqlQueryEqualityPre CommitValidator`. Along with other related configurations, the Hudi writer will execute SQL commands and validate the results as configured. Refer to the Hudi documentation (*https://oreil.ly/sLkP9*) for more details.

Summarize the Upsert Flow

Having discussed each step in the writer flow using `upsert` as an example, we will now summarize the entire process (see Figure 3-3 for a comprehensive diagram):

1. *Start the commit:* A Hudi write client initiates the commit process by first ensuring a clean state on the table's timeline, rolling back any failed actions. It then creates a "requested" instant (either a `commit` for COW or a `deltacommit` for MOR) on the timeline.

2. *Prepare the records:* Incoming records are prepared for writing. This involves wrapping them in the `HoodieRecord` model, merging records based on their `HoodieKey` and ordering values, and performing indexing.

3. *Partition the records:* Prepared records are then partitioned in memory for distributed processing. The small-file handling mechanism will be used for `upsert` and `insert` operations to keep the table storage layout optimized.

4. *Write to storage:* Hudi uses different kinds of "write handle" operations to process partitioned records and perform I/O to the storage.

5. *Commit the changes:* In this final step, the Hudi writer performs various tasks to complete the transaction and bookkeep the table.

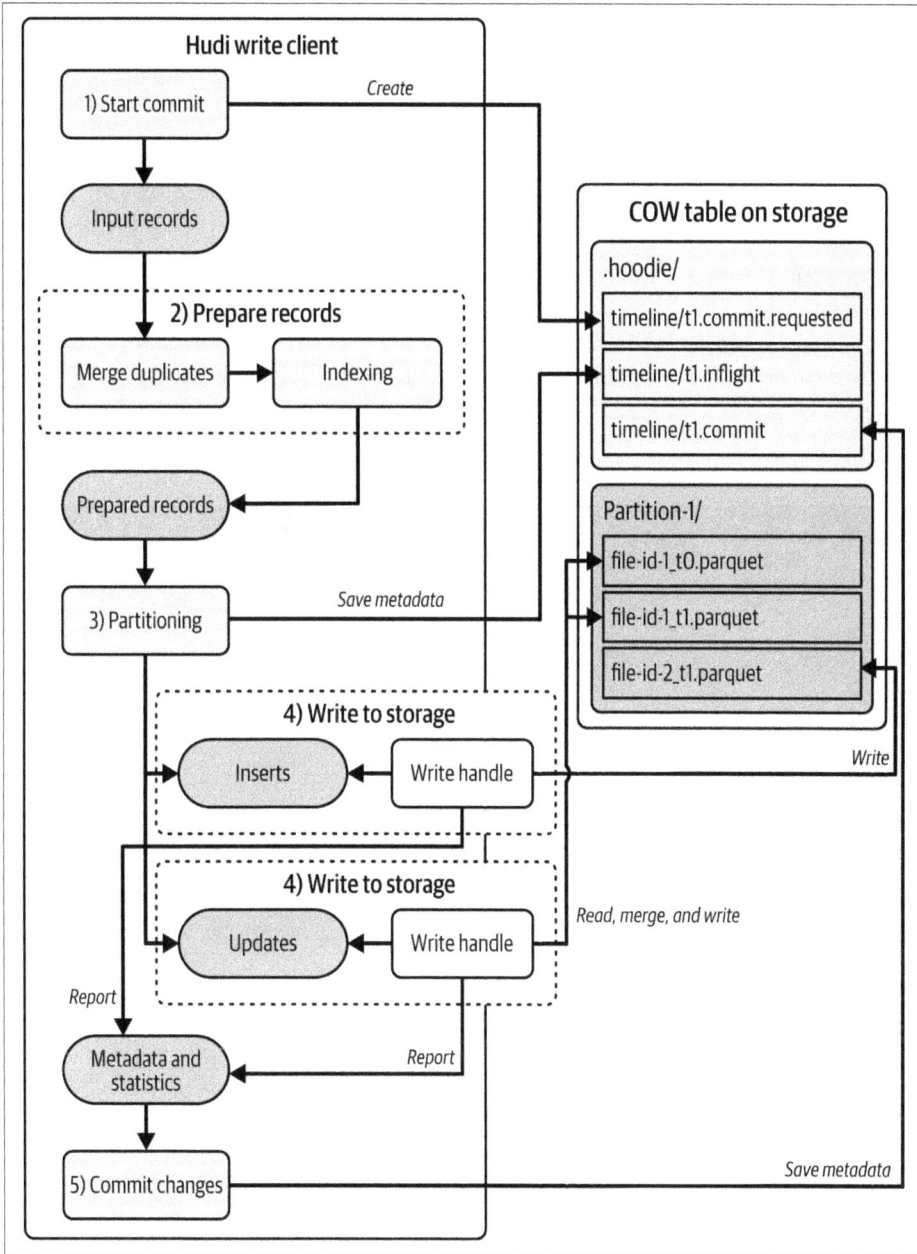

Figure 3-3. Hudi upsert *flow on a COW table*

Exploring Write Operations

In the previous section, we explored the detailed internal workings of Hudi's write operations, using the default `upsert` operation as a representative example. While `upsert` is fundamental, Hudi offers a variety of other write operation types. In this section, we will shift to a more practical approach, demonstrating these operations with Spark SQL code examples and explaining their behaviors and related concepts.

Our examples in this section will be based on an imagined company, DataCentral, Inc. DataCentral is a data provider specializing in collecting sensor data from IoT devices and offering analytics services through its platform. The primary table used by its data collection module is `sensor_data`, which has the schema shown in Table 3-1.

Table 3-1. The schema of `sensor_data` used by DataCentral, Inc.

Field name	Data type	Description
id	STRING	A unique identifier for the sensor device
type	STRING	The type of sensor data collected (e.g., TEMP for temperature, HUM for humidity, and PRES for pressure)
ts	BIGINT	The epoch timestamp in milliseconds when the sensor data was sampled
emit_ts	BIGINT	The epoch timestamp in milliseconds when the sensor data was emitted
value	FLOAT	The sampled sensor data value
org_id	STRING	A unique identifier for the organization that owns the sensor device

The subsequent sections will focus on using this table to illustrate various scenarios that can occur during sensor data processing.

Define Table Properties

Let's first create the `sensor_data` table according to the schema described in Table 3-1:

```
CREATE TABLE sensor_data (
    id STRING,
    type STRING,
    ts BIGINT,
    emit_ts BIGINT,
    value FLOAT,
    org_id STRING
) USING HUDI
TBLPROPERTIES (
    type = 'mor', ❶
    primaryKey = 'id,type,ts', ❷
    preCombineField = 'emit_ts' ❸
)
PARTITIONED BY (org_id); ❹
```

❶ We choose MOR as the table type to handle high-throughput writes from a large number of IoT devices.

❷ We define a composite record key based on the sensor ID, sensor data type, and sampling timestamp to uniquely identify each sensor data record.

❸ We use the emit timestamp (`emit_ts`) to determine the order of records via the `preCombineField` property, which is crucial for handling late-arriving or out-of-order data.

❹ We partition the table by `org_id` to optimize queries that commonly filter data by the organization that owns the sensor devices.

When working with Hudi tables that allow updates or deletes, it's essential to establish a clear logic for ordering records that share the same record keys. This is critical because when an update occurs, Hudi must select the correct version of the record based on this order. Similarly, for delete operations, Hudi uses this ordering to determine if the incoming delete request is newer, in which case the deletion proceeds; otherwise, the delete should be skipped. The pre-combine field, also referred to as the *ordering field*, allows you to designate a specific field for comparison, where a greater value signifies a more recent record version.

> Since Hudi 1.1, you can specify multiple fields as ordering fields. Hudi will use these fields in the specified order for comparison, moving to the next field only if the preceding ones are identical, to jointly determine the record order.

However, simply picking the newest version isn't always sufficient. Depending on business needs, you might want to implement custom merging logic. This could involve selectively updating only certain fields or performing calculations like summing or averaging values from both old and new records. The merging behavior of an incoming record with an existing one is determined by how you configure the merge mode, a topic that will be discussed later in this chapter. For the examples in this section, just keep in mind that `emit_ts` dictates the record order; thus, during data correction processes where sensors might emit records with the same data keys but different values at a later time, Hudi will select the record with the greater `emit_ts` as the most current version.

Use INSERT INTO

Typically, we append new sensor data to the table. Periodically, when sensors emit corrected data, we perform an upsert operation. This ensures that existing records are updated and that new records are inserted. Hudi supports both insert and upsert semantics through three distinct write operations: insert, bulk_insert, and upsert. All these operations can be executed using the standard SQL INSERT INTO syntax.

Let's write an initial batch of data to the sensor_data table using the insert operation:

```
SET hoodie.spark.sql.insert.into.operation=insert; ❶

INSERT INTO sensor_data VALUES
('SENSOR_001', 'TEMP', 1797649200010, 1797649200050, 296.65,  'ORG_A'),
('SENSOR_001', 'HUM',  1797649200020, 1797649200050, 65.2,    'ORG_A'),
('SENSOR_001', 'PRES', 1797649200030, 1797649200050, 1013.25, 'ORG_A'),
('SENSOR_002', 'TEMP', 1797649200040, 1797649200100, 297.25,  'ORG_B'),
('SENSOR_002', 'HUM',  1797649200050, 1797649200100, 62.8,    'ORG_B');
```

❶ Specifies the write operation for INSERT INTO statements

This example uses the insert operation to write five sensor data records into two partitions, one for organization A and one for organization B. The sensors detect three types of data: temperature, humidity, and pressure. As you may have noticed, despite being sampled at different timestamps for different data types, the records for each sensor were emitted at the same timestamp, which is later than the sampling time.

To achieve the same result using the bulk_insert operation, you can set the configuration as follows before executing the same INSERT INTO command:

```
SET hoodie.spark.sql.insert.into.operation=bulk_insert;
```

Insert versus bulk insert

Both the insert and bulk_insert operations follow the same append-only semantics, but they have some differences in their write flow implementation. The comparison is summarized in Table 3-2.

Table 3-2. Comparison of insert and bulk_insert operations

	insert	bulk_insert
Merges duplicates	No by default; enabled by setting hoodie.combine.before.insert=true	
Has indexing step	No	
File-sizing mechanism	Automatic small-file handling	Tunable via sort mode and partitioning
Suitable scenario	Incremental, small-batch writes	Initial bootstrap, large-batch writes

It is important to note that neither of these operations modifies any existing records in the table, as no indexing is performed. Furthermore, although both can be configured to merge duplicates in the incoming data, this merging does not occur between the incoming data and existing records in the table. Understanding these implications of the append-only semantics is crucial.

The subsequent two sections will delve into the file-sizing mechanisms used by these two operations.

Small-file handling for insert and upsert operations

In both batch and stream processing systems, data is written to the file system in batches of varying sizes. This can lead to a proliferation of small files over time, especially with smaller batches or low-volume stream ingestion. This problem is detrimental to query performance, as engines must open, read, and close numerous files during query planning and execution. Additionally, a large number of small files increases metadata overhead, can increase write latency due to slower indexing, and results in inefficient storage utilization due to lower compression ratios (fewer records in each compressible data file). Therefore, maintaining optimal data file sizes is crucial for preserving both query performance and storage efficiency.

Hudi maintains configured target file sizes automatically when performing insert and upsert operations. Before writing new records, Hudi identifies eligible small-sized files in the target partitions and routes incoming data to these files, adding enough records to bring them closer to the configured maximum size limit. The remaining records are then written to new files. This intelligent bin-packing approach ensures that small files eventually grow to approach the target file size limit, effectively mitigating the small-file problem without requiring manual intervention.

For COW tables, as illustrated in Figure 3-4, Hudi employs a straightforward approach where any file slice (consisting of one base file) smaller than the configured threshold (the default is 100 MB via `hoodie.parquet.small.file.limit`) becomes a candidate for expansion. New inserts are distributed among these candidates to grow them toward the target file size (the default is 120 MB via `hoodie.parquet.max.file.size`). A file slice that exceeds the small-file limit will not be considered a candidate to receive new records; it will be rewritten only when updates or deletes to its existing records are received.

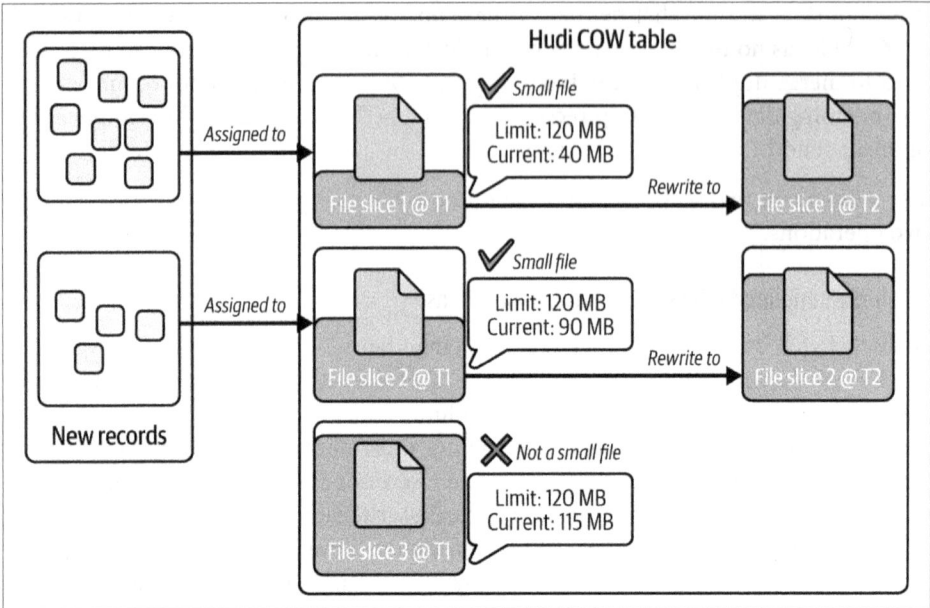

Figure 3-4. New records go through small-file handling in a COW table

MOR tables handle small files a bit differently to optimize for write performance. When new records are added to a file group as determined by the small-file handling algorithm, they'll trigger the rewriting of the latest file slice in that group. This is acceptable for COW tables, as rewriting base files is an expected part of update and delete operations, so a rewrite for new inserts does not worsen the overall time complexity. However, because MOR tables are designed for lower write latency, frequent rewrites would defeat the purpose. Therefore, by default, only one small-file group per partition is selected for expansion during each write operation (this is configurable via hoodie.merge.small.file.group.candidates.limit) to minimize the impact on write latency. Additionally, file groups whose latest file slice already contains log files from previous updates are excluded from small-file candidacy. This is because incorporating new inserts would require merging the base files and log files, which incurs additional compute overhead and increases write latency. The rationale behind the different small-file handling behavior in MOR is that, by spreading small-file handling across multiple write operations and improving the size for one file group (or more, as per configuration) per partition at a time, the table's overall file size distribution will eventually become optimal. Using MOR usually implies more frequent writes, so these file size improvements can be realized in a timelier manner.

For MOR tables with certain writer index types that allow new records to be appended directly to log files, this different small-file handling behavior does not apply. In these cases, inserts can be appended to any file group that meets the small-file threshold, just like with COW, which helps accelerate the file size optimization process. The bucket index, which will be discussed in more detail in Chapter 5, is one such common index type.

The small-file handling process requires finding candidate file groups and running a bin-packing algorithm for input records, which incurs some latency to write operations. You can completely turn off small-file handling by setting `hoodie.par` `quet.small.file.limit` to 0 to improve write performance. To mitigate the file sizing issue, you can instead configure an asynchronous clustering service that is dedicated to rewriting file groups with more optimized file sizes. This topic will be discussed further in Chapter 6.

Sort modes in bulk_insert

Distributed engines divide large workloads into smaller tasks, which are then assigned to workers across multiple machines. In a data-writing scenario, each worker processes a portion of the input data. When writing to nonappendable file formats like Apache Parquet, a single task typically writes to one output file in a nonpartitioned table. However, for a partitioned table, a single task may write multiple output files as its records are routed to different partition paths based on the values of the partition fields (as shown in Figure 3-5).

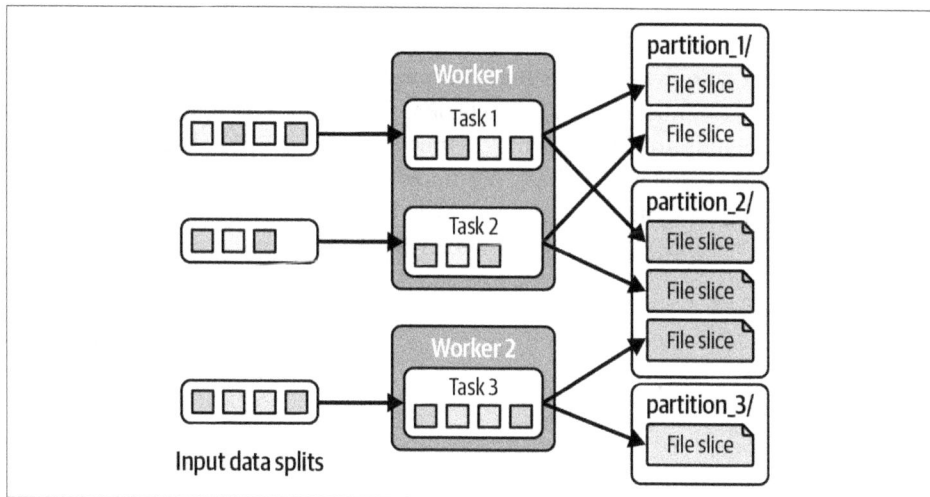

Figure 3-5. Tasks writing file slices in different partitions

Unless the input data is specifically controlled or pre-transformed, tasks can randomly process records belonging to distinct partition paths. This can result in a large number of small files, particularly when having a large number of tasks. To address this, the bulk_insert write flow does not use small-file handling like insert does. This is because bulk_insert is primarily designed for initial data bootstrapping, where no small files exist to be filled. The small-file handling process is also inefficient for the large volumes of data that are typical of bulk inserts. Instead, bulk_insert uses sort modes to control how data is sorted and partitioned, and assigned to tasks. This approach enables the creation of well-sized output files, provided that a suitable sort mode is chosen. We will introduce two common ones: GLOBAL_SORT and PARTITION_PATH_REPARTITION.

The GLOBAL_SORT mode sorts the entire input batch of records, first by partition path and then by record key. This process colocates records from the same physical partition, enabling each task to write to fewer, larger files. The globally sorted records can be evenly split and distributed by the execution engine, which helps mitigate data skew and prevent the waste of compute resources. Additionally, sorting by record key (especially when keys are temporal or have business significance) improves data locality within the file groups, which can improve the efficiency of subsequent updates. While this strategy offers benefits such as well-sized files, evenly distributed workloads, and improved data locality, its main drawback is the substantial overhead from the full data sorting and shuffling, which can significantly increase write latency and memory consumption. Furthermore, the data locality benefit is not applicable when record keys are completely random (such as UUIDs), which makes the sorting overhead less worthwhile.

On the other hand, the PARTITION_PATH_REPARTITION mode, as shown in Figure 3-6, assigns all records with the same partition path to the same task without sorting. This approach provides a similar benefit to the GLOBAL_SORT mode by writing fewer, larger files. Because it avoids sorting the entire input batch, it is faster and less memory intensive. However, its main drawback occurs when data is skewed on certain partition paths. In such cases, the corresponding tasks can become a bottleneck, leading to resource wastage as some workers remain idle while others handle significantly larger workloads.

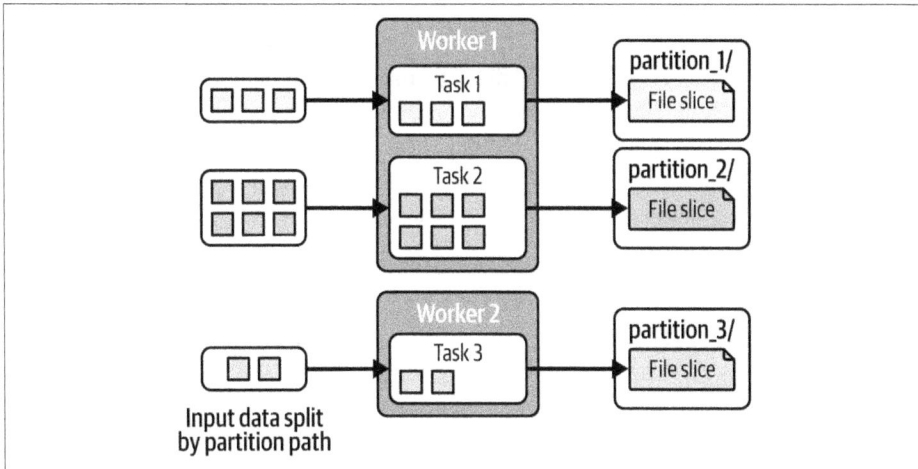

Figure 3-6. Using the `PARTITION_PATH_REPARTITION` *mode*

> By default, `bulk_insert` uses a no-op `NONE_SORT` mode. This mode relies entirely on the execution engine to distribute workloads to tasks, without interfering with task splitting and assignment. While this approach has no overhead and provides the fastest write performance, it can also lead to a severe small-file problem, as illustrated in Figure 3-5. The choice of sort mode significantly impacts `bulk_insert` performance, memory consumption, and the storage pattern of the resulting table. Therefore, it is crucial to thoroughly analyze the data patterns for your tables and select the most appropriate strategy for your `bulk_insert` operations.
>
> To fully customize the sorting and partitioning behavior, you may also implement Hudi's `BulkInsertPartitioner` interface to optimize `bulk_insert` for your use cases.

Execute as upsert

Returning to the `sensor_data` example, we can also perform an `upsert` using the `INSERT INTO` syntax. In this case, any existing records will be updated, while new records will be inserted. Because we have defined the record keys and an ordering field for the `sensor_data` table, Hudi will automatically instruct the `INSERT INTO` to perform an `upsert` operation. This auto-inferring behavior is designed to reduce configuration efforts. You can, however, override this behavior for a specific Spark SQL session by setting `hoodie.spark.sql.insert.into.operation` to `insert` or `bulk_insert`. The `upsert` operation, like `insert`, employs the small-file handling process to maintain optimal file sizes, as both are designed for smaller, incremental data batches rather than the large-volume processing typical of `bulk_insert`.

Perform Partial Merge with MERGE INTO

There might be scenarios where you need to manually update a batch of corrected sensor data in a Hudi table for a specific organization, rather than relying on the standard INSERT INTO upsert flow. In such cases, you can leverage the MERGE INTO syntax (introduced in Chapter 2) to load the batch of data for updates and apply them to the target table, as shown in the following example:

```
MERGE INTO sensor_data t
USING (
  SELECT
    'SENSOR_001'  AS id,
    'TEMP'        AS type,
    1797649200010 AS ts,
    1797649300000 AS emit_ts,
    300.2         AS value,
    'ORG_A'       AS org_id
) s
ON t.id = s.id AND t.type = s.type AND t.ts = s.ts AND t.org_id = s.org_id
WHEN MATCHED THEN UPDATE SET
  emit_ts = s.emit_ts,
  value = s.value;
```

The SQL statement demonstrates that when the composite record keys and the partition value from the source table s match those in the target table t, the corresponding records in t will be updated with the new emit_ts and value from s. While this example uses a hardcoded sample record for demonstration, in a real-world scenario, you would typically SELECT data from an external source table containing the updates.

A key advantage of using MERGE INTO with Hudi, especially for MOR tables, is its support for *partial merge*. As we learned in Chapter 2, updates to a Hudi table are saved as log files within their respective file groups. Partial merge specifically records only the changed columns and their new values in these log files. This approach offers multiple benefits. First, it reduces the amount of data that is written, leading to faster writes and lower storage consumption. Furthermore, during query execution, the merging process of base files and log files becomes more efficient, improving query performance.

Partial merge is particularly crucial for wide tables, which are common in various data lakehouse scenarios. For instance, in streaming processing, it's typical for multiple stream writers to process and write small batches of updates to a "super wide" fact table that consolidates data from numerous streams and may contain hundreds or even thousands of columns. Similarly, in the AI domain, a wide table might store multimodal features sourced from various origins. In such patterns, where numerous updates involve only a small fraction of the total table columns, enabling partial merge is essential. If writing updates with the full schema instead, the efficiency of write, storage, and read operations would be severely degraded.

> Currently, the partial merge feature is only available when using MERGE INTO as the writer. As the project evolves, this powerful feature will be enabled across all sorts of Hudi writers; for example, through the UPDATE SQL command or through the Hudi Streamer introduced in Chapter 8.

Perform Deletion

As a quick recap from Chapter 2, records can be deleted using the DELETE FROM syntax with filtering on either record key fields or other fields:

```
DELETE FROM sensor_data
WHERE id = 'SENSOR_001' AND type = 'HUM' AND ts = 1797649200020; ❶

DELETE FROM sensor_data
WHERE org_id = 'ORG_A'; ❷
```

❶ Delete a specific sensor data record.

❷ Delete all records of organization A.

Delete partitions efficiently

Hudi also supports the ALTER TABLE DROP PARTITION SQL syntax to delete an entire partition:

```
ALTER TABLE sensor_data
DROP PARTITION (org_id = 'ORG_A');
```

This method is considerably more efficient than using DELETE FROM for deleting entire partitions. By leveraging Hudi's timeline and file group design, the operation generates a replacecommit action. This action logically marks all file groups and slices within the target partition as deleted on the timeline, without physically removing the data from storage.

This metadata-only approach is significantly faster and does not interfere with subsequent read or write operations. Data processing engines first consult the timeline, where they will no longer see any data files for the dropped partitions—thanks to the logical segregation achieved through file groups and unique file IDs. The engines then proceed with their tasks as if the partitions were empty.

This also provides a "grace period" for time travel queries (introduced in Chapter 2). Because the timeline retains action timestamps associated with past data files, you can still read records that existed before the partition was dropped. It's important to note, however, that this past data will not be retained indefinitely; it will be permanently removed after a configured period by the cleaning table service, a topic covered in detail in Chapter 6.

Overwrite Partition or Table

Hudi supports inserting a batch of new data and overwriting one or more partitions, or the entire table at the same time. The corresponding write operation types in Hudi are `insert_overwrite` and `insert_overwrite_table`. Using the INSERT OVERWRITE TABLE SQL syntax, you can perform these operations. Here are examples to overwrite specific partitions:

```
INSERT OVERWRITE TABLE sensor_data PARTITION(org_id = 'ORG_A') ❶
SELECT 'SENSOR_003', 'TEMP', 1797649200010, 179764920050, 290.8; ❷

SET hoodie.datasource.write.operation = insert_overwrite; ❸
INSERT OVERWRITE TABLE sensor_data
SELECT
'SENSOR_003', 'TEMP', 1797649200010, 179764920050, 290.8, 'ORG_A'; ❹
```

❶ This explicitly specifies a target partition to be overwritten with the new data.

❷ The partition field value must be omitted as all the records are deemed for the partition specified by the PARTITION clause.

❸ This is the extra Hudi config to instruct INSERT OVERWRITE TABLE to work on affected partitions dynamically.

❹ The partition field values should be included in the source data if the table is partitioned.

For illustration, we have only inserted one record into the target partition. In a practical scenario, you would typically run the SELECT statement against an external table that contains the source data to be inserted. By omitting the PARTITION clause, you can overwrite multiple partitions based on the partition field values of the source data.

To overwrite the whole table, you can set Hudi's write operation to `insert_over write_table`:

```
SET hoodie.datasource.write.operation = insert_overwrite_table; ❶
INSERT OVERWRITE TABLE sensor_data
SELECT 'SENSOR_003', 'TEMP', 1797649200010, 179764920050, 290.8, 'ORG_A';
```

❶ This instructs INSERT OVERWRITE TABLE to truncate the entire table and then insert the new source data.

When the config `hoodie.datasource.write.operation` is set to `insert_overwrite_table`, the INSERT OVERWRITE TABLE command will always replace the *entire table*, regardless of whether you specify a PARTITION clause. You should unset this configuration when you intend to perform a partition-specific overwrite.

When running any of these operations using INSERT OVERWRITE TABLE, whether it works on partitions or on the whole table, Hudi generates a `replacecommit` action on the Hudi timeline, similar to when you delete a partition using ALTER TABLE DROP PARTITION. You can effectively view this action as a series of one or more partition deletes followed by a `bulk_insert`. What will actually happen is that within the same `replacecommit` action, Hudi records which partitions were marked as deleted and which new data files have been written to the table.

The SQL syntax INSERT OVERWRITE is functionally equivalent to INSERT OVERWRITE TABLE, with the latter being more commonly seen in documentation for engines like Spark or Apache Hive. It is important, however, not to confuse these SQL syntaxes with Hudi's write operation types, `insert_overwrite` and `insert_overwrite_table`. Running INSERT OVERWRITE TABLE does not implicitly set the Hudi write operation to `insert_overwrite_table`, and the same applies to running INSERT OVERWRITE.

Highlighting Noteworthy Features

Having covered the internal write flow and demonstrated common write operations using SQL in the previous two sections, we will now turn our attention to additional advanced features. This section highlights three particularly noteworthy capabilities related to writing data to Hudi. For each feature, we will discuss its usage, provide guidance on when to apply it, and explain the specific benefits it offers.

Key Generators

Hudi pioneered the concept of primary keys in lakehouses, a feature long established in traditional databases. The ability to uniquely identify records is fundamental to Hudi's core capabilities, including efficient updates and deletes, high-performance point lookups (Chapter 4), and fast indexing (Chapter 5). As we saw earlier in this chapter, the `HoodieKey` struct represents the unique identifier for a record, containing both the record key and the partition path. Hudi's `KeyGenerator` API serves the purpose of using the original record key and partition path fields (introduced in Chapter 2) to create the `HoodieKey` (see Figure 3-7).

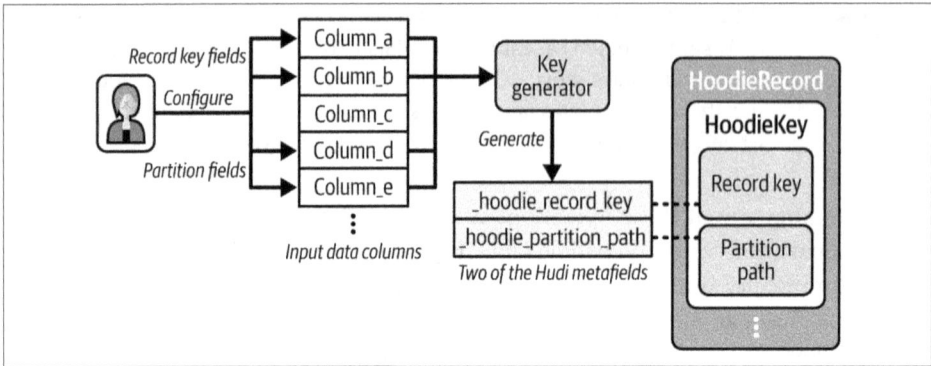

Figure 3-7. Key generation process

Hudi prepends several metafields, all of which are of the string type, to each record in the table to facilitate efficient processing. These include _hoodie_record_key and _hoodie_partition_path, which store the values that constitute the HoodieKey. While the record key and partition field configurations allow Hudi to locate the relevant values within the original input data, these raw values may not always be sufficient to create a globally unique identifier. The KeyGenerator API addresses this by ensuring the HoodieKey correctly functions as a primary key, a crucial capability for Hudi's data management features. It is important to note that the KeyGenerator API consistently returns the record key and partition path values as strings, converting them from their original data types to match the types of their corresponding metafields.

Hudi provides some built-in key generators to handle most common scenarios:

SIMPLE

> This generator is designed for tables with a single record key field and a single partition field.

COMPLEX

> This is used for partitioned tables with one or more record key fields and one or more partition fields. It constructs the record key and partition path by concatenating field names and their corresponding values. It uses a colon (:) to delimit the field name and value, and a comma (,) to separate each field-value pair.

NON_PARTITION

> This is for nonpartitioned tables that have one or more record key fields. It operates similarly to the COMPLEX generator for the record key but always produces an empty string for the partition path, which places all records directly in the table's base path.

TIMESTAMP

An extension of the COMPLEX generator, the TIMESTAMP type is used for partitioned tables where the partition path must be a formatted timestamp string (e.g., a date- or hour-based string). It generates the record key using the COMPLEX logic but formats the partition path according to this key generator's specific timestamp configurations.

CUSTOM

The most flexible of the built-in generators, CUSTOM is ideal for partitioned tables that require advanced transformations. It automatically infers the record key generation logic, applying the SIMPLE strategy for a single record key field and the COMPLEX strategy for multiple fields. Its key advantage is the ability to combine multiple partition path generation strategies. For example, you can configure different transformations for individual partition fields, such as setting hoodie.data source.write.partitionpath.fields=country:SIMPLE,date:TIMESTAMP. This configuration applies SIMPLE logic for the country partition field and TIMESTAMP logic for the date field, resulting in a multilevel partition path.

> You don't need to explicitly set a key generator type in your writer configuration. Hudi automatically infers the appropriate key generator based on the configured values for the record key and partition fields.

For more usage examples of the KeyGenerator APIs, you can refer to the official documentation page (*https://oreil.ly/Eu551*).

All of the CREATE TABLE examples we have seen thus far required you to set the primaryKey to specify the record key fields. However, there are times when the source dataset may not contain a natural primary key field, and you only want to append new data to the table. Hudi addresses this by allowing you to omit the record key configuration, at which point it will automatically generate a globally unique key for each record. This key is constructed using a combination of 1) the write action timestamp, and 2) the sequence numbers of the distributed task and the record within that task.

Returning to the sensor_data example from the "Exploring Write Operations" on page 52, if you do not have corrected data and only need to insert all incoming records as new data, you can define a COW table without specifying record key or ordering fields. In this case, the CREATE TABLE statement can be simplified as follows:

```
CREATE TABLE sensor_data (
    id STRING,
    type STRING,
    ts BIGINT,
```

```
    emit_ts BIGINT,
    value FLOAT,
    org_id STRING
) USING HUDI
PARTITIONED BY (org_id);
```

You can still partition the table based on fields like org_id and leverage the Key Generator API to define the partition paths. While the partition paths will be generated according to the KeyGenerator settings, the record keys will be auto-generated.

Beyond simplifying the table setup, the main advantage of automatic key generation is the ability to efficiently process delete requests. Even if you initially only perform append-only operations for your sensor_data table, you may later be legally required to delete specific records, such as for GDPR compliance. By having properly populated record keys, you can leverage Hudi's efficient write processes to perform these deletions effectively.

Merge Modes

Many real-world data pipelines require record merging to ensure business logic is processed correctly. Hudi features a first-class design for merging mechanics, using *merge mode* to define common semantics and the record merger API for full customization. Record merging in Hudi occurs at multiple stages—record preparation, storage writes, querying (Chapter 4), and compaction (Chapter 6)—with the standardized API ensuring consistent behavior throughout.

Hudi supports two merge modes out of the box, COMMIT_TIME_ORDERING and EVENT_TIME_ORDERING:

COMMIT_TIME_ORDERING
    Merges the records based on arrival order and picks the latest version as the merged result

EVENT_TIME_ORDERING
    Merges the records based on a user-specified ordering field and picks the version with the highest ordering value

The COMMIT_TIME_ORDERING mode is, for instance, suitable for processing database change logs, where the records are in strict order of a logical sequence number (LSN) that denotes the ordering of the writes in the upstream database. The EVENT_TIME_ORDERING mode works for use cases with late-arrival events such as user activities being sent out with delay due to a signal blackout. You can set the hoodie.write.record.merge.mode configuration to pick the right merge mode for your use cases. If you don't set it, COMMIT_TIME_ORDERING will be used if the table has not set any ordering field, and EVENT_TIME_ORDERING will be used for the table that has set one or more ordering fields.

If a full customization of the merging logic is needed, you may implement the record merger API and set these configurations:

```
hoodie.write.record.merge.mode=CUSTOM
hoodie.write.record.merge.custom.implementation.classes=<your implementations>
hoodie.write.record.merge.strategy.id=<ID of the implementation to use>
```

The configurations for a merge mode will be persisted in the table as table properties, and they cannot be altered after the table is created to ensure consistent merging behavior. You may read more about this feature in the documentation page (*https://oreil.ly/yiX0i*).

Schema Evolution on Write

We have been showcasing Hudi's write capabilities using SQL examples, but this is not the only way to write to Hudi tables. Execution engines like Spark or Flink also support programmatic APIs that allow you to write code (e.g., Python or Java) to perform the same operations as SQL. Hudi seamlessly integrates with these programmatic APIs.

Here is an example of using PySpark to upsert records to the `sensor_data` table:

```
columns = ["id", "type", "ts", "emit_ts", "value", "org_id"]
data = [("SENSOR_004", "TEMP",  1797649200050, 1797649200100, 70.1, 'ORG_C')]
df = spark.createDataFrame(data).toDF(*columns)

hudi_options = {
    "hoodie.table.name": "sensor_data",
    "hoodie.datasource.write.recordkey.field", "id,type,ts",
    "hoodie.datasource.write.partitionpath.field": "org_id",
}

df.write.format("hudi"). \
    options(**hudi_options). \
    mode("append"). \
    save(basePath)
```

For the purposes of this section, we do not need to understand every line of this code. The key takeaway is that programmatic APIs offer greater flexibility than SQL. For instance, you can transform the input data using any functions you need, provided the necessary library is installed. This flexibility, however, introduces additional considerations for handling schema evolution during writes.

When using `INSERT INTO`, SQL engines validate that your input data conforms to the schema defined during table creation; missing columns will result in a validation failure. In contrast, with programmatic APIs like the PySpark example, you create a Spark DataFrame where the input records conform to the columns you define. At the API level, there is no inherent validation for mismatches between the input data's schema and the table's schema. This is where Hudi's capabilities become essential, as its table format defines the behavior for handling such schema evolution.

Hudi supports backward-compatible schema evolution, which means the incoming schema can add new columns or promote the data type of an existing column (e.g., from INT to LONG). Although incompatible schema evolution, such as dropping existing columns, is also supported by enabling hoodie.data source.write.schema.allow.auto.evolution.column.drop (which is false by default), this practice is not recommended. It can lead to numerous downstream compatibility issues and migration efforts.

By default, the Hudi writer will fail if the incoming schema is backward incompatible with the latest table schema. To provide more flexibility in handling incoming data, you can set hoodie.write.set.null.for.missing.columns to true. This triggers a reconciliation process between the incoming and existing schemas, which works as follows:

- Any new columns in the incoming schema are added to the table's schema.
- Any columns present in the table's schema but missing from the incoming schema are populated with null values for the incoming records.
- Any matching columns where the incoming type is a promoted version of the table's type (e.g., incoming LONG versus table INT) will cause the table's schema to be promoted to the new type.

This reconciliation process allows Hudi tables to gracefully handle schema mismatches, preserving backward compatibility for downstream pipelines.

> The Hudi project is constantly evolving. While the principle of recommending backward-compatible changes remains consistent, there are many nuances to how schema evolution is handled. It is recommended to consult the latest official documentation page for the full list of cases (*https://oreil.ly/gfH7s*).

Bootstrapping

Imagine you have a large dataset of plain Parquet files in a cloud storage service (e.g., Amazon S3), partitioned by specific fields. You want to import this dataset into a new Hudi table in a new directory and preserve the exact same records so that you can leverage Hudi's advantages like efficient upsert or incremental queries. The most intuitive approach would be to load the Parquet files using Spark and then perform a bulk_insert into a new Hudi table, which the CREATE TABLE AS SELECT example from Chapter 2 demonstrates. However, for a huge data volume, this approach can be time-consuming and costly, as it requires nontrivial operational effort, such as scaling out a properly sized cluster, and results in numerous data read and write operations that can lead to high cloud bills.

The Hudi `bootstrap` operation is designed to make this import process more efficient in terms of both time and cost. A high-level overview is depicted in Figure 3-8.

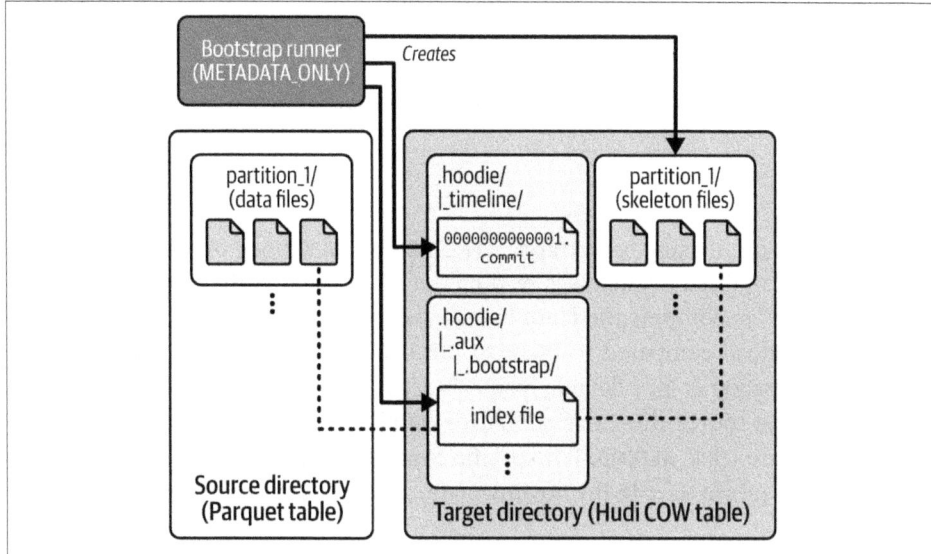

Figure 3-8. METADATA_ONLY bootstrap process

The METADATA_ONLY bootstrap process follows these three main steps:

1. A bootstrap runner reads a source directory of Parquet files to bootstrap a new Hudi table at a target directory. For each source file, it creates a "skeleton" file that contains only Hudi's metafields, such as _hoodie_record_key and _hoodie_partition_path, which are derived from the original records based on write configurations.

2. The runner creates bootstrap index files, stored under *.hoodie/.aux/.bootstrap/*, that map the skeleton files to their corresponding source data files. These index files are a key component, enabling subsequent Hudi writers and readers to "stitch" the metafield values from the skeleton files with the original records. This allows the skeleton files to be treated as normal base files within file groups.

3. The `bootstrap` operation is a transactional write action, recorded on the table's timeline. As it is the first write operation for a table, a special action timestamp is reserved. For METADATA_ONLY bootstrapping, the action timestamp is always 00000000000001.

Another mode of the `bootstrap` operation is called `FULL_RECORD`, which is essentially a bulk insert. It reads the original data and writes it to the target table, with the write action recorded on the timeline with the timestamp `00000000000002`.

Once a table has been bootstrapped, it functions as a normal Hudi table. Subsequent writes will be performed on the target table, leaving the source directory untouched.

> The feature of doing partial merge as introduced earlier in this chapter is not yet supported for bootstrapped tables.

The key advantage of using bootstrap is its `METADATA_ONLY` mode. As you can see, creating the skeleton files only involves reading a small fraction of the original data—the columns needed to compute the Hudi metafields—which drastically reduces the read and write workload compared to the `FULL_RECORD` or a standard `bulk_insert`. The `bootstrap` operation is also flexible; you can use regular expressions to select which partitions in the source directory should be handled by `METADATA_ONLY` mode and which should use `FULL_RECORD`. For specific commands and the full list of bootstrap configurations, please refer to the documentation (*https://oreil.ly/JlUZR*).

Summary

This chapter provided a comprehensive exploration of Hudi's write capabilities, covering both the internal mechanics and practical applications of writing data to Hudi tables. The knowledge presented serves as a foundation for building efficient and reliable data lakehouse pipelines.

Hudi's write flow follows a systematic five-step process: initiating commits, preparing records with optional duplicates merging and indexing steps, partitioning data for distributed processing, writing to storage through specialized write handles, and finalizing commits on the timeline. This structured approach ensures data consistency and enables Hudi's core capabilities, such as efficient updates and deletes.

Hudi offers a variety of write operations:

- The `insert` operation appends new data with small-file handling, ideal for incremental batch processing.

- The `bulk_insert` operation handles large-volume data loads efficiently through repartitioning strategies, perfect for initial data bootstrapping.

- The `upsert` operation combines inserts and updates in a single operation, automatically handling both new and existing records, and also leveraging small-file handling to optimize file sizes.

- Using `MERGE INTO` to leverage the partial merge feature significantly improves your Hudi table's efficiency in write, read, and storage.

- Using `DELETE FROM` is good for record-level deletions, and `ALTER TABLE DROP PARTITION` is ideal for efficient partition deletes.

- The `insert_overwrite` and `insert_overwrite_table` operations combine the efficiency of partition deletion and bulk insert to realize efficient data overwrite.

Understanding when to use each operation type is crucial for optimal performance and storage efficiency.

Hudi provides several powerful features that enhance write operations:

- Key generators create unique record identifiers from your data fields, with built-in options to handle single or multiple record key and partition fields, plus automatic key generation for append-only tables.

- Merge modes support common ordering semantics and fully customizable merging logic to facilitate consistent and efficient merging processes.

- Schema evolution allows tables to adapt to changing data structures over time, supporting backward-compatible changes like adding columns and promoting data types without breaking existing pipelines.

- Bootstrapping enables efficient migration of existing datasets into Hudi tables by creating metadata-only references to original files, dramatically reducing time and cost compared to full data rewrites.

By mastering the concepts in this chapter—from understanding the write flow and selecting the right operation to leveraging Hudi's advanced features—you are now fully equipped to build efficient and reliable data lakehouse pipelines tailored to your specific needs.

## CHAPTER 4

Reading from Hudi

The ability to efficiently read and query data is the ultimate purpose of any data lakehouse, directly impacting the speed and flexibility of analytics and machine learning. A deep understanding of Hudi's read-side capabilities—and how they integrate with various query engines—is therefore paramount for building a performant and reliable data platform. Building upon the foundational concepts of table layouts from Chapter 2 and the write operations we explored in Chapter 3, this chapter combines technical deep dives and practical examples, serving as your definitive guide to reading data from Apache Hudi.

This chapter is organized into three sections to provide a comprehensive exploration of Hudi's read capabilities. *"Integrating with Query Engines"* explains how popular query engines interact with Hudi. We will introduce the Hudi read flow, discuss the integration mechanisms for seamless and efficient querying of your Hudi tables, and examine the role of data catalogs in this process.

To ground our discussion in practical application, "Exploring Query Types" showcases Hudi's diverse read capabilities with examples. We will explore different query types and discuss the related behaviors and configuration options that enable you to solve a wide range of analytical challenges.

The flexibility and power of Hudi's read operations are enhanced by several important features designed for advanced data lakehouse patterns. "Highlighting Noteworthy Features" will explore these more involved features and designs.

By completing this chapter, you will be able to effectively read data from Hudi. You will gain a clear understanding of the read flow, learn how to apply various query types for different scenarios, and know how to use advanced features to architect an efficient and reliable data platform for your downstream applications.

Integrating with Query Engines

In a data lakehouse architecture, the query engine is the computational powerhouse responsible for processing user queries against data stored in the lakehouse. Think of it as a master librarian for your data. It interprets your requests—typically expressed in SQL—and efficiently retrieves the precise information you need from the vast archives of your storage layer (like Amazon S3, GCS, or HDFS). Engines such as Apache Spark, Presto, and Trino are the workhorses that provide the APIs and distributed execution capabilities to read, process, and return data from tables. They effectively decouple the compute layer from the storage layer, providing the flexibility to choose the right tool for your specific analytical needs.

Query Lifecycle

To appreciate how Hudi integrates with query engines, it's helpful to first understand the typical lifecycle of a query. While specific implementations vary between engines like Spark or Trino, they all follow a similar multiphase process to transform a user's SQL statement into a result set. This process ensures that the query is not only understood correctly but also executed in the most efficient way possible across a distributed cluster. Let's walk through the key phases of this lifecycle, shown in Figure 4-1.

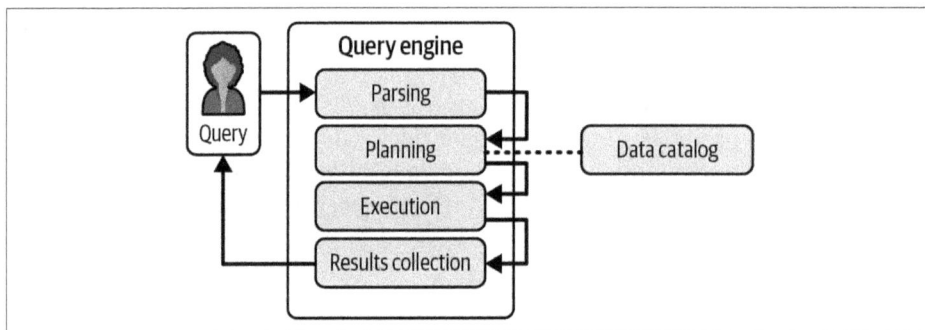

Figure 4-1. Query lifecycle in a distributed query engine

The journey begins when a user submits a query, most commonly through a SQL statement. The query engine's first task is *parsing*, where it breaks down the SQL string to verify its syntax and structure. It identifies the distinct components of the query—such as the SELECT columns, FROM table, and WHERE clause predicates—and organizes them into a logical representation, often called an abstract syntax tree (AST).

Next comes the crucial *planning* phase, which is typically split into two steps. First, in logical planning, the engine takes the parsed table and database names and consults a central data catalog (e.g., Apache Hive Metastore or AWS Glue). This catalog provides vital metadata about the table, including its storage location, data format (e.g., Apache Parquet), schema, and partitioning details. Using this information, the engine builds a logical plan—a high-level, abstract recipe for fetching the data. Following this, the engine performs physical planning. The query optimizer evaluates various strategies for executing the logical plan, such as different join algorithms or filter pushdown opportunities, and selects the most efficient physical plan based on a cost model. The output is a highly optimized execution plan, often represented as a directed acyclic graph (DAG), that details the exact sequence of operations to be performed.

With a plan in hand, the engine moves to the *execution* phase. It translates the physical plan into concrete tasks that are distributed across the physical resources of the cluster. Worker nodes execute these tasks in parallel, reading the necessary data files from the underlying storage concurrently.

Finally, in the *results collection* phase, the partial results computed by each worker node are gathered and aggregated by a central coordinator or driver node. After any final processing, the complete result set is returned to the user, concluding the query lifecycle.

Data Catalog

In the context of a data lakehouse, a data catalog is a centralized metadata management service that acts as an inventory of all your data assets. It is the linchpin that connects query engines to the underlying data, making the data discoverable and queryable. By maintaining a registry of tables, schemas, partitions, and file locations, the catalog provides the critical information that query engines need during the planning phase of the query lifecycle.

A data catalog is indispensable for organizing the vast number of tables in a modern data lakehouse. It allows users to search for tables and browse metadata, such as schemas and column descriptions, to understand the datasets available within their own teams or across the organization. This capability serves two primary, complementary functions: it provides a technical registry for developers and data scientists to discover and access datasets, while also offering a business-centric platform for governance, security, and comprehensive data management.

In practice, many organizations operate a federated ecosystem of catalogs. This often includes technical catalogs, such as Hive Metastore, AWS Glue, Databricks Unity Catalog, and Apache Polaris Catalog, which are tightly integrated with the data platform's execution engines. Complementing these are specialized data governance and metadata management catalogs—like DataHub, Alation, Atlan, and Collibra—that offer advanced capabilities such as schema evolution tracking, data lineage, and data quality profiling. Together, these tools facilitate robust governance and ensure data reliability and consistency across a diverse landscape.

Hudi supports seamless integration with multiple data catalogs (a topic we will discuss in detail in Chapter 9). The key takeaway here is that by registering your Hudi tables with a data catalog, you enable query engines to connect to it, fetch the necessary metadata, and efficiently execute the query planning phase.

Although a data catalog is not a strict prerequisite for querying Hudi tables—you can always use the programmatic APIs offered by engines like Spark or Apache Flink to read a table from its storage location directly—it is far more common to establish a central catalog for your data lakehouse. This approach unlocks the benefits of data discovery and governance and, importantly, allows you to leverage the power and expressiveness of SQL, the lingua franca of data analytics. For this reason, the examples throughout the rest of this chapter will use SQL to demonstrate Hudi's read capabilities.

Hudi Integration

Now that we have a clear picture of the standard query lifecycle, we can examine how Hudi fits into this process. Hudi's integration with query engines is not about replacing this lifecycle but enhancing it. By providing specialized connectors and logic, Hudi injects its own intelligence into the planning and execution phases, enabling engines to efficiently navigate its unique file layout and transactional guarantees. This ensures that queries on Hudi tables are both fast and accurate.

As illustrated in Figure 4-2, Hudi's deep integration with query engines occurs primarily during the planning and execution phases. This is made possible through engine-specific artifacts, such as the hudi-spark-bundle for Spark or the dedicated connectors for Presto and Trino. The integration acts as a bridge between the query engine's generic processing logic and Hudi's specific storage format.

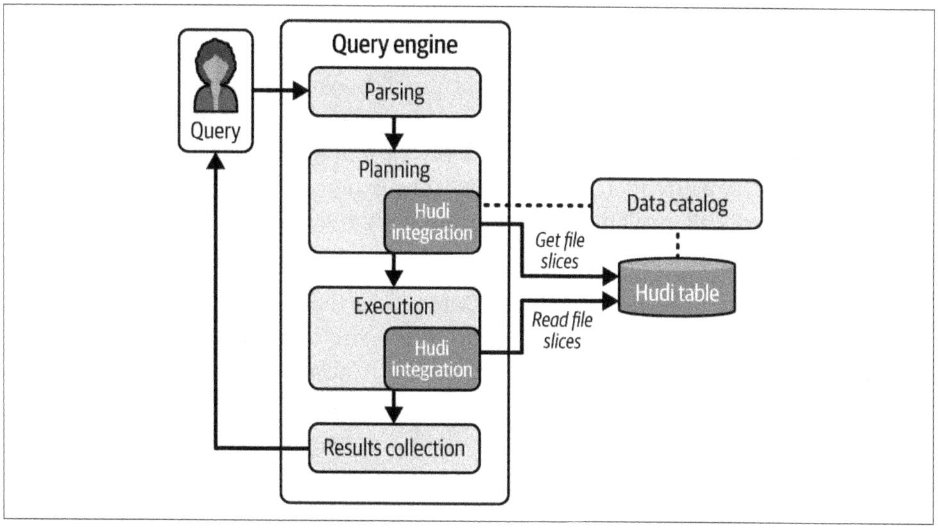

Figure 4-2. Hudi integration in the query engine read flow

Get pruned file slices

During the planning phase, the Hudi integration is responsible for a critical optimization: identifying the minimal set of file slices required to satisfy the query. This is achieved through the coordinated work of an index reader and a timeline reader (see Figure 4-3).

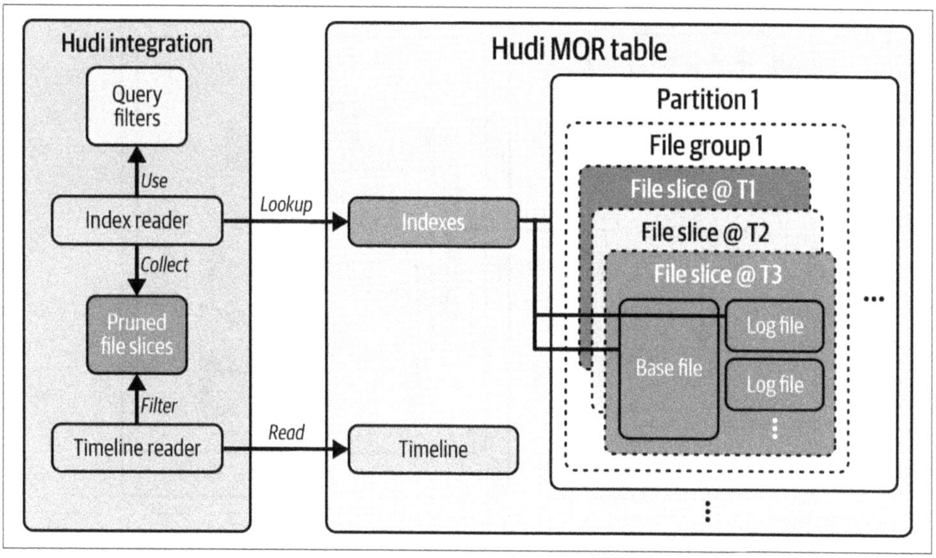

Figure 4-3. Getting pruned file slices in the planning phase

The *index reader* uses the query's filter predicates to perform data skipping. It queries the indexes stored in the metadata table, an indexing subsystem within the Hudi table, to find only the file slices that could possibly contain the requested records. The metadata table provides powerful indexing capabilities and can efficiently prune both partitions and individual files based on various filter types, including range comparisons and equality matches—a topic to be explored deeply in Chapter 5. This lookup process uses all available filters to drastically reduce the number of candidate file slices.

The *timeline reader* loads the timeline instants to further refine this list. For a time travel query, for instance, the timeline reader uses the target timestamp to find the closest file slices created earlier than that point. It also filters out those file slices that have been rewritten by a `replacecommit` action (such as an INSERT OVERWRITE operation, introduced in Chapter 3), provided that `replacecommit` is in the target timestamp range for the query. Overall, these steps produce a list of pruned file slices to be processed in the next phase.

Read file slices efficiently

In the subsequent execution phase, the query engine distributes the task of reading these identified file slices across its worker nodes. As records are read from the files by a file group reader, the engine applies any applicable row-level filters and performs column projections to select only the requested fields (see Figure 4-4).

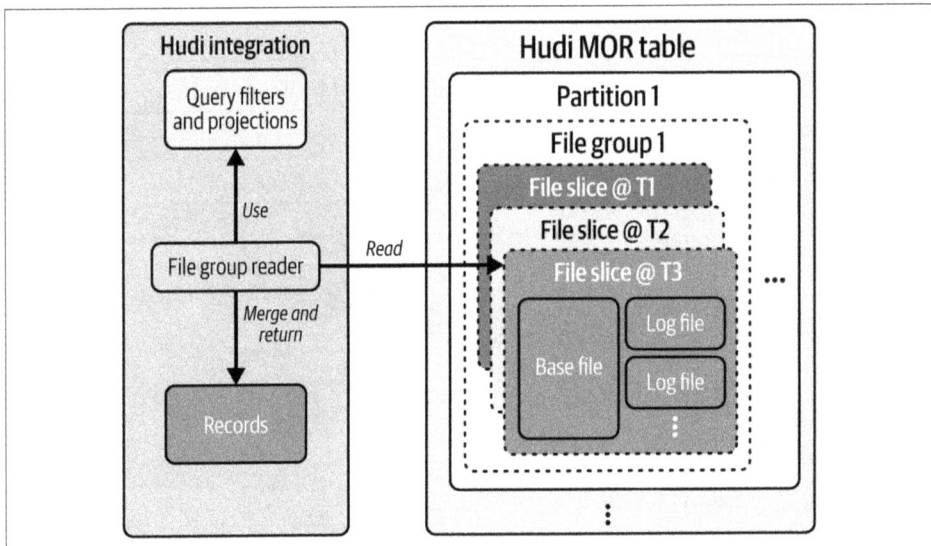

Figure 4-4. Reading a file slice in the execution phase

Reading a file slice is straightforward when it only consists of a base file, which is always the case for Copy-on-Write (COW) tables. For Merge-on-Read (MOR) tables, however, a file slice may also contain several log files holding new or updated records. In these situations, the file group reader uses the configured merge mode (introduced in Chapter 3) for the table to merge records from the log files with those in the base file on the fly. This highly optimized merge process ensures that the query engine can efficiently receive and return the correct version of each record from the target file slices.

In summary, Hudi's integration with query engines enhances the standard query lifecycle. By injecting its logic into the planning and execution phases, Hudi ensures that queries are highly optimized, leveraging its indexing capabilities for efficient data pruning, and timeline filtering based on transaction boundaries for data consistency. This seamless integration is what allows users to query Hudi tables with ease and performance.

With this foundational understanding of how Hudi and query engines work together, we can now shift our focus to the different types of queries that Hudi supports, each designed to address specific analytical needs.

Exploring Query Types

To make the concepts in this chapter more tangible, we will use a running example centered on a fictional ridesharing company called LetsMotor. Initially founded to help city dwellers hire drivers for short-to-mid-distance travel, LetsMotor has since expanded its services and, consequently, its data needs. Throughout this section, we will work with one of its core Hudi tables, trips. This table contains detailed customer trip records, with attributes such as a unique trip identifier, trip start timestamp, fare, rider, trip record update timestamp, and driver names, and the city where the ride was initiated.

Let's first set up the table:

```
CREATE TABLE trips (
    uuid STRING,
    start_ts BIGINT,
    rider STRING,
    driver STRING,
    fare DOUBLE,
    update_ts BIGINT,
    city STRING
) USING HUDI
TBLPROPERTIES(
    type = 'mor',
    primaryKey = 'uuid',
    preCombineField = 'update_ts'
```

```
)
PARTITIONED BY (city);
```

And insert some sample data:

```
INSERT INTO trips VALUES
('ride-001', 1672531200, 'rider-A', 'driver-1', 15.75, 1672531260, 'SF'),
('ride-002', 1672534800, 'rider-B', 'driver-2', 22.50, 1672534860, 'NYC'),
('ride-003', 1672538400, 'rider-C', 'driver-3', 8.25,  1672538480, 'SF'),
('ride-004', 1672542000, 'rider-D', 'driver-4', 31.80, 1672542120, 'LA'),
('ride-005', 1672545600, 'rider-E', 'driver-5', 12.40, 1672545720, 'SEA');
```

Given the high volume of data writes and updates on the LetsMotor platform, the MOR table type is a more suitable choice. The query types we will discuss in the following sections are applicable to both MOR and COW table types, and their behavior is consistent regardless of which type you're using.

Snapshot Query

A *snapshot query* is the default query type when reading Hudi tables. As its name suggests, it provides a snapshot of the table's data as of the latest commit. This type of query is used to read the most up-to-date committed data, and it can be achieved with a standard SELECT SQL statement:

```
SELECT rider, driver, fare, city
FROM trips
WHERE fare > 20;
```

As discussed in Chapter 2 on table type trade-offs, a snapshot query on an MOR table takes longer to complete compared to a COW table when log files are present. This is because the query engine must perform an on-the-fly merge of the base files and log files to provide the most current data.

If you require optimal query performance and are willing to sacrifice some data freshness, you can still use an MOR table for its fast ingestion capabilities by running a read optimized query. To do this, simply set the following configuration before running your SELECT statement:

```
SET hoodie.datasource.query.type=read_optimized
```

This MOR-only setting instructs the query engine to read only the base files and skip the merging of recent updates from the log files. While this can speed up queries to a level comparable with COW tables, it is important to remember that the results will not include the most recent records from the log files.

To use read-optimized queries, you should also consider running the compaction table service (covered in Chapter 6). This service merges log files with base files and produces new base files, allowing read-optimized queries to return more-recent data. Using a targeted strategy, you can run compaction specifically on partitions that are queried most frequently.

Time Travel Query

While we briefly touched upon the time travel query in Chapter 2, let's now take a closer look. Consider a scenario where we need to update a record in the trips table to adjust the fare due to a promotion. We can specifically update that record using the following SQL statement:

```
UPDATE trips
SET fare = fare - 5,
    update_ts = unix_timestamp()
WHERE uuid = 'ride-002';
```

The finance team at LetsMotor may need to run analytical queries on the fare data *before* this promotion was applied. A time travel query is perfect for this use case. By using the TIMESTAMP AS OF clause, you can retrieve the record's value from a specific point in time:

```
SELECT rider, driver, fare, city
FROM trips TIMESTAMP AS OF '202301010091628123' ❶
WHERE uuid = 'ride-002';
```

❶ A timestamp in the form of the Hudi timeline timestamp format yyyyMMddHHmmssSSS

By providing a timestamp with the query, users can effectively travel back in time to retrieve the table's state at that specific moment. Internally, the Hudi timeline reader compares the provided timestamp against the table's timeline to find either an exact match or the closest earlier commit. The reader then uses the timestamp from this found commit to filter out any file slices created after that point, thereby reconstructing the table's historical snapshot. If the specified timestamp precedes the first commit on the timeline, the query will yield no results. Conversely, if the timestamp is more recent than the latest commit, the query will simply return the most current snapshot of the data.

You can think of the snapshot query as a special case of the time travel query, where the query timestamp always points to the latest commit on the Hudi timeline.

For ease of use, Hudi time travel queries support other common standard timestamp formats like:

```
SELECT * FROM trips
TIMESTAMP AS OF '2023-01-01 09:16:28.123' ❶
WHERE uuid = 'ride-002';

SELECT * FROM trips
TIMESTAMP AS OF '2023-01-01' ❷
WHERE uuid = 'ride-002';
```

❶ Time travel query using the yyyy-MM-dd HH:mm:ss.SSS format

❷ Time travel query using the yyyy-MM-dd format

Time travel queries are useful for many downstream analytics use cases like compliance audits, as well as for internal data debugging and troubleshooting.

Incremental Query: The Latest-State Mode

A common use case for Hudi is to power multistage data pipelines, where data is progressively transformed and normalized as it moves from its raw state to a more refined one. Consider the platform team at LetsMotor, which needed to model how trips data moves through such a pipeline.

Before adopting Hudi, the team's process was highly inefficient. At each stage, its ETL jobs had to reprocess the entire dataset from the previous stage. This brute-force approach was necessary because, in a traditional data lake, there was no straightforward way to identify which specific records had been added or changed since the last processing run.

Hudi's incremental queries fundamentally solve this problem. By providing a view of only the records that have changed between two points in time, Hudi allows the team to build highly efficient pipelines that process only the delta, significantly speeding up downstream processing.

This is the primary use case for an incremental query in its default *latest-state mode*. Given a start and end commit time, this query will return the complete and most up-to-date record for every key that was inserted or updated within that time window. It effectively answers the question: "What is the latest state of all the records that changed since I last checked?"

Record-level change tracking

So, how does Hudi efficiently isolate just the changed records? The process involves a two-phase filtering mechanism. First, much like a time travel query, an incremental query filters file slices based on time. However, instead of using a single timestamp,

---

it uses the specified time range to select all file slices that were created within that window.

This initial pass is not sufficient on its own. A single base file can contain records associated with many different commits, especially when older data is carried over into new file slices during write operations. To ensure precision, Hudi performs a second filtering pass at the record level during the execution phase. This is where Hudi's metafields become crucial. In Chapter 3, we introduced _hoodie_record_key and _hoodie_partition_path. For incremental queries, a third metafield, _hoodie_commit_time, plays the key role. This field, embedded within every record, stores the timestamp of the commit that last modified it. As the query engine scans the data files, it uses this field to select only those records whose commit time falls within the target time window. For MOR tables, Hudi's log files also encode this commit time information within their metadata blocks, serving the same filtering purpose.

The parameters

Here's a SQL template of an incremental query that the platform team at LetsMotor can use to figure out which updates need to be applied to downstream views of the data:

```
SELECT * FROM
    hudi_table_changes(table or path, query_type, start_time [, end_time]);
```

This table-valued function takes four parameters, which are detailed in Table 4-1.

Table 4-1. Parameters of the table-valued function for incremental query

Parameter name	Description	Notes
table or path	Table identifier or the base path to the table.	If it's a table identifier, it'll usually be in the form *<database name>.<table name>*. If it's a path, it'll be the storage system's absolute path.
query_type	The incremental query mode to use.	The valid value is latest_state or cdc. The cdc mode will be discussed in the next section.
start_time	The timestamp used to mark the incremental change window's start (exclusive).	The valid value is earliest or a supported timestamp format. The earliest value denotes the earliest available commit timestamp from the timeline. The supported timestamp format is the Hudi timeline's timestamp format yyyyMMddHHmmssSSS.
end_time	The timestamp used to mark the incremental change window's end (inclusive). This is an optional parameter.	When end_time is omitted, the function returns the changes up to the latest commit (inclusive) in the timeline.

To get the latest state of all records changed since the beginning of the table's history, you can specify 'earliest' as the start time and omit the end time. This query is equivalent to running a snapshot query on the table's current state:

```
SELECT * FROM hudi_table_changes('trips', 'latest_state', 'earliest');
```

Now, let's say we have detected a data issue with a batch of updates applied after 2024-05-19, and we want to see the state of the table before those changes. The following query retrieves the latest state of all records committed since the beginning and up to the 2024-05-19 start (0 o'clock, inclusive), effectively performing a time travel query to that specific point in time:

```
SELECT * FROM hudi_table_changes(
  'trips', 'latest_state', 'earliest', '20240519000000000'
); ❶
```

❶ Return the states of the changed records starting from the earliest and ending at 2024-05-19 0 o'clock (inclusive). The states correspond to 2024-05-19 0 o'clock.

We can also isolate the changes to a certain time window. The following query retrieves the latest state of all records that were updated from 2024-05-18 start (0 o'clock, exclusive) up to 2024-05-19 start (0 o'clock, inclusive):

```
SELECT * FROM hudi_table_changes(
  'trips', 'latest_state', '20240518000000000', '20240519000000000'
); ❶
```

❶ Return the states of the changed records starting from 2024-05-18 (0 o'clock exclusive) and ending at 2024-05-19 0 o'clock (inclusive). The states correspond to 2024-05-19 0 o'clock.

Incremental Query: The Change Data Capture Mode

While the latest-state mode is excellent for propagating the final state of records, some use cases require a deeper understanding of *how* the data changed. Consider LetsMotor's real-time driver leaderboard. A trip's rating or tip amount can be updated long after the trip is complete. To keep the leaderboard accurate, a downstream process needs to know the exact nature of each modification. For example, it must distinguish between a newly added tip, a correction to an existing one, or a deletion of an invalid trip record—details that the latest-state mode cannot provide.

Those are perfect scenarios for change data capture (CDC). In Hudi, you can enable CDC mode for incremental queries to get a richly detailed log of all record-level changes. Instead of just returning the latest state, a CDC query provides the operation type (`insert`, `update`, `delete`) for each change. Furthermore, for updates, it provides both the "before" and "after" images of the record, giving you the complete context of the modification (see Figure 4-5). This granular insight is invaluable for building sophisticated downstream applications that need to react to specific data transformations.

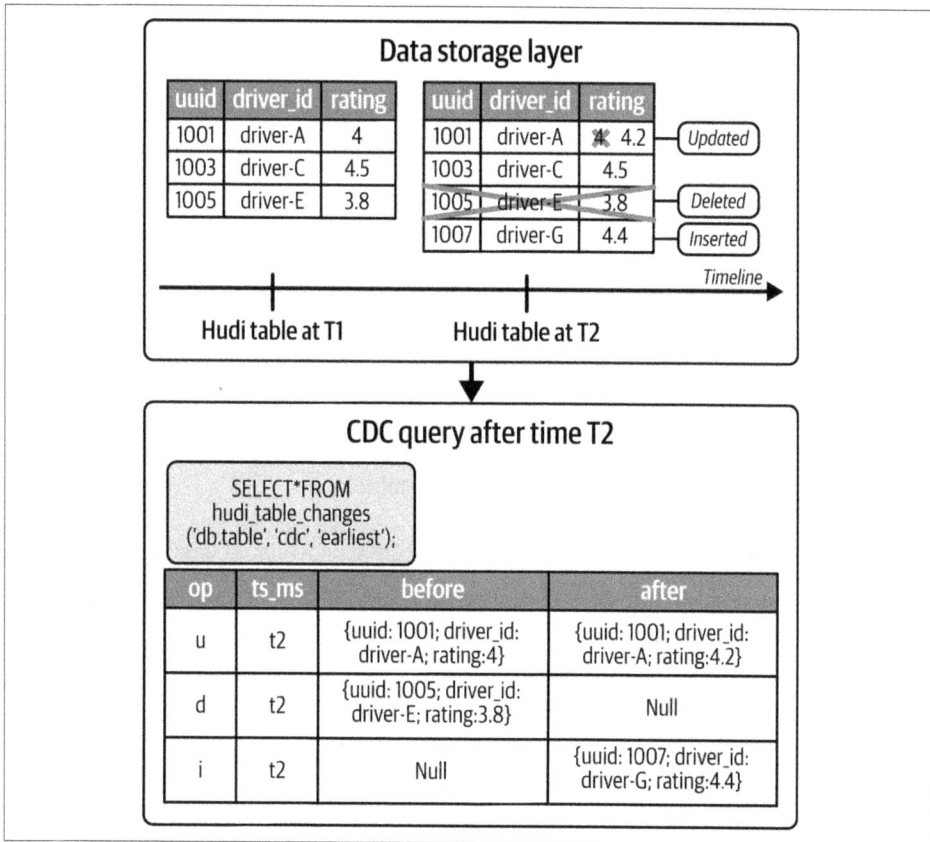

Data storage layer

uuid	driver_id	rating
1001	driver-A	4
1003	driver-C	4.5
1005	driver-E	3.8

uuid	driver_id	rating	
1001	driver-A	4.2	Updated
1003	driver-C	4.5	
1005	driver-E	3.8	Deleted
1007	driver-G	4.4	Inserted

Timeline →

Hudi table at T1   Hudi table at T2

CDC query after time T2

```
SELECT*FROM
hudi_table_changes
('db.table', 'cdc', 'earliest');
```

op	ts_ms	before	after
u	t2	{uuid: 1001; driver_id: driver-A; rating:4}	{uuid: 1001; driver_id: driver-A; rating:4.2}
d	t2	{uuid: 1005; driver_id: driver-E; rating:3.8}	Null
i	t2	Null	{uuid: 1007; driver_id: driver-G; rating:4.4}

Figure 4-5. Typical CDC scenario

Figure 4-5 illustrates two snapshots of a Hudi table at times t1 and t2. Between these two timestamps, one record is inserted, another is updated, and a third is deleted. An incremental query in CDC mode for this time window will return a detailed log of these operations. The returned records contain an operation type column op that can be i for insert, u for update, or d for delete to indicate the types of changes happened. For insert, the before column will be null, and the after column will contain the inserted record. For update, the before column will contain the version of the record before the update, and the after column will contain the updated record. For delete, the before column will contain the version of the record before the delete, and the after column will be null, indicating the deletion.

To enable CDC queries, you must first activate the feature at the table level. This is done using two key table properties, as shown in the following example for creating a new trips table:

```
CREATE TABLE trips (
    uuid STRING,
    start_ts BIGINT,
    rider STRING,
    driver STRING,
    fare DOUBLE,
    update_ts BIGINT,
    city STRING
) USING HUDI
TBLPROPERTIES(
    primaryKey = 'uuid',
    preCombineField = 'update_ts',
    'hoodie.table.cdc.enabled' = 'true', ❶
    'hoodie.table.cdc.supplemental.logging.mode' = 'OP_KEY_ONLY' ❷
)
PARTITIONED BY (city);
```

❶ This option enables the CDC feature for the table.

❷ This option sets the logging mode for persisting CDC-related data.

Once CDC is enabled, Hudi writers will begin generating CDC log files (with a *.cdc* suffix) alongside the base files and regular log files within each file group. These specialized files record detailed information about the changes made during each write operation, which query engines can then read and interpret.

The configuration `hoodie.table.cdc.supplemental.logging.mode` controls the content of the CDC data logged. Table 4-2 describes each mode's behaviors.

Table 4-2. Supplemental logging modes for using CDC in Hudi

CDC logging mode	Description
OP_KEY_ONLY	The CDC log files store only the changed record keys and the corresponding operations.
DATA_BEFORE	The CDC log files store the full changed records before the change, and the corresponding operations.
DATA_BEFORE_AFTER	The CDC log files store the full changed records before *and* after the change, and the corresponding operations. This is the default mode.

As the table indicates, OP_KEY_ONLY is the most storage-efficient option. This means that it requires the query engine to perform additional lookups to reconstruct the full before and after images. In contrast, DATA_BEFORE_AFTER maximizes query performance by logging both images directly, albeit at a higher storage cost. DATA_BEFORE offers a balance between these two extremes. The choice of logging mode, therefore, represents a direct trade-off between storage overhead and CDC query performance.

It is critical to understand that both `hoodie.table.cdc.enabled`
and `hoodie.table.cdc.supplemental.logging.mode` are perma-
nent, table-level configurations. Once set for a table, they cannot be
changed or disabled.

After configuring your table for CDC, querying the change stream uses the same
`hudi_table_changes` function we introduced previously for the `latest-state` mode.
The only difference is setting the second query parameter to `cdc`.

Highlighting Noteworthy Features

Having explored multiple types of queries, we've seen how Hudi supports several key
analytical read needs. We will now turn our attention to three additional read-related
features, providing insights on their use cases and benefits.

Streaming Read

Hudi's timeline is the core component that enables its powerful incremental processing capabilities, making it a natural fit for streaming read patterns. In essence, a
streaming read involves processing data in small, continuous batches based on offsets
in the source. This model aligns perfectly with Hudi's incremental query mechanism,
which leverages action timestamps on the timeline to fetch only the data that has
changed since the last read.

Out of the box, Hudi provides robust integrations with leading stream processing frameworks, most notably Spark' Structured Streaming and Flink, which were
designed with a streaming-first philosophy. This native support simplifies the development of real-time data pipelines. To illustrate, let's consider how to implement a
streaming read using PySpark:

```
from pyspark.sql import functions as F

base_path = "/base/path/to/the/table"

def func(batch_df, batch_id):
    # Simple aggregation logic - return the aggregated DataFrame
    return batch_df.groupBy("column_name") \
        .agg(
            F.count("*").alias("record_count"),
            F.sum("numeric_column").alias("total_amount"),
            F.avg("numeric_column").alias("avg_amount"),
            F.max("timestamp_column").alias("max_timestamp")
        )

spark.readStream.format("hudi") \
    .option("hoodie.datasource.query.type", "incremental") \
    .option("hoodie.datasource.query.incremental.format", "cdc") \
```

```
    .load(base_path) \
    .writeStream.format("console") \
    .foreachBatch(func) \
    .start()
```

The example demonstrates a common use case: performing a continuous CDC incremental query on a CDC-enabled Hudi table. In this code example, we set up a streaming source that reads incrementally from the Hudi table, performs an aggregation on each microbatch of changes, and prints the results to the console. You don't need to explicitly set the start and end timestamps for the incremental query here, as Hudi internally manages them for the continuous query execution.

While this example simply prints the output, a more practical application would be to write the transformed stream to another Hudi table, forming a chain of streaming transformations. This ability to daisy-chain streaming jobs allows for the creation of sophisticated multistage data pipelines. Hudi's fundamental design, which combines a detailed timeline for tracking changes with the MOR table type's ability to absorb high-throughput writes, makes it an excellent foundation for modern streaming architectures. To see more examples, please check out the documentation page (*https://oreil.ly/b-cfD*) for streaming read.

Schema Evolution on Read

In Chapter 3, we discussed schema evolution on write, which handles schema mismatches while ensuring backward compatibility. However, data systems are dynamic, and there are scenarios where more-drastic, backward-incompatible schema changes are necessary. For example, you might need to rename, delete, modify, or even move columns, including those nested within complex types.

Hudi addresses this need with *schema evolution on read*. By enabling the configuration hoodie.schema.on.read.enable=true, you can perform these complex schema alterations without rewriting the underlying data. Let's examine what happens when you rename a column using an ALTER TABLE command with this feature enabled:

```
SET hoodie.schema.on.read.enable=true;
ALTER TABLE trips RENAME COLUMN driver TO driver_id;
```

Instead of launching a massive data rewriting job, Hudi performs an alter_schema operation, which creates a special *.schemacommit* file in the *.hoodie/.schema/* directory. This file acts as a ledger. It assigns a unique ID to each column in the original schema and then records the change—in this case, the new name for the corresponding column ID.

When a query engine reads the table, it sees the new schema. However, the underlying base files and log files still contain data written with the old schema. Hudi bridges this gap by using the information in the *.schemacommit* file to map the new schema back to the old one at read time. This metadata-only approach is efficient, avoiding costly data migration.

> While powerful, using ALTER TABLE to make backward-incompatible changes carries significant operational risks. Because the command permanently modifies the table schema, you are responsible for ensuring that all upstream writers and downstream readers can handle the new structure. For instance, if you drop a column, an existing write job still producing records with the old schema will likely fail. Similarly, if another team relies on the previous schema for a dashboard, you must coordinate with that team to prevent its reports from breaking. Given these practical challenges, Hudi does not recommend making backward-incompatible changes unless absolutely necessary.

Hudi also supports other incompatible changes, like dropping a column, changing a column's data type, and reordering columns. For a comprehensive list of supported operations and more examples, we recommend consulting the documentation page (*https://oreil.ly/gfH7s*).

Read Using Rust or Python

Although Hudi began its journey in the JVM world, with deep integrations into JVM-based engines like Spark and Flink, its ecosystem is rapidly expanding. To support native integration with non-JVM frameworks, the community has introduced Hudi-rs (*https://oreil.ly/Yfkck*), a new implementation written in Rust.

The goal of Hudi-rs is to standardize core Hudi APIs and broaden its adoption across a more diverse range of data systems. Implemented in Rust and providing Python language bindings, Hudi-rs allows engines from the Rust and Python ecosystems to work with Hudi tables natively. This initiative has already led to integrations with modern data frameworks like Ray and Daft.

For example, you can now run a snapshot query on a Hudi table directly with the Rust-based query engine Apache DataFusion, as shown in the following code snippet:

```
let ctx = SessionContext::new();
let hudi = HudiDataSource::new("/base/path/to/the/table").await?;
ctx.register_table("trips", Arc::new(hudi))?;
let df: DataFrame = ctx.sql("SELECT * from trips where city = 'SF'").await?;
df.show().await?;
```

Currently, Hudi-rs is focused on providing read support. However, the long-term vision is to achieve feature parity with the Java implementation, which will significantly expand Hudi's capabilities and use cases within these growing ecosystems.

Ecosystem Integration

Hudi has a wide range of support across the data ecosystem. Table 4-3 lists all the projects and products that support read and/or write with Hudi at the time of writing.

Table 4-3. Hudi's ecosystem integrations

Project/Product	Support
Onehouse.ai	Read, write
Apache Spark	Read, write
Apache Flink	Read, write
Presto	Read
Trino	Read
Apache Hive	Read
DBT	Read, write
Apache Kafka, Kafka Connect	Write
Apache Kafka	Write
Apache Pulsar	Write
Debezium	Write
Apache Kyuubi	Read, write
ClickHouse	Read
Apache Impala	Read, write
AWS Athena	Read
AWS EMR	Read, write
AWS Redshift	Read
AWS Glue	Read, write
Google BigQuery	Read
Google DataProc	Read, write
Azure Synapse	Read, write
Azure HDInsight	Read, write
Databricks	Read, write
Vertica	Read
Apache Doris	Read
StarRocks	Read
Daft	Read
Ray	Read

As Hudi continues to actively expand its integration across the ecosystem, this list will keep growing. Please refer to the official page of ecosystem support (*https://oreil.ly/y5Ijb*).

Summary

In this chapter, we dissected the rich and versatile read capabilities that make Hudi a powerful framework for the data lakehouse. We began by exploring how Hudi integrates with query engines, leveraging a data catalog to provide the necessary table schema and file locations. This integration plugs into both the planning phase, where Hudi determines the exact file slices to read based on the query type, and the execution phase, where it supports reading the file slices correctly and efficiently.

With that foundation, we reviewed the full spectrum of query types Hudi supports. We covered snapshot queries for accessing the latest version of records, and time travel queries, which enable auditing and debugging by allowing reads of past record versions. We also covered incremental queries, a fundamental feature for building chained data pipelines that efficiently propagate changes. This query type supports both latest-state and CDC modes, with CDC providing rich, row-level insights about every change.

Finally, we highlighted several advanced features that complete Hudi's read capabilities. We discussed streaming reads, which fit naturally with Hudi's incremental-first design; schema evolution on read, which addresses the need for backward-incompatible changes; and the Hudi-rs project, which extends Hudi's reach into the Rust and Python ecosystems. Together, these features provide a robust and flexible set of tools for extracting value from your data.

Achieving Efficiency with Indexing

Lakehouses must be able to manage petabyte-scale datasets with complex, often unpredictable mutation patterns while maintaining both write efficiency and query performance. These systems operate at a massive scale on distributed storage and need to support a mix of analytical and transactional workloads. To meet these demands, lakehouse tables require versatile indexing capabilities, similar to OLTP databases. On the write path, the indexes have to be maintained as new writes happen, and then they will be used to efficiently locate existing records for updates and deletes across massive datasets. On the read path, the indexes need to handle diverse query patterns with equal efficiency: range predicates benefit from file statistics pruning, equality predicates benefit from index lookups, and function-based predicates need specialized expression handling.

As of this writing, Apache Hudi is the only lakehouse storage system that natively supports indexing capabilities. In this chapter, we discuss how Hudi keeps read and write operations performant at scale, by employing indexing techniques. We will also see why getting your indexing strategy right is what makes near-real-time lakehouse performance possible. We'll cover:

- The essentials of indexing for lakehouse tables, with a look at how indexing techniques in readers and writers optimize performance

- How multimodal indexing works via the Hudi metadata table, along with the different types of indexes supported

- Writer-side indexes specifically designed to optimize write operations without much storage overhead, with guidance on when to choose each one

By the end of this chapter, you will have a comprehensive understanding of Hudi's powerful and versatile indexing capabilities. More importantly, you will learn how to analyze your specific workload and select the optimal index by carefully weighing the trade-offs between performance, cost, and operational complexity. Hudi abstracts away the formidable engineering challenge of implementing indexing on distributed storage, allowing you to focus on making higher-level choices that deliver the best performance for your use case.

Overview of the Indexes in Hudi

Hudi's indexes can be broadly categorized into two groups. The first is the multi-modal indexing subsystem, housed within the metadata table, which provides a variety of indexes that jointly enhance both read and write performance. The second category consists of specialized writer-side indexes designed specifically to accelerate write operations in particular scenarios. Table 5-1 summarizes the most commonly used index types in Hudi.

Table 5-1. Overview of the most common Hudi index types

Category	Index type	Where is it stored?	Where is it used?	How does it work?
Multimodal index	Files	Metadata table	Reader & writer	Provides partition and file lists to support writer, indexing, and query planning
	Partition stats	Metadata table	Reader	Provides partition-level statistics for pruning partitions during query planning
	Column stats	Metadata table	Reader	Provides file-level statistics for pruning files during query planning
	Bloom filter	Metadata table	Reader & writer	Provides Bloom filters on record key fields to speed up the process of locating records for both SQL DMLs and queries
	Record	Metadata table	Reader & writer	For reads, provides exact matching of file groups for equality-matching predicates on record key fields

For writes, checks record-to-file mappings to identify updates/deletes and inserts |
	Secondary	Metadata table	Reader	Provides exact matching of files for equality-matching predicates on specified nonrecord key fields
	Expression	Metadata table	Reader	Provides pruning capabilities based on designated expressions on columns
Writer-side indexes	Simple	Implicitly with file slices	Writer	Performs join operations on incoming and existing records to locate the file groups for updates and deletes
	Bloom	Implicitly with base files	Writer	Performs an efficient search for incoming record keys against existing records using Bloom filters built on the keys and key ranges for file slices
	Bucket	Implicitly with file groups	Writer	Locates the exact file groups for incoming records using a consistent hashing technique

In the sections that follow, we will first examine indexing from the perspective of the write path. We will begin by recapping the high-level write flow, then delve into the specific index types that optimize write operations, discussing their ideal scenarios and trade-offs. Subsequently, we will shift our focus to the read path, where we will review the read flow and explore the indexes designed to accelerate query planning, again analyzing their suitable use cases and trade-offs.

Index Acceleration for Writes

When Hudi processes an incoming batch of records, it must efficiently determine whether each record is a new addition or a modification of an existing one. This process of mapping an incoming record to its physical location within the table is effectively what indexing accomplishes for writes. For updates and deletes, indexing for writes is a critical first step, as the writer must correctly locate the specific file group containing the record to be modified.

As illustrated in Figure 5-1, indexing during a write operation consists of two primary steps:

1. *Lookup:* The index is queried with the record keys from the incoming batch to determine the current location of any existing records.
2. *Update:* During data writing, the indexes are also updated to reflect the latest information about the written records.

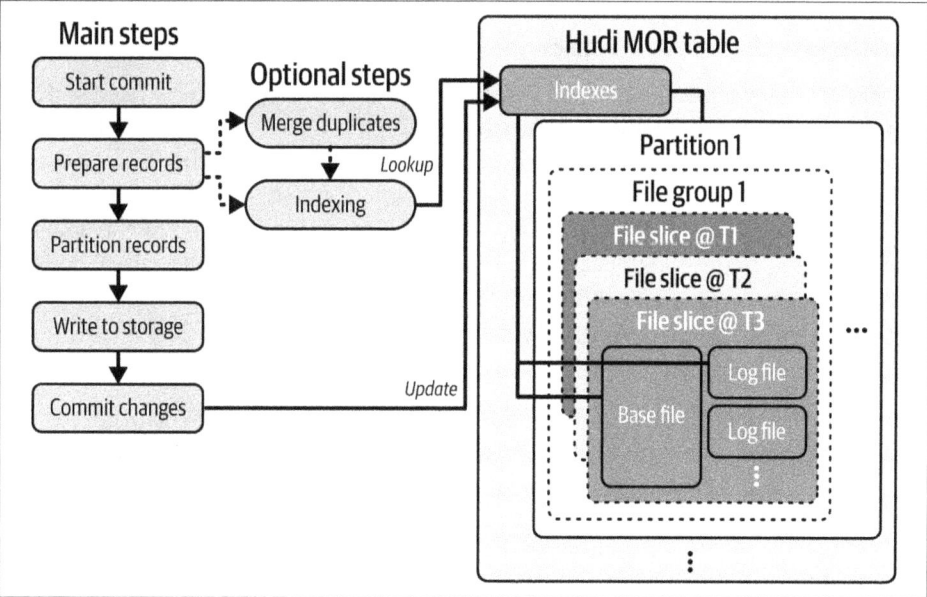

Figure 5-1. Indexing steps in the write flow

Writer-side indexes are stored implicitly as part of the data files in the table, requiring no explicit maintenance step. However, they cannot be leveraged by queries in a general-purpose manner.

Because indexing is an integral part of the write path, the choice of indexing strategy directly impacts overall write performance. An inefficient index can also create unnecessary overheads, prolonging the entire write process. Therefore, selecting the optimal index for your workload is essential for building high-performance data pipelines that can deliver timely business insights.

In the following sections, we will discuss the most commonly used indexes and demonstrate how to select the best index for various real-world scenarios.

General-Purpose Multimodal Indexing

An index that provides a direct mapping from a record key to its physical location offers the fastest possible lookup. To achieve this, Hudi pioneered the *record index* in data lakehouses, a general-purpose, high-performance indexing solution suitable for most real-world scenarios, especially at large scale. The record index resides within Hudi's metadata table, a component we first introduced in Chapter 2. A thorough understanding of the metadata table is essential for grasping the mechanics of the record index and other concepts covered in this chapter. Therefore, we will begin by examining its structure and functionalities.

Index storage with the metadata table

Located at *.hoodie/metadata/* (see Figure 5-2), the metadata table is itself a Hudi Merge-on-Read (MOR) table. It contains specially designed partitions, each serving some specific indexing purposes and supporting operations in the read path, the write path, or both. The metadata table is enabled by default when a Hudi table is created, and it automatically creates three types of indexes in three partitions: files in `files/` partition (tracks the partition list and file lists in the table), column stats in `column_stats/` partition (provides file-level statistics), and partition stats in `partition_stats/` partition (provides partition-level statistics). The record index resides in the `record_index/` partition and will need to be enabled explicitly.

To ensure that data and its corresponding index entries remain synchronized, any write to the main data table also updates the metadata table within the same atomic transaction. Reading from and writing to the metadata table follows the same flow as any standard MOR table.

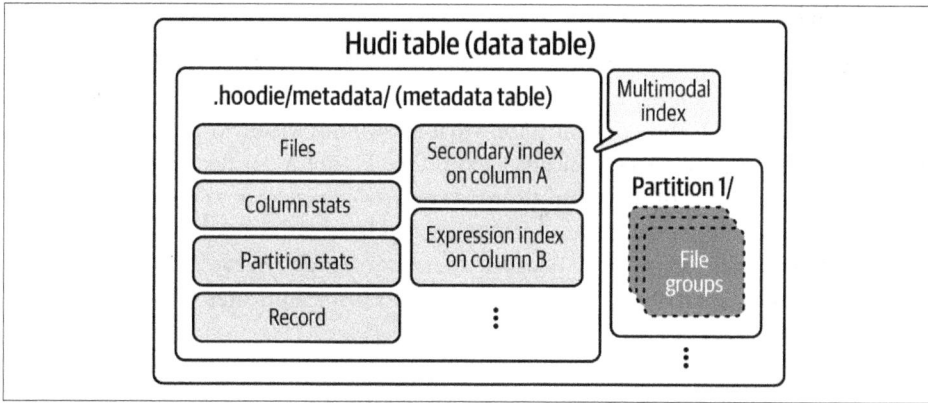

Figure 5-2. Organization of the metadata table

The metadata table uses a row-optimized format (HFile) for its base files. HFile is a sorted immutable key-value file format, similar in structure to a Sorted String Table (SSTable), that is optimized for high-performance lookups. It stores records sorted by key and includes an internal, multilevel index, which allows for retrieving a value without scanning the entire file. This format is ideal for the metadata table's typical query patterns, which often involve batched lookups. For instance, when ingesting a large batch of records, the record keys can be looked up in batches efficiently against the sorted data in the HFiles, significantly improving indexing performance.

As an MOR table, the metadata table is well suited to handling high-frequency writes. To access the most up-to-date index information, index readers must perform snapshot queries, which merge base files with the log files. However, an excessive number of log files can degrade read performance. To mitigate this, Hudi automatically runs compaction on the metadata table, just as it does for a standard MOR data table. This process, which we first discussed in Chapter 4, ensures that snapshot query performance remains optimal. By default, compaction is triggered every 10 writes, a setting that can be adjusted using the `hoodie.metadata.compact.max.delta.commits` configuration.

The metadata table is often called a *multimodal index* because it houses diverse types of indexes in its various partitions. As shown in Figure 5-2, some of the supported index types include files, column stats, partition stats, record, and secondary. It also supports building indexes using expressions on specified columns. In the following sections on writer indexing, we will take a closer look at the record index and other writer-side indexes. Other indexes that primarily benefit read operations will be covered in detail in "Index Acceleration for Reads" on page 109.

The record index

Hudi's record index stores the location mappings in the `record_index/` partition for every record in the data table. Each entry contains essential metadata—including the partition path, file ID, and commit time—that allows the writer to pinpoint the exact file slice containing the corresponding record (see Figure 5-3). Because writes to the metadata table are part of the same atomic transaction as writes to the data table, the index is automatically updated for any inserted, updated, or deleted records, ensuring that it remains fully consistent. Because the record index serves as the source of truth for record locations, a lookup that returns no result indicates that the incoming record is a new insert.

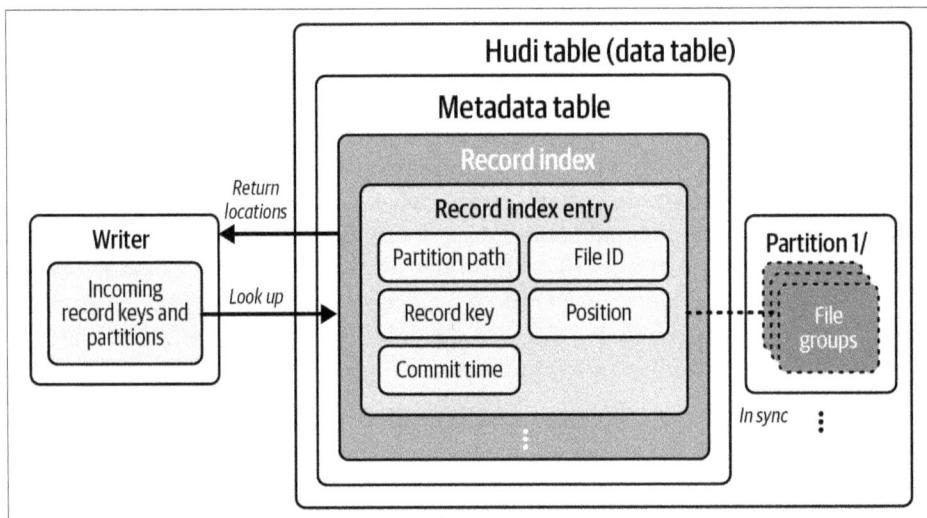

Figure 5-3. Record index lookups return the record location for incoming updates or deletes

In addition to benefiting writers, the record index also drastically boosts read performance when equality-matching predicates are present; a scenario we'll discuss in "Equality Matching" on page 113. The record index entries use a fixed schema and are compressed, resulting in an average size of approximately 48 bytes. To put this into perspective, for a 100 TB table with one billion records, the record index would also contain one billion entries but would only consume about 48 GB of storage—less than 0.05% of the total table size. This low-ratio storage overhead is a modest investment for the significant performance gains the record index provides, making it a highly cost-effective solution.

You can enable the record index by setting a table property when you first create the table:

```
CREATE TABLE user_profile (
    id STRING,
    name STRING,
    age INT,
    update_ts BIGINT,
    country STRING
) USING hudi
TBLPROPERTIES(
    primaryKey ='id',
    preCombineField = 'update_ts',
    'hoodie.metadata.record.index.enable' = 'true'
)
PARTITIONED BY (country);
```

You can also enable or disable the record index for an existing table using the following SQL commands:

```
CREATE INDEX record_index ON user_profile (id); ❶
DROP INDEX record_index ON user_profile; ❷
```

❶ You must specify the correct record key fields (id in this example) for creating the record index. The CREATE INDEX command will trigger a process to build the record index and bring it into sync with the data table.

❷ The DROP INDEX command permanently removes the index files and the record_index/ partition from the metadata table.

> For very large tables, the initial indexing process can be time-consuming. To avoid blocking subsequent write operations, you can build indexes asynchronously using the indexing table service, which will be discussed in more detail in Chapter 6.

Writer-Side Indexes

In the following sections, we'll explore the choice of writer-side indexes for different write patterns. But first, we'll take a deep dive into the bucket index, which is a great choice for real-time write speeds.

The bucket index

Like the record index, Hudi's *bucket index* provides a direct record-to-file mapping, delivering excellent lookup performance. However, instead of persisting index entries in the metadata table, the bucket index uses a hashing mechanism to route records to a specific file group. Each record's key is hashed to deterministically map it to a "bucket," which corresponds to a single file group (see Figure 5-4). This ensures that a given record key always lands in the same file group, making lookups a constant-time, in-memory hash computation.

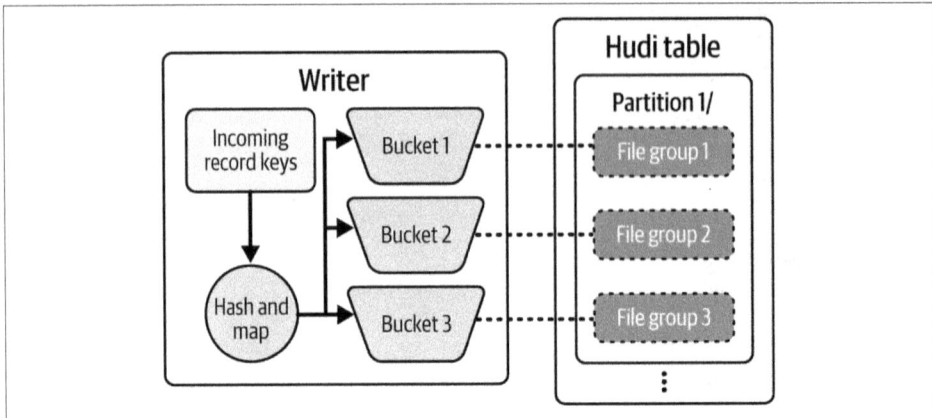

Figure 5-4. Bucket index hashes and maps records to buckets and file groups

The bucket index comes in two variants:

Simple bucket index
> This is the default variant, which uses a fixed number of buckets per partition. It is well suited to handling workloads with predictable data volumes and works for both Copy-on-Write (COW) and MOR tables.

Consistent hashing bucket index
> This variant dynamically resizes the number of buckets to adapt to data growth or skew, offering greater flexibility for evolving workloads. However, it is only available for MOR tables.

To use the bucket index, you must set the appropriate configurations before a write operation. For example:

```
-- use the simple bucket index
SET hoodie.index.type=BUCKET;
SET hoodie.index.bucket.engine=SIMPLE;
SET hoodie.bucket.index.num.buckets=64;

-- use the consistent hashing bucket index
SET hoodie.index.type=BUCKET;
SET hoodie.index.bucket.engine=CONSISTENT_HASHING;
SET hoodie.bucket.index.min.num.buckets=32;
SET hoodie.bucket.index.max.num.buckets=128;
```

The primary advantage of the bucket index is its lightweight design, which relies on in-memory hash computation rather than lookups against an on-disk index. Because the hashing function is deterministic, a record's location is calculated on the fly, ensuring that the same key is always mapped to the same file group. This makes the bucket index *implicit*, eliminating the need for a separate update step and keeping it perpetually in sync with the data.

However, being lightweight comes with trade-offs. With the simple bucket index, the number of buckets is fixed up front, which can lead to data skew if not chosen carefully. The consistent hashing variant mitigates this by resizing buckets, but it is only for MOR tables and requires running the clustering table service (covered in Chapter 6) to rebalance the data, adding operational complexity. On another note, neither variant has been integrated with the read path to accelerate equality-matching predicates in the same way the record index is.

The simple index

In a data warehouse, a dimension table stores descriptive reference data about business entities, such as user profiles, merchant information, or product attributes. These tables are typically much smaller than the main transactional data tables (called *fact tables*) and change less frequently, though they may receive small, scattered (random) updates or occasional deletes (Figure 5-5). Because dimension tables are usually small, they are often left unpartitioned, though partitioning may be considered based on factors like query patterns, update frequency, and platform capabilities, not just table size alone.

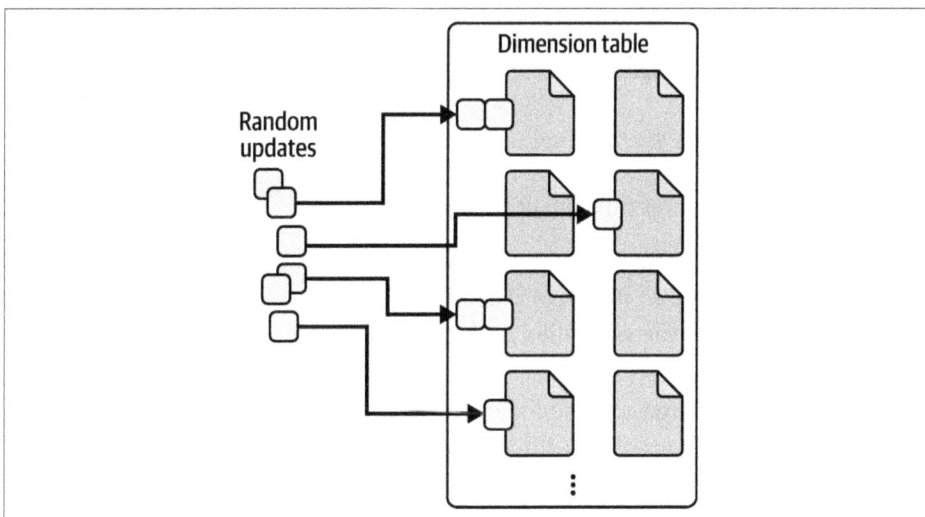

Figure 5-5. Random updates in a dimension table

For small to medium-sized dimension tables, the simple and global simple indexes offer a straightforward and effective solution. As their names imply, these indexes use a simple mechanism to locate existing records: they perform a left join between the incoming batch of records and the current table. While both indexes share this fundamental approach, they differ in their operational scope. The simple index confines its search for matching record keys to the relevant data partitions, whereas the global simple index expands the search across the entire table. For brevity, we will refer to them collectively as *the simple indexes*. The mechanics of this process are illustrated in Figure 5-6.

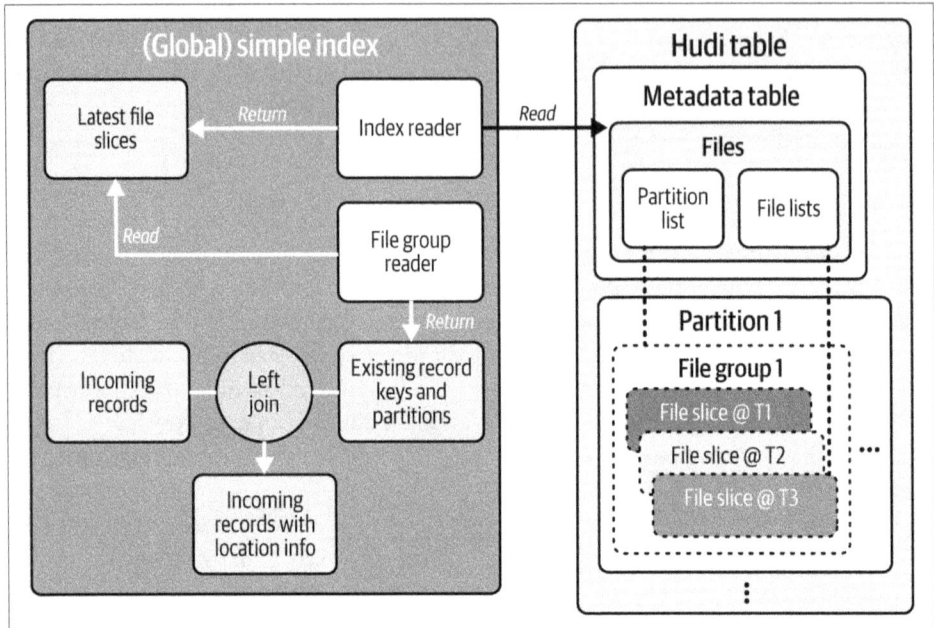

Figure 5-6. Indexing flow for the simple indexes

The indexing flow involves three main steps:

1. *File slice discovery:* The index reader queries the files index of the metadata table to get the latest list of file slices. For the simple index, it retrieves only the file slices in partitions corresponding to the incoming records. For the global simple index, it retrieves all file slices across the entire table.

2. *Key extraction:* File group readers process the relevant file slices, extracting only the record key and partition path for each record. This creates a minimal dataset needed for the join operation.

3. *Location tagging:* The incoming batch of records is left-joined against the extracted keys and/or partitions. A successful join indicates a match, signifying an update or delete, and the record's location is tagged. Records that do not find a match are identified as new inserts.

The effectiveness of this join-based approach hinges on the *hit rate*—the proportion of file slices scanned that contain records matching the incoming batch. For random updates and deletes, which are scattered across many different file slices, the likelihood that any given file slice contains a matching record is high. This widespread distribution makes the cost of scanning all relevant partitions worthwhile, as the broad scan is more likely to yield matches. In essence, the more randomly distributed the updates are, the more efficient the simple indexes become.

While the simple index is the default, you can explicitly configure it or the global simple index before a write operation:

```
-- use simple index (default)
SET hoodie.index.type=SIMPLE

-- use global simple index
SET hoodie.index.type=GLOBAL_SIMPLE
```

The simple indexes, like the bucket indexes, are also implicitly stored with data—as long as the file slices are created properly, they are ready for future indexing lookups, which simply load the files themselves.

However, the performance of the join-based indexing process can degrade for tables with large numbers of file slices. This is particularly true for the global simple index, which must scan every file group in the table for the latest file slices. Even though the operation only loads record keys and partition paths, performing a large-scale join against even a small input batch can be time-consuming and become a bottleneck for the entire write operation.

The bloom index

Fact tables, which typically store transactional data, are often partitioned by temporal fields like a creation date. For example, an orders table might be partitioned by the day the order was created. In such scenarios, writes are often heavily skewed: most new data, including updates and deletes, targets the most recent partitions (e.g., the current day), while a smaller volume of late-arriving data might be written to older partitions (Figure 5-7).

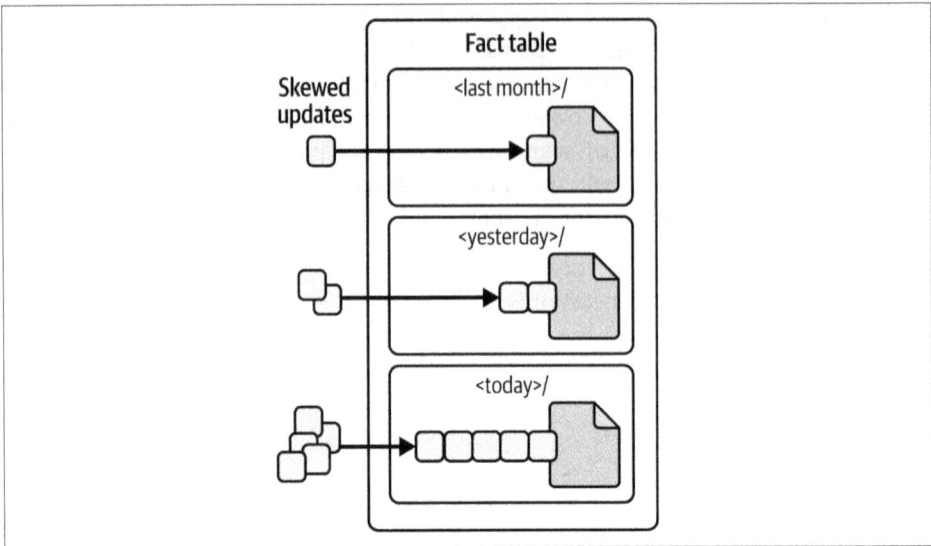

Figure 5-7. Skewed updates in a fact table

For workloads with this skewed write pattern, the bloom and global bloom indexes offer an effective solution. These indexes leverage a probabilistic data structure called a *Bloom filter* to quickly determine a key's nonexistence in a target file, avoiding unnecessary file reads. Additionally, they use the minimum and maximum values of record keys stored with the data files to further narrow down the candidate files whose Bloom filters need to be checked. Similar to the simple and global simple indexes, the bloom index operates on relevant partitions, while the global bloom index works across the entire table. For brevity, we will refer to them collectively as *the bloom indexes*. The detailed flow is shown in Figure 5-8.

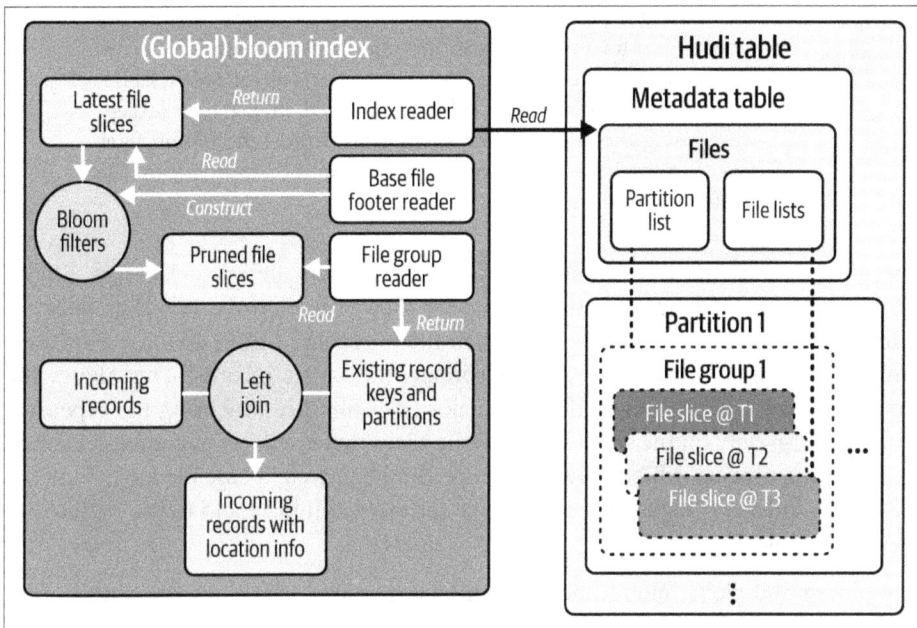

Figure 5-8. Indexing flow for bloom indexes

The indexing flow involves these main steps:

1. *File slice discovery*: This step is the same as for the simple indexes. The files index in the metadata table is queried to retrieve a list of relevant file slices—either from matching partitions for the bloom index or from the entire table for the global bloom index.

2. *File slice pruning*: This is the key step where the Bloom filters are used. For each of the candidate file slices narrowed down using record key ranges, a Bloom filter is read from the footer of the base file. A Bloom filter is a space-efficient probabilistic data structure that can say whether an element is *definitively not* in a set or *may be* in the set, with a tunable false-positive rate. By checking the incoming record keys against these filters, Hudi can create a pruned list of file slices that is guaranteed to contain the incoming updating and deleting records.

3. *Key extraction*: This step is the same as for the simple indexes. File group readers will extract the record keys and partitions from the pruned file slices for the next step.

4. *Location tagging*: This step is the same as for the simple indexes. The incoming records are left-joined against the record keys and/or partitions extracted from step 3. A successful join tags the record as an update/delete, while a failed join indicates a new insert.

Only the base file in a file slice uses its footer block to store the Bloom filter for the records in that file. When pruning file slices, we do not need to consider log files in the case of MOR tables, because only updates and deletes are saved in log files (except when using the bucket indexes). In other words, the Bloom filter saved for the base file can represent the file slice and perform the existence check correctly.

The efficiency of the bloom indexes comes from their ability to leverage Bloom filters to dramatically improve the hit rate for skewed workloads. When updates are concentrated in a few partitions, the Bloom filters retrieved from all other partitions can quickly confirm that they do not contain the target records. This allows the bloom indexes to skip reading the vast majority of file slices, focusing the expensive join operation only on the small subset of file slices that are likely to contain matches. This filtering process, which only involves reading lightweight base file footers, makes the bloom indexes a highly efficient choice for skewed update and delete patterns in even large tables.

The bloom and global bloom indexes can be configured before a write operation as follows:

```
-- use bloom index
SET hoodie.index.type=BLOOM

-- use global bloom index
SET hoodie.index.type=GLOBAL_BLOOM
```

Like the simple indexes, the bloom indexes are updated implicitly. The Bloom filter for a given base file is stored in its footer and written as part of the same operation that writes the data, ensuring that the index is always synchronized.

In workloads with random update patterns, the bloom indexes' performance can be worse than that of the simple indexes. This is because the widespread distribution of record keys across many file groups increases the probability of the Bloom filter saying that an element *may be* in a set, causing less file slice pruning. When this occurs, the index still has to read and join against a large number of file slices, making the Bloom filter loading and pruning step an unnecessary overhead.

Furthermore, the bloom indexes can incur performance overhead with tables that contain a very high number of file slices. While the Bloom filters can be effective at pruning the search space, the initial step of reading the footers from every candidate base file can itself become a bottleneck. This is especially true for the global bloom index, which must consider every file group in the table. The cumulative I/O from reading numerous file footers can slow down the overall write operation.

Comparison of Writer Indexing Choices

So far, we have explored four main writer index types: record, bucket, simple, and bloom. Understanding their respective strengths, weaknesses, and ideal use cases is critical for achieving optimal write efficiency for your Hudi tables. Each index type offers a unique approach to locating records, with distinct trade-offs in performance, cost, and operational complexity.

To help guide your selection process, Table 5-2 provides a side-by-side comparison of their key characteristics.

Table 5-2. Writer index summary

Index type	Pros	Cons
Record	• General-purpose, high-performance indexing • Works well for tables at all sizes and all workload patterns • Helps speed up equality-matching queries • Easy management with SQL commands	• Incurs some storage overhead • Requires additional index maintenance overhead
Bucket	• Fastest option for update-heavy write workloads • Works well for tables of all sizes • No storage overhead	• Can result in a table storage layout that is not optimal for queries (e.g., losing temporal locality for queries) • Consistent hashing bucket index only works for MOR
Simple	• Simple and has no storage or index maintenance overhead • Leverages all the join optimizations in the query engine • Applicable for random update/delete patterns	• Does not perform well for skewed update/delete patterns • Not suitable for large-scale tables
Bloom	• Performs well for skewed update/delete patterns • Suitable even for very large tables because index lookup scales proportionally to incoming write patterns and not table size • Incurs small storage and index maintenance overhead to store Bloom filters and key ranges	• Does not perform well for random update/delete patterns

As the table illustrates, the optimal choice depends heavily on your specific workload, including table size, update patterns, and performance requirements.

Hudi also offers the *flink state index*, which works similarly to the record index. The difference is how the indexing data is stored. Unlike the record index, which uses the metadata table that leverages the same storage space as the data lakehouse uses, the flink state index stores the record location mappings in the Apache Flink writer job's storage backend database.

We have briefly discussed global and nonglobal indexes, a concept rooted in the scope of a record key's uniqueness. When configuring a Hudi table for upserts, you must define the record key fields, which Hudi uses to uniquely identify records. For partitioned tables, you also define partition path fields. The scope of a record's uniqueness is determined by whether the record key is unique across the entire table or only within its specific partition. This distinction is critical, as it dictates which type of index—global or nonglobal—is appropriate for your workload. Lakehouse tables can be 10 to 100 times bigger than Relational Database Management System/online transaction processing (RDBMS/OLTP) tables, and for such large data volumes, nonglobal indexes help scale index lookups with knowledge of the partition a record key resides in. Depending on your data's characteristics, your table will fall into one of two scenarios:

Scenario 1

The record key can be solely used to determine the record's uniqueness; that is, there won't be more than one record with the same record key across all partitions in the table.

Scenario 2

The record key and partition path fields need to be used jointly to determine the record's uniqueness; that is, the same record key may appear in different partitions. This also means that the user is expected to supply both the key and partition path for write operations.

Because both scenarios are dependent on data, Hudi introduces the notion of global and nonglobal indexes: if scenario 1 applies to you, choose a global index for your writer, and if scenario 2 applies to you, choose a nonglobal index. Table 5-3 summarizes this property for the writer indexes.

Table 5-3. Global and nonglobal writer indexes

Index type	Is it global?
Simple	No
Global simple	Yes
Bloom	No
Global bloom	Yes
Bucket (simple)	No
Bucket (consistent hashing)	No
Record	Yes

A global index expects uniqueness across all partitions, and therefore its lookup process may involve scanning files over the whole table. The performance may degrade when the table size grows for global simple index, while record index won't be impacted too much due to its design of providing direct key-to-file mappings.

A nonglobal index expects uniqueness only within partitions; hence, simple and bloom indexes are generally more performant than their global counterparts, because the lookup scanning space is reduced to relevant partitions of the incoming records.

> The notion of global and nonglobal indexes is only applicable to writer indexes. There is no such notion for reader indexes, because when we read data, we always want to fetch the matching records (including partition matching) across the table.

If scenario 1 applied to you and you chose a nonglobal index like simple or bloom, it could lead to data correctness issues as the index lookup would only involve the partitions relevant to the incoming records. If scenario 2 applied to you and you chose a global index like global simple or global bloom, you would waste compute resources scanning unnecessary files during lookup. The rule of thumb is to understand your data so that you can make the right choice between global and nonglobal indexes.

> For nonpartitioned tables, the entire table can be seen as having a single partition with an empty string as the partition path. Therefore, either a global index or its nonglobal counterpart will work for it as they are functionally equivalent.

Index Acceleration for Reads

As we discussed in Chapter 4, Hudi's integration with query engines leverages its indexing component to optimize the list of file slices returned during the query planning phase (Figure 5-9). In most cases, this indexing component is the metadata table, which is enabled by default. If the metadata table is disabled explicitly by setting `hoodie.metadata.enable` to `false` when creating the table, you will not benefit from the powerful read-size indexing capabilities we are about to discuss.

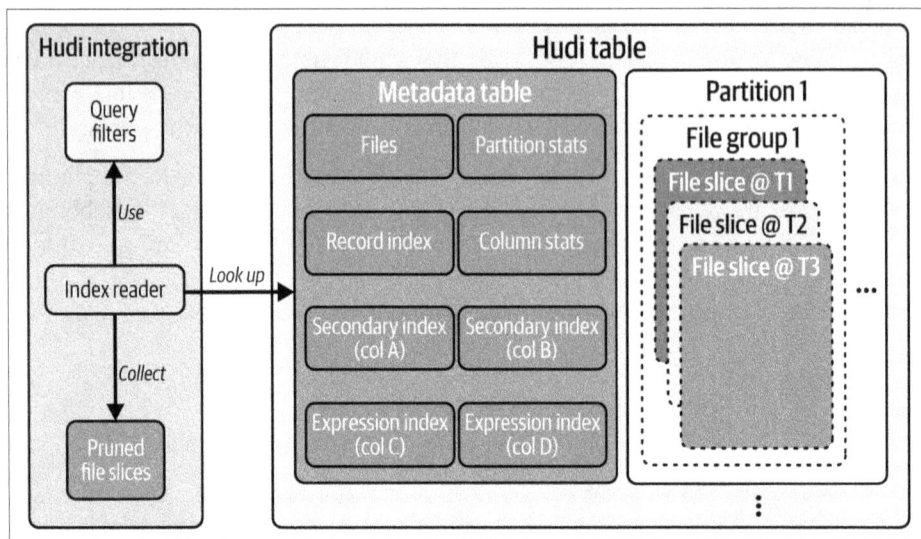

Figure 5-9. Query engine integration uses the metadata table to optimize planning

In the previous sections on writer indexes, we introduced the metadata table as a multimodal index. Its true multimodal nature comes from its ability to provide versatile indexes that maximize optimization opportunities based on the available query filters, jointly enhancing the read process.

Data Skipping

Analytical SQL queries in production environments almost always contain predicates to filter data, such as A >= X or B BETWEEN Y AND Z. Query engines can push these predicates down to Hudi's query engine integration layer, which then uses indexes in the metadata table to optimize the query plan by minimizing the number of files to be read.

Three indexes—files, column stats, and partition stats—work in concert to achieve this file pruning. We will examine each one individually before demonstrating how they collaborate in the optimization flow.

The files index

As we saw in the write path, the files index provides writers with a list of file slices for lookups. It serves a similar function in the read path, offering a complete and up-to-date list of all partitions in the table and the file slices within each. This list serves as the initial candidate set that will be pruned using the applicable query predicates.

Without the files index, both readers and writers would need to perform expensive and time-consuming file system listing operations to discover the table's contents. Because this partition and file information is fundamental to nearly all Hudi operations, the files index is always available whenever the metadata table is enabled.

The column stats and partition stats indexes

The column stats and partition stats indexes store statistics that enable data skipping, a powerful optimization for accelerating queries. For example, if the statistics for a data file show that the maximum value for column A is 100, the query planner can safely skip reading that file entirely when processing a query with the predicate A > 100.

The column stats index maintains file-level statistics, including the minimum and maximum values, total value count, and null count for columns within each file slice. The partition stats index stores similar statistics but aggregated at the partition level.

Both indexes are enabled by default and are updated automatically with each write operation, ensuring that the statistics remain synchronized with the data. You can, however, disable them during table creation or for a specific write job by setting the following properties to `false`:

```
hoodie.metadata.index.column.stats.enable
hoodie.metadata.index.partition.stats.enable
```

> The partition stats index depends on the column stats index. Therefore, you must enable column stats to use partition stats, although you can use column stats independently.

The pruning process

Putting all three indexes together, we can get a full picture of how files are pruned during the optimization process (Figure 5-10):

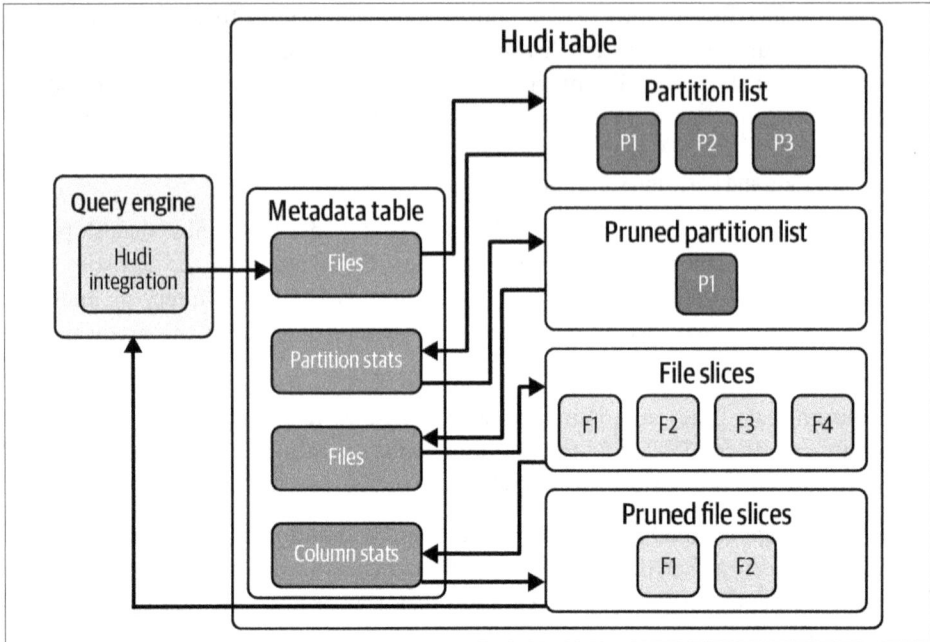

Figure 5-10. File pruning process

1. The files index is queried to get a list of partitions.
2. Based on the passed-down predicates, partition stats is queried to prune out the partitions whose statistics fall out of the ranges. If partition values are available in the predicates, those partitions will be selected or filtered out directly.
3. The pruned partitions are then used as arguments for the files index to get file lists for those partitions.
4. Similar pruning logic is applied based on the predicates to the files using column stats.
5. The final pruned file list is returned to the query engine for further processing.

By default, the first 32 columns will be indexed and stored in column stats and partition stats. This is to avoid unnecessary indexing overhead for wide tables with hundreds of columns. You can change this cap number by setting this config:

```
hoodie.metadata.index.column.stats.max.columns.to.index=20
```

It often makes more sense for you to choose specific columns for indexing. For a table order that contains customer order information such as price and shipping date, you may configure just the `price` and `shipping_date` to speed up frequent queries asking for `price > 300` or `shipping_date BETWEEN Date'2025-06-01' AND Date'2025-06-30'`:

```
hoodie.metadata.index.column.stats.column.list=price,shipping_date
```

> When hoodie.metadata.index.column.stats.column.list is
> set, the config hoodie.metadata.index.column.stats.max.col
> umns.to.index will be ignored.

Equality Matching

Your queries may contain equality-matching predicates like A = X or B IN (X, Y,
Z). While file pruning will also be effective for these, a more efficient approach is to
find the exact file slices that contain those column values.

The record index

In earlier sections, you learned that the record index stores the exact mappings for a
record key and its enclosing file slice. This is efficient not just for Hudi writers to find
file groups for writing data, but also for Hudi readers to speed up queries that contain
equality-matching predicates with the record key field being the left operand.

As long as the configured record index is active, queries with the applicable equality-
matching predicates will be optimized by it—the mapped file slices will be directly
used for any further pruning, speeding up the whole planning process.

The secondary index

When a query predicate uses an equality match on a nonrecord key field (e.g., name
= 'X'), the record index cannot be used to locate the relevant files. To address this,
Hudi provides the *secondary index*. A secondary index functions as an inverted index,
storing a mapping from the values in a nonrecord key field to their corresponding
record keys.

For a query with an applicable predicate, Hudi first queries the secondary index to
retrieve the set of matching record keys. It then uses the record index to find the
specific file slices containing those keys. Because of this, you must have the record
index enabled to use a secondary index.

For example, consider a user_profile table where a record has id = '001' and name
= 'X'. If you create a secondary index on the name column, an entry mapping 'X' to
'001' is created. A lookup for name = 'X' will efficiently find the record key '001'
in the secondary index and then use the record index to locate the exact file slice
containing that user's record.

You can create multiple secondary indexes, each on a different nonrecord key field:

```
CREATE INDEX idx_on_name ON user_profile (name);
```

For each secondary index, Hudi creates a dedicated partition in the metadata table, prefixed with `secondary_index_`, to store the index entries. The name you provide in the `CREATE INDEX` command (e.g., `idx_on_name`) is used as part of the partition name, making it easy to manage multiple indexes. The name `record_index` is reserved and cannot be used.

To remove a secondary index, you can use the `DROP INDEX` command:

```
DROP INDEX idx_on_name ON user_profile;
```

The use of HFile for the metadata table's base files is particularly advantageous for secondary indexes. The lexicographically sorted keys in HFile allow for efficient prefix lookups, which works well when multiple record keys map to the same secondary key value. However, the secondary index delivers the best performance on high-cardinality columns, where there are many unique values, leading to more selective 1-to-1 mappings. For low-cardinality columns (e.g., a Boolean field), a secondary index is less effective, as it will not significantly narrow down the candidate file slices. The Hudi community is actively developing a bitmap index to better handle these low-cardinality scenarios.

Indexing on Expressions

Queries often apply inline transformations to columns within their predicates, such as:

```
SELECT * FROM user_profile
WHERE from_unixtime(update_ts, 'yyyy-MM-dd') = '2025-06-01';
```

In this scenario, a standard column stats index on the `update_ts` column would be ineffective, as the predicate operates on the *result* of the `from_unixtime` function, not the raw column value. Adding a new, derived column to the table just to support this query is inefficient, as it adds storage overhead and becomes useless if a different date format is needed.

To solve this, Hudi provides the *expression index*, which extends the power of data skipping to predicates that contain functions.

The expression index with column_stats

By creating an expression index of type `column_stats`, you instruct Hudi to compute and store statistics on the transformed column values. For the example with `user_profile`, you could create the following index:

```
CREATE INDEX update_date ON user_profile
USING column_stats(update_ts)
OPTIONS(expr='from_unixtime', format='yyyy-MM-dd');
```

With this index in place, Hudi will pre-compute the min/max values for `from_unixtime(update_ts, 'yyyy-MM-dd')` for each file slice. When a matching query is executed, the file pruning process can use these specialized statistics to effectively perform skipping, just as it would with a standard column stats index.

Each expression index creates a dedicated partition in the metadata table, prefixed with `expr_index_`. You can manage them using the `DROP INDEX` command:

```
DROP INDEX update_date ON user_profile;
```

This type of index supports a wide range of functions, including `lower`, `regexp_extract`, and `concat`. For a complete list, refer to the documentation page (*https://oreil.ly/phcem*).

The expression index with bloom filter

Expression indexes can also be of type `bloom_filter`. This creates a Bloom filter for each file slice based on the transformed values of a column, which is useful for accelerating equality checks. For example, you could build an index to support case-insensitive lookups:

```
CREATE INDEX idx_bloom_name ON user_profile
USING bloom_filters(name) OPTIONS(expr='lower');

DROP INDEX idx_bloom_name ON user_profile;
```

This index stores a Bloom filter of the lowercase `name` values for each file. A query with a predicate like `WHERE lower(name) = 'x'` can then use this index to quickly eliminate file slices that do not contain the value x.

Like the secondary index, the `bloom_filter` expression index is most effective on high-cardinality columns. The more unique the values are, the higher the probability that a given value does not exist in a file slice, which is the ideal scenario for Bloom filter pruning. The effectiveness of this index can be further enhanced by using the clustering table service (a topic covered in Chapter 6) and sorting the data by the indexed column. This concentrates similar values into fewer file slices, increasing the number of file slices that can be skipped during a query.

Build the Right Indexes

The metadata table provides a powerful and versatile indexing framework to help query engines fully optimize their query plans. However, it is crucial to select and build indexes judiciously based on your data and query patterns. Creating unnecessary indexes can slow down the write process, as each index must be updated with every commit, without providing a corresponding benefit to read performance.

Pay special attention to storage overhead with indexes like the record index and secondary indexes, which grow in proportion to the number of records in the table. Creating secondary index on too many columns can lead to excessive storage consumption.

Furthermore, be aware of overlapping capabilities. Both the secondary index and the bloom_filter expression index can accelerate equality-matching predicates. For a given column, you typically only need one. The secondary index generally offers superior performance by narrowing the search to the exact file slices containing the data. In contrast, the bloom_filter only enhances the pruning of candidate file slices. The trade-off is storage: the secondary index is more precise but consumes more space with O(number of records) complexity, whereas Bloom filters at the file level are more space efficient.

Summary

This chapter began with a deep dive into writer indexes, starting with the need for general-purpose, high-performance indexing. This led us to the metadata table, the foundation for Hudi's most powerful indexing solutions. We explored the record index as a fast, scalable option for most workloads and compared it with the lightweight, hashing-based bucket index. We then addressed specific write patterns, introducing the join-based simple indexes for random updates and the filter- and join-based bloom indexes for skewed updates. Finally, we summarized the writer indexes, comparing their characteristics and discussing the important distinction between global and nonglobal scopes.

Shifting to the read path, we continued our exploration of the metadata table's multimodal capabilities. We demonstrated how the files, column stats, and partition stats indexes work together to enable effective file pruning for range-based queries. For equality-matching predicates, we noted that the record index also accelerates reads, and we introduced the secondary index to provide fast lookups on nonrecord key fields. Lastly, we extended Hudi's pruning power to predicates with functions by introducing the expression index, which supports both column_stats and bloom_fil ter types to optimize for an even wider range of predicates.

Hudi's indexing capabilities are continuously evolving to meet new challenges. The community is actively developing new indexes, such as bitmap index to provide efficient filtering on low-cardinality columns, and vector search index to support similarity searches on unstructured data for AI applications. The metadata table's flexible architecture provides a robust and extensible foundation, ensuring that Hudi can readily incorporate these and other versatile indexes in the future.

Maintaining and Optimizing Hudi Tables

Just as we regularly maintain a house to keep it in optimal condition, maintaining Apache Hudi tables is essential for a well-functioning data lakehouse. Just as a house requires regular sorting, decluttering, and reorganization to remain spacious and easy to navigate, tables must also be periodically reviewed and organized to keep them efficient and accessible.

When writing data, users often focus more on minimizing read and write delays than on perfectly organizing the data, and this is a serious oversight, especially for high-throughput tables. As we discussed at the beginning of Chapter 1, Hudi is conceived as a data lakehouse platform that can anticipate such pitfalls and guard against them from the get-go. This saves users from inefficiencies and difficulties in operating their data lakehouses later on.

For instance, unmaintained Hudi tables can suffer from:

Increased storage costs
Too many small files lead to high storage access latencies and inefficient compression on storage, increasing storage costs for the lakehouse. Too many objects in cloud storage can also balloon storage API costs.

Slow query performance
Suboptimal table organization can result in long query execution times, due to an unclustered and poorly partitioned data layout. Large numbers of small files also contribute to metadata bloat, especially for lakehouses retaining multiple versions of a table.

Increased compute costs
Without index maintenance, writers and queries can end up scanning the entire table to locate records of interest, holding compute resources for long durations and contributing to extremely high compute cluster charges.

High read amplification

> Without frequent compaction to control log file growth, queries on Merge-on-Read (MOR) tables can suffer from having to read too much data each time.

Just as you shouldn't let your home become completely disorganized before taking action, proactive table maintenance is crucial for ensuring optimal data accessibility and query performance.

This is where table services come into play. These services perform regular maintenance operations to keep the data lakehouse clean, organized, and efficient. Without them, our data lakehouse could become an inefficient data swamp—technically containing everything we need but making it frustratingly difficult to find and access specific items quickly.

In this chapter, we will explore the world of Hudi's table services, automated built-in platform services that render the essential maintenance operations for your data lakehouse. We will begin by defining what these services are and explaining their fundamental role in maintaining healthy, high-performance tables. Next, we will examine the various ways these services can be deployed to suit different operational needs. The core of the chapter is a deep dive into four key table services—compaction, clustering, cleaning, and indexing—that work together to keep your data lakehouse running at peak efficiency. By the end of this chapter, you will have a comprehensive understanding of how to maintain and optimize your Hudi tables effectively.

Table Service Overview

Table services in Hudi are a suite of software services designed to optimize and manage data *after* it has been written or based on a configurable table service strategy. For example, one strategy can define that the table be periodically sorted based on a particular column often used in common queries.

Unlike regular write operations that add new records, table services focus on housekeeping tasks that improve storage layout, streamline the table's structure, and enhance future query performance. Figure 6-1 shows a high-level overview of the table service workflow.

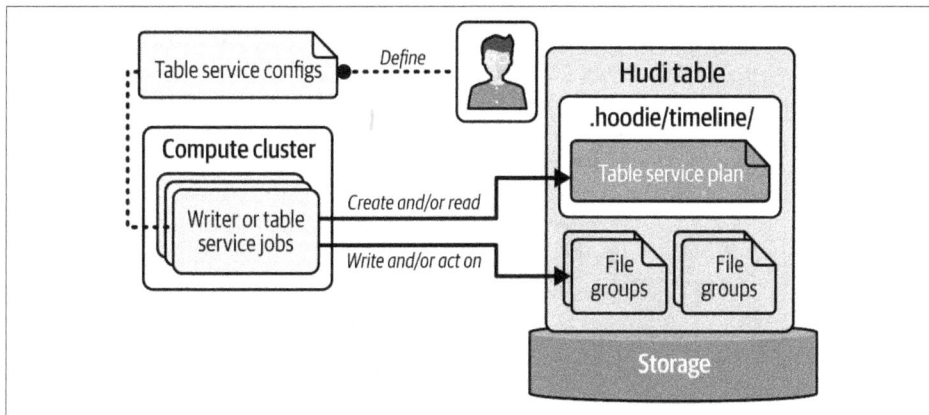

Figure 6-1. Overview of the table service workflow

A typical table service operation is a two-step process: first, *scheduling* creates a comprehensive maintenance plan detailing how to achieve the maintenance goal, and then, *execution* carries out that plan to make actual changes to the table. To accommodate different operational needs and constraints, Hudi offers three deployment modes for table services: inline, async execution, and standalone. Let's explore the characteristics of each mode to help you choose the right approach for your use case.

Deployment Mode: Inline

With the *inline mode*, table services run synchronously within the same writer job, immediately following the triggering write operation (Figure 6-2). This is the simplest deployment model, as it bundles the table service tasks—first scheduling, then execution—with the data write, ensuring that the table is consistently optimized without requiring separate jobs or infrastructure. Think of it as an all-in-one process where housekeeping happens automatically with every write commit.

It's important to understand that while the table service runs inline or in any other mode, it's making changes to the table, which will be recorded as actions on the Hudi timeline. For example, after a `commit` action from the write operation is completed, the configured cleaning table service under the inline mode will begin, creating its own `clean` action. This distinction clarifies that the table service operation is a distinct transaction, not part of the triggering write.

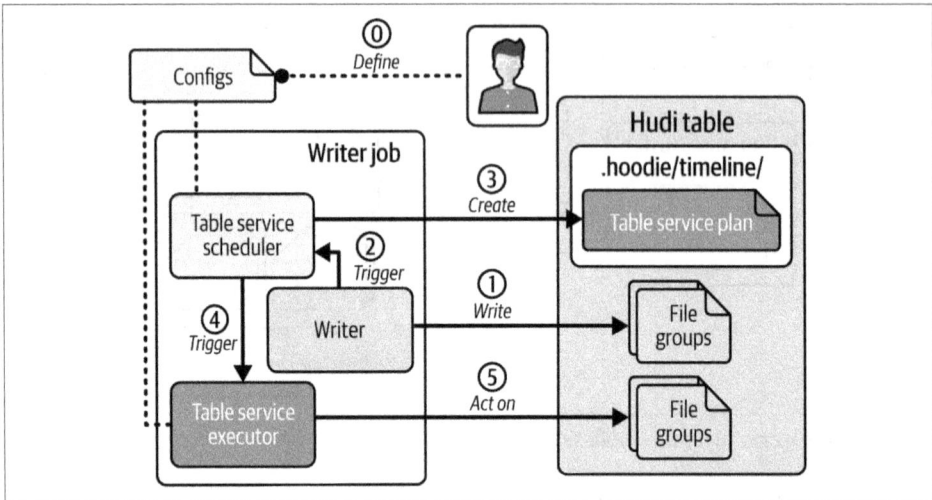

Figure 6-2. Table service inline deployment mode

The actions made by a table service also go through the same states as any Hudi actions do: requested => inflight => completed. The maintenance operation plan, containing information like which file groups to work with, is written in the requested instant of the table service action, making the execution step idempotent in the case of retries, as the retries execute prior to pending operation plans, before new ones are scheduled or executed. The action will be transitioned to a completed state after the execution finishes successfully.

The inline mode keeps things very simple, sidestepping all concurrency between the writer and table services. The simplicity of using the inline mode comes with a trade-off. Because table services run sequentially after the write, they can introduce latency to the overall write process. Furthermore, because both writing and maintenance share the same compute resources, this may not be the most efficient allocation. For instance, a large cluster provisioned for a heavy write workload might be under-utilized when performing a lightweight table service, leading to wasted resources.

Deployment Mode: Async Execution

The *async execution mode* takes a hybrid approach by keeping the scheduling part inline with writes while executing the table service plan asynchronously (Figure 6-3). That is, the table service plan will be made synchronously after the write operation, while the execution is to be conducted by a separate job. This option makes a lot of sense when you consider the fact that scheduling, which is about reading the metadata of file groups and creating a plan, is typically a lightweight operation compared to the I/O-intensive execution. By keeping scheduling inline, we maintain tight coordination with write operations and simplify orchestration. Meanwhile, the heavier execution workload runs separately, allowing you to:

- Optimize resource allocation by using dedicated compute resources for the execution workloads.
- Unblock your write pipeline for faster data writes.
- Scale execution resources independently of your write resources.

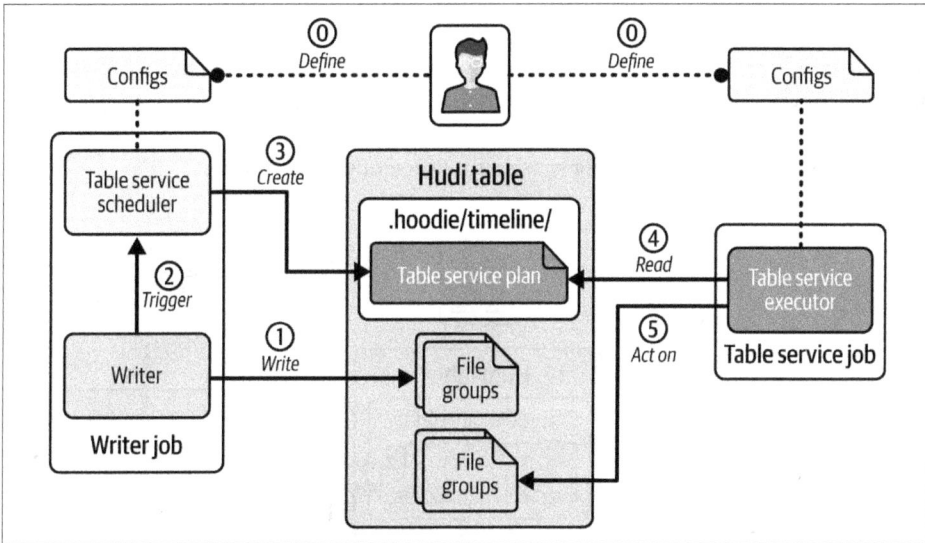

Figure 6-3. Table service async execution deployment mode

By striking this balance between coordination and resource optimization, the async execution mode offers a practical middle ground for many production deployments. Still, the scheduling time of gathering file groups' metadata and composing a plan based on the configured table service strategy won't be negligible and will inevitably slow down the writer process to some extent. For applications that aim for the most optimal write latency, the async execution mode may not be the best choice. Hudi tools like Hudi Streamer and Hudi Flink Streamer for Apache Flink offer convenient built-in async execution that executes table services in separate resource pools within the same compute cluster.

Deployment Mode: Standalone

The standalone mode offers the highest level of flexibility by fully decoupling both table service scheduling and execution from writer processes (Figure 6-4). In this mode, you can:

- Run the scheduling and execution completely independent of the write processes.
- Implement sophisticated scheduling strategies that consider resource availability and table priorities.
- Scale your table service infrastructure separately from your data pipeline.

This approach recognizes that housekeeping operations don't need to be tied to write frequency or be run on the same compute resources. Instead, they can be managed as a centralized platform maintenance effort, running on a custom cadence—such as every few minutes, every few hours, or nightly—to optimize tables across the lakehouse. Think of the standalone mode as a dedicated maintenance crew that operates independently from the regular ingestion/ETL team. This crew can assess, plan, and execute optimization tasks across all the tables on its own schedule and using its own resources, ensuring maximum efficiency and control.

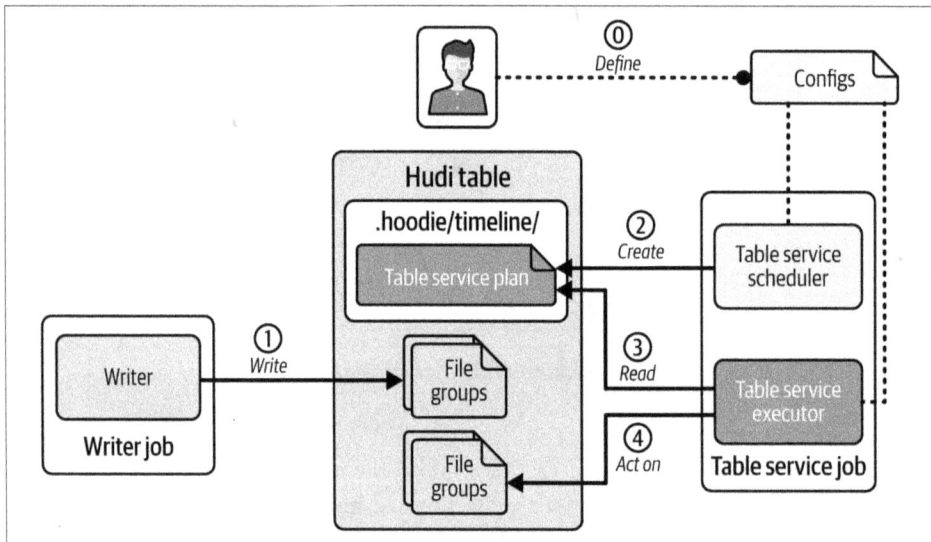

Figure 6-4. Table service standalone deployment mode

The flexibility of standalone mode does come with additional operational complexity—you'll need to manage separate infrastructure and set up a lock provider to coordinate the concurrent write and table service jobs to ensure proper transactionality in those actions. We will discuss lock providers in Chapter 7. For large-scale lakehouse deployments, this investment often pays off through better resource utilization and more optimized maintenance schedules.

Choosing a Suitable Mode

Choosing a deployment mode is a matter of providing the right configurations to your Hudi writer and table service jobs:

Inline mode

Supply all table service configurations directly to your writer job. This instructs the writer to handle both scheduling and execution.

Async execution mode

Provide scheduling-related configurations to the writer job. The writer job then submits another job with execution-related configurations to execute the table service plan asynchronously.

Standalone mode

Provide all scheduling and execution configurations to a dedicated, runnable application supplied by Hudi, which operates independently of any writer job. Additionally, for both writer and table service jobs, you will need to provide configurations to specify the lock provider's properties.

Each deployment mode represents a different point on the spectrum between operational simplicity and flexibility. While the inline mode offers a straightforward "set it and forget it" approach that is perfect for smaller deployments, the async execution and standalone modes provide increasingly sophisticated options for larger-scale operations where resource optimization becomes crucial. Table 6-1 provides a quick comparison of the deployment modes.

Table 6-1. Deployment modes comparison

Feature	Inline	Async execution	Standalone
Operational complexity	Minimal	Medium	High
Scheduling and execution flexibility	Low	Medium	High
Increased write latency	High	Low	Minimal
Facilitates resource optimization	Low	Medium	High

With a clear understanding of these trade-offs, you can select the deployment mode that best aligns with your operational needs and data processing requirements. The upcoming sections will explore Hudi's four primary table services in detail. For each service, we will cover its purpose and mechanics, provide sample configurations for inline mode, and point to the official documentation for additional examples.

Compaction

As we discussed in previous chapters, MOR tables excel at fast ingestion by writing updates and deletes to row-based log files. However, this design introduces a query-time trade-off. As log files accumulate, snapshot queries must merge them with the base file on the fly, a process that can degrade read performance.

Compaction is the table service designed to solve this problem specifically for MOR tables. It merges a base file with its corresponding log files to produce a new, versioned base file containing the latest state of the data (Figure 6-5). This process effectively converts any row-based updates and deletes into an optimized, columnar format, dramatically improving snapshot query performance while preserving the high write throughput of MOR tables.

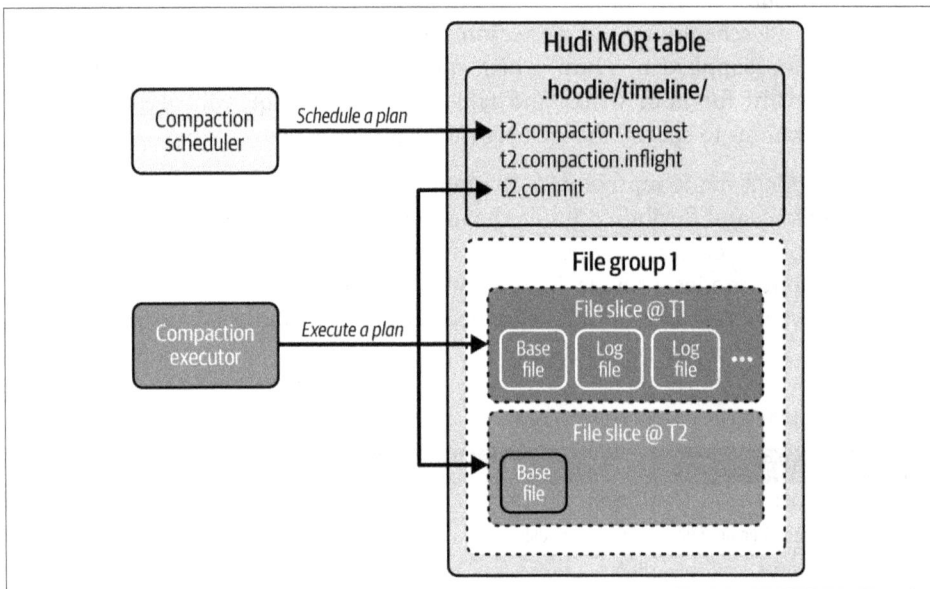

Figure 6-5. Compaction process

Comparing the MOR compaction process with the Copy-on-Write (COW) write process provides a clear perspective on their fundamental differences (Figure 6-6). In COW tables, any update or delete triggers a commit action that rewrites the entire file slice. In contrast, MOR tables efficiently append these changes to log files, and compaction runs periodically to merge them with the base file, optimize the file slice for reading, and produce a commit action. In essence, a COW table performs an implicit compaction with every write, which is functionally equivalent to an MOR table configured to run inline compaction after every deltacommit action.

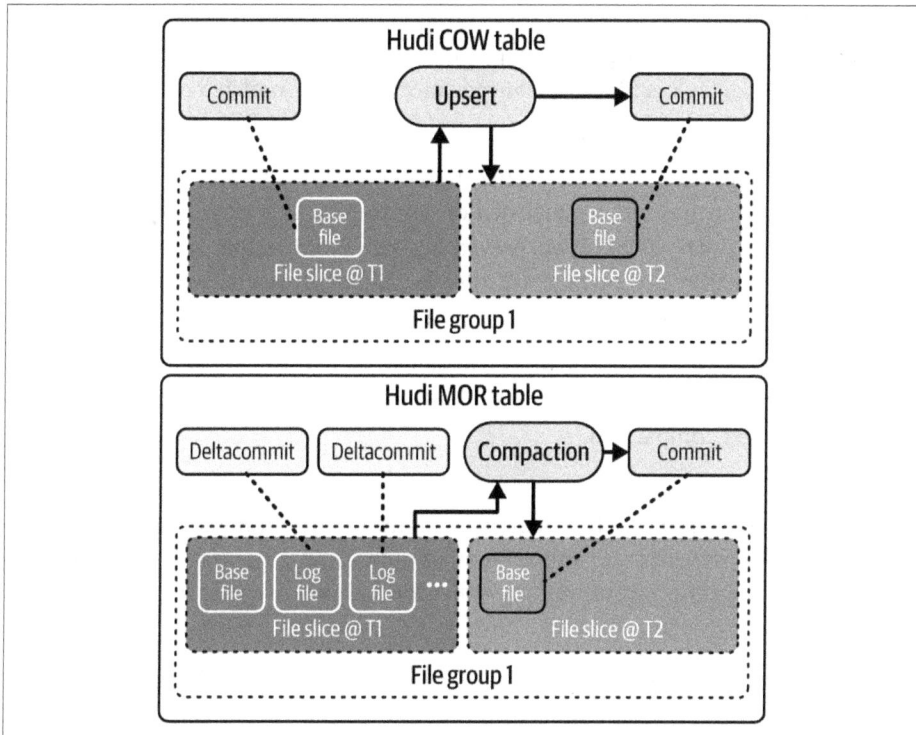

Figure 6-6. Compaction in an MOR table versus write (upsert) in a COW table

You can tune the compaction process by selecting a cadence and strategy that align with your table's update frequency and volume. Let's explore the available configuration options.

> As of this writing, Hudi is the only lakehouse storage system capable of asynchronously compacting files without blocking or failing a concurrent writer process that is also updating the same record in the same file group. This makes Hudi stand out as the preferred choice for near-real-time replication of mutable data streams like Relational Database Management System (RDBMS) change data capture (CDC) logs or frequently updating incremental ETL pipelines.

Schedule Compaction

Compaction is triggered based on a configurable strategy that is set using `hoodie.compact.inline.trigger.strategy`. Hudi offers several options to control when compaction is scheduled:

NUM_COMMITS

The default strategy. Triggers compaction after a specified number of `deltacommit` actions (default is 5) have occurred since the last completed compaction.

NUM_COMMITS_AFTER_LAST_REQUEST

Triggers compaction after a specified number of `deltacommit` actions since the last compaction was either requested or completed. This provides a more stable cadence than `NUM_COMMITS` by preventing new compaction plans from being scheduled if a previous one has failed or is still pending, thus avoiding a backlog of compaction requests.

TIME_ELAPSED

Triggers compaction after a configured number of seconds have elapsed since the last completed compaction.

NUM_AND_TIME

Triggers compaction only when both a minimum number of `deltacommit` actions have occurred *and* a minimum amount of time has passed. This strategy prevents compaction from running either too frequently or too infrequently.

NUM_OR_TIME

Triggers compaction when *either* a minimum number of `deltacommit` actions have occurred *or* a minimum amount of time has passed. This flexible approach ensures that compaction runs regularly, preventing long delays.

Once triggered, the execution of the compaction plan is guided by a specific strategy, which you can define using `hoodie.compaction.strategy`. This setting determines how Hudi identifies and prioritizes file slices for compaction. Some commonly used strategies are:

LogFileSizeBasedCompactionStrategy

The default strategy; prioritizes file slices with the largest total size of log files, targeting those with the most unmerged data. It includes a configurable threshold to select file slices based on a minimum log file size (default is 0) and caps the total data to be processed (default is 500 GB) in a single run to manage I/O and memory consumption.

LogFileNumBasedCompactionStrategy

Prioritizes file slices with the largest number of log files. This approach is effective for targeting file slices that have accumulated many small updates. Like the size-based strategy, it provides a threshold to select file slices but based on a minimum log file count (default is 0). It also caps the total data to be processed (default is 500 GB) to control resource usage.

PartitionRegexBasedCompactionStrategy

Selects partitions for compaction by matching their path against a regular expression. This allows you to run targeted compaction jobs on specific groups of partitions, which is useful for applying different maintenance policies across your data.

The following example shows a sample configuration set for inline compaction. Using this, compaction is triggered after 10 `deltacommit` actions. It uses the `LogFileNum` `BasedCompactionStrategy` to prioritize file slices with the highest number of log files, selecting any file slice with at least one log file. Finally, it caps the total I/O (including both reading and writing file slices) for the compaction run at 100 GB to manage resource consumption:

```
hoodie.compact.inline=true
hoodie.compact.inline.max.delta.commits=10
hoodie.compact.inline.trigger.strategy=NUM_COMMITS_AFTER_LAST_REQUEST
hoodie.compaction.strategy=\
org.apache.hudi.table.action.compact.strategy.LogFileNumBasedCompactionStrategy
hoodie.compaction.logfile.num.threshold=0
hoodie.compaction.target.io=102400
```

To provide more flexibility, Hudi also offers `CompositeCompactionStrategy` to chain multiple strategies together, applying `AND` logic to select candidate file slices. For full customization, you may also implement the `CompactionStrategy` API and supply your own strategy for the compaction scheduler.

Execute Compaction

If you configured the compaction for inline mode, the execution will start immediately after the plan being generated by the scheduler. The same writer job, like Apache Spark or Flink, will continue to run the compaction. If you configured it for async execution mode, the writer job will submit another job for the execution to run asynchronously. If you configured it for standalone mode, you'll need to set up another job, leveraging Hudi's utility application, like `HoodieCompactor` for Spark or `HoodieFlinkCompactor` for Flink, to execute the compaction plan. For more examples, please refer to the documentation page (*https://oreil.ly/cnfhk*).

Compaction is inherently resource intensive for several reasons:

- The merge process is compute intensive, requiring substantial CPU resources to combine and sort records.
- It could involve reading large volumes of data from both base files and log files.
- Depending on the plan, it could generate many new base files simultaneously during the rewrite process.

These characteristics make compaction fundamentally different from regular write operations that are typically performed on MOR tables. While writes tend to be frequent, smaller operations that can run efficiently on a modest cluster, compaction behaves more like a batch processing job that benefits from dedicated computing resources. Understanding this distinction is crucial for resource planning at scale.

Clustering

Clustering in Hudi optimizes data layout by grouping similar records together to improve query performance and storage efficiency in your data lakehouse. It addresses the challenges of small files and record organization by consolidating and sorting data based on specified columns.

When writing data at high velocities, especially in streaming scenarios, we often accumulate many small files to maintain low latency. While this approach helps achieve faster data freshness, it can significantly degrade query performance as systems need to open and process many small files instead of fewer larger ones. Even with the small-file handling feature introduced in Chapter 3, tables may still suffer from under-optimized storage layout due to having undesired initial file group allocation and the small-file handling not being able to improve the data proximity by sorting. Clustering solves this by intelligently consolidating small files into optimally sized ones while sorting records based on specified columns to maintain good proximity.

This principle of "proximity" means that records sharing common values for columns are physically stored together. For instance, in a sales dataset, clustering by region would place all sales records for California into the same file or a small set of nearby files. As a result, a query filtering for sales in that region can read a minimal amount of data to dramatically improve performance.

The clustering process in Hudi reorganizes data by identifying eligible file slices, reading the records, sorting them based on specified columns, and rewriting them into new, optimized file groups (Figure 6-7). This provides two key benefits:

Enhanced data skipping
> By physically grouping related records, clustering allows query engines to bypass entire files that do not contain relevant data. For example, if your queries frequently filter by date ranges, clustering by date significantly increases the chance that records from the same day are stored together, enabling the engine to quickly skip files outside the requested range.

Improved compression
> Storing similar data together improves the efficiency of columnar formats like Apache Parquet. When values in a column are alike, they can be compressed more effectively, reducing storage costs.

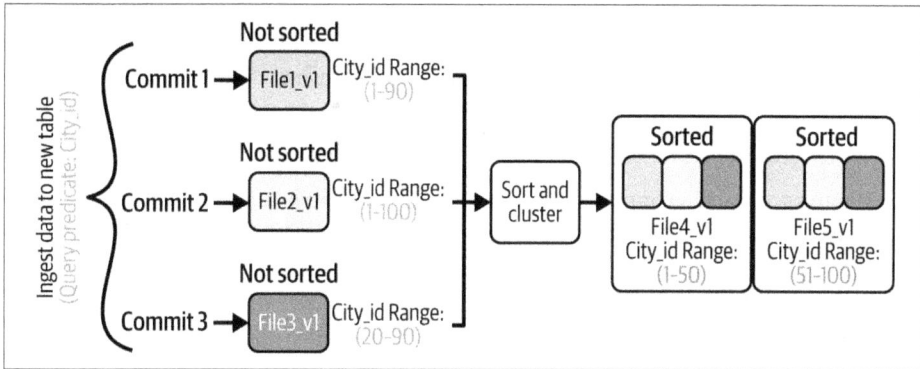

Figure 6-7. Clustering process

Just as with compaction, you can configure the clustering process by selecting from various strategies. Let's examine these options.

Schedule Clustering

Triggering clustering is based on the number of `commit` or `deltacommit` actions accumulated since the last clustering process. As an example, you could configure these settings for your writer job for inline mode:

```
hoodie.clustering.inline=true
hoodie.clustering.inline.max.commits=4
```

Once the settings are triggered, Hudi uses its clustering plan strategy to identify candidate file slices for clustering. By default, Hudi provides a size-based clustering plan strategy, which creates clustering groups based on the maximum size allowed per group and considers the following key thresholds:

```
# Target maximum file size for clustering output
hoodie.clustering.plan.strategy.target.file.max.bytes=1073741824  # 1GB

# Small file size limit for clustering
hoodie.clustering.plan.strategy.small.file.limit=314572800  # 300MB

# Maximum number of groups in clustering plan
hoodie.clustering.plan.strategy.max.num.groups=30

# Maximum bytes per group
hoodie.clustering.plan.strategy.max.bytes.per.group=2147483648  # 2GB
# Columns to sort
hoodie.clustering.plan.strategy.sort.columns=a,b
```

Based on this example configuration, the clustering plan would be as follows:

1. Within each partition, identify all file slices smaller than 300 MB.

2. Group these small file slices together, ensuring that each group's total size does not exceed 2 GB, and create no more than 30 such groups in total.

3. Finally, for each group, sort the records by columns a and b before rewriting them into new, larger file slices, each targeting a maximum size of 1 GB.

The plan can also be configured by setting `hoodie.clustering.plan.partition.fil ter.mode` to filter which partitions to include using different partition filtering modes:

- `NONE`, to include all partitions that have clustering candidates
- `RECENT_DAYS`, to include partitions from a specific date range
- `SELECTED_PARTITIONS`, to include only specified partition paths
- `DAY_ROLLING`, to include partitions based on a rolling daily schedule

Execute Clustering

If you configured the clustering for inline mode, the execution will start immediately after the plan being generated by the scheduler. The same writer job, like Spark or Flink, will continue to run the clustering. If you configured it for async execution mode, the writer job will submit another job for the execution to run asynchronously. If you configured it for standalone mode, you'll need to set up another job, leveraging Hudi's utility application, like `HoodieClusteringJob` for Spark or `HoodieFlinkClus teringJob` for Flink, to execute the clustering plan. For more examples, please refer to the documentation page (*https://oreil.ly/dOMCe*).

Layout Optimization Strategies

While Hudi's default strategy uses linear (lexicographical) sorting of records based on specified columns, it may not be optimal for all use cases. Let's explore why and when you might want to use alternative layout strategies.

Linear sorting

The linear strategy is often highly effective for datasets in which record proximity relies on just one column. For instance, consider a table containing transaction records with a timestamp column. Analysts often run queries to fetch all records between transaction time A and transaction time B. Given that the records are considered proximally close as long as the transaction timestamps are close, linear sorting by timestamp is a perfect strategy to preserve locality.

However, the linear strategy may not perform well with datasets that require two or more columns to determine record proximity. For example, consider a house inventory dataset with columns for latitude and longitude. Lexicographical sorting of latitude followed by longitude would group geographically distant house records together simply based on the proximity of latitude. In such cases, sorting algorithms that are capable of handling *N*-dimensional records are needed. This is where Z-order and Hilbert optimization strategies can be applied.

Space-filling curves

The mathematical term *space-filling curve* describes a curve that traverses a space, intersecting with all possible points in that space and thereby filling it entirely. Once the curve is straightened, all the multidimensional points are mapped to a one-dimensional space and are assigned a single-value coordinate. Among the various curve-drawing methods, Z-order and Hilbert, as shown in Figure 6-8, are two approaches that can effectively preserve spatial locality through this mapping, as the majority of nearby points on the curve are also close to each other in the original space.

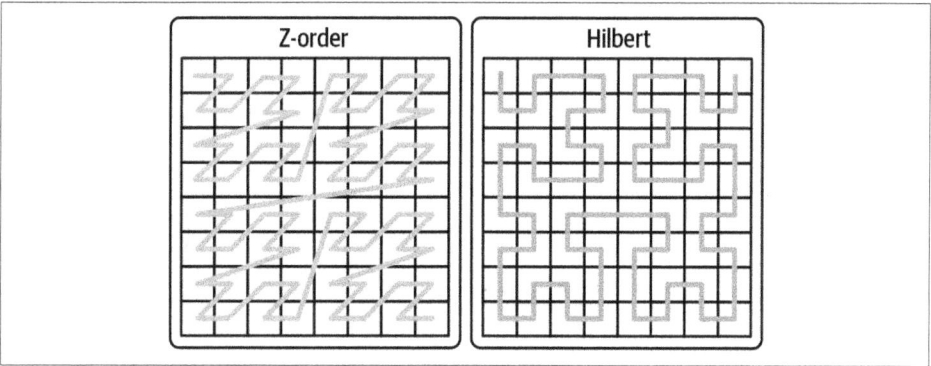

Figure 6-8. Z-order and Hilbert curves in a two-dimensional plane

When we treat records as multidimensional points, drawing a Z-order or Hilbert curve essentially defines the way to sort them. Given that spatial locality is well preserved, actual "nearby" records are more likely to be stored in the same files. This fulfills the proximity condition and could significantly enhance read efficiency by skipping more files to scan.

By setting `hoodie.layout.optimize.strategy` to `ZORDER` or `HILBERT`, you can instruct the clustering process to sort the records based on these advanced sorting algorithms. This ensures that records that are close in multidimensional space (e.g., nearby geographical coordinates) are also physically co-located on disk, enabling highly efficient range and radius queries.

Clustering Versus Compaction

While both clustering and compaction rewrite data to optimize table performance, they serve different purposes and operate differently. Here are the key distinctions.

First, clustering works with both COW and MOR tables, while compaction only applies to MOR tables. This makes clustering a more versatile optimization tool across different table types.

Second, they differ in how they handle record organization. Compaction operates within a file group, merging log files with their base file to create a new file slice that represents a newer version of records in that file group. In contrast, clustering reorganizes records across file groups, creating entirely new ones with both optimized sizes and sorted records.

Cleaning

Hudi achieves snapshot isolation between writers and readers through MVCC, which maintains multiple versions of data files. While these versioned files enable powerful features like time travel and incremental queries, they can significantly impact storage costs over time. As new data arrives, Hudi tables continuously create file slices to represent newer versions, inevitably consuming more storage space. This is where the cleaning service comes in. It reclaims storage space by removing older, unnecessary versions of data files, effectively keeping storage costs in check (Figure 6-9).

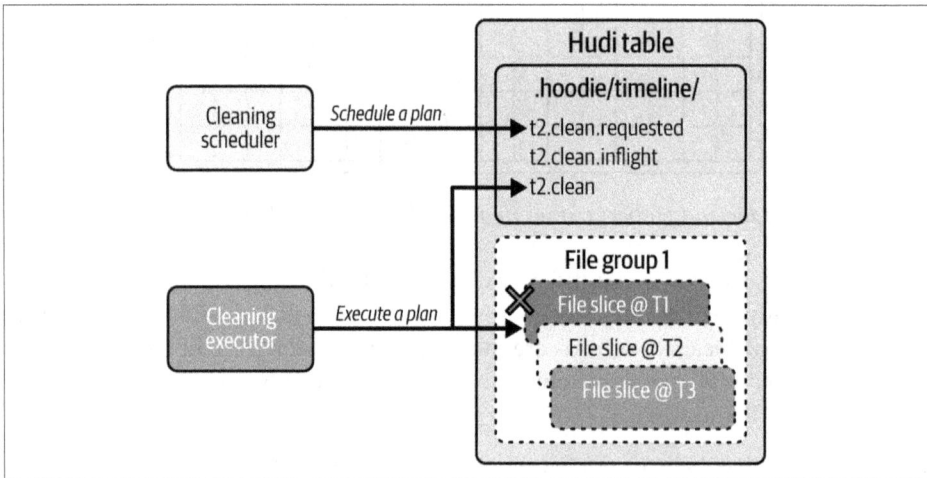

Figure 6-9. Cleaning process

The cleaning service is most relevant for tables with updates or deletes, where each modification creates a new version of the affected data. By leveraging this service, we can control the retention period for historical versions while optimizing storage costs, effectively balancing between storage efficiency and the time window available for time travel queries and incremental processing.

Append-only tables do not need the cleaning table service, as they never generate multiple versions of the same data. Running cleaning on these tables would be a no-op because there are no outdated versions to clean. It's also worth noting that the cleaning table service serves a distinct purpose from time-to-live (TTL) operations. While TTL might delete entire date partitions older than a threshold, the cleaning service specifically manages and removes outdated versions of modified records.

Schedule Cleaning

When scheduling cleaning operations, Hudi uses a trigger-based approach to determine when maintenance is needed. Let's explore how we can configure and control this scheduling process to match our table maintenance requirements.

The configurations for inline cleaning are:

```
hoodie.clean.automatic=true
hoodie.clean.async.enabled=false
```

This is the default mode for using Spark as the writer. For Flink, the default is the async execution mode.

The cleaning service is triggered by setting the `CleaningTriggerStrategy`, which currently supports triggering based on commits. We can configure how frequently cleaning should be scheduled by specifying the number of commits between cleaning operations. For example, if we set this to 10 commits, Hudi will evaluate whether cleaning is needed after every 10th commit:

```
# Configure cleaning trigger interval
hoodie.clean.trigger.strategy=NUM_COMMITS
hoodie.clean.trigger.commits=10
```

Once triggered, the cleaning planner scans relevant partitions to identify file slices that meet the cleaning criteria. These criteria are defined by our chosen `Hoodie CleaningPolicy`.

We can choose from three cleaning policies based on our specific needs:

Commit-based retention
    For example:

    ```
    # Keep last 24 commits
    hoodie.cleaner.policy=KEEP_LATEST_COMMITS
    hoodie.cleaner.commits.retained=24
    ```

    This is ideal when we need to ensure that our long-running queries have access to historical data. For instance, if we ingest data every 30 minutes and our longest query takes 12 hours, we should retain at least 24 commits to maintain a safe window for query execution.

Version-based retention

For example:

```
# Keep last 3 versions of each file
hoodie.cleaner.policy=KEEP_LATEST_FILE_VERSIONS
hoodie.cleaner.fileversions.retained=3
```

This works well when we want to maintain a fixed number of versions regardless of time, such as keeping only the most recent version for storage optimization.

Time-based retention

For example:

```
# Keep versions from last 72 hours
hoodie.cleaner.policy=KEEP_LATEST_BY_HOURS
hoodie.cleaner.hours.retained=72
```

This provides a straightforward way to retain data based on age, making it easy to implement time-based retention policies.

Execute Cleaning

Once we have our cleaning schedule and policies in place, the execution phase carries out the actual cleaning operations, in this case, deleting the old file slices.

If you configured the cleaning for inline mode, the execution will start immediately after the plan being generated by the scheduler. The same writer job, like Spark or Flink, will continue to run the cleaning. If you configured it for async execution mode, the writer job will submit another job for the execution to run asynchronously. If you configured it for standalone mode, you'll need to set up another job, leveraging Hudi's utility application HoodieCleaner for Spark (there is no utility for Flink at the time of writing), to execute the cleaning plan. For more examples, please refer to the documentation page (*https://oreil.ly/V9f_g*).

By properly configuring both scheduling and execution parameters, we can maintain optimal storage efficiency while ensuring that our data remains accessible for all necessary operations.

Indexing

As discussed in Chapter 5, Hudi offers a variety of indexing options. The metadata table, in particular, serves as a multimodal index and is the core indexing subsystem within a Hudi table, improving both read and write performance.

However, for indexes such as the record index and secondary index, the metadata table stores entries that grow with the number of records in the table. Consequently, enabling these indexes on a large, existing table requires scanning a large number of file slices to build the index from scratch—a process that can be time-consuming. In addition, it will not be acceptable to fail writers or queries for the duration of the index building process; rather, readers and writers should continue to operate normally and should gracefully degrade in performance. Furthermore, when indexing completes, the indexing process should ensure that the index is consistent with the latest writes on the table. These challenges are the primary motivation for the indexing table service.

The indexing operation creates an `indexing` action in the data table's timeline to record the operation. In the same transaction, it also performs a `deltacommit` action on the metadata table, writing index data to the partition for the new index (Figure 6-10). In Chapter 5, we used the `CREATE INDEX` SQL command to build multiple index types in the metadata table. Using this command essentially runs the indexing table service in the inline mode. This approach requires stopping all writers to the table while the indexing is in progress, which can cause service interruptions and a negative business impact, as we noted earlier.

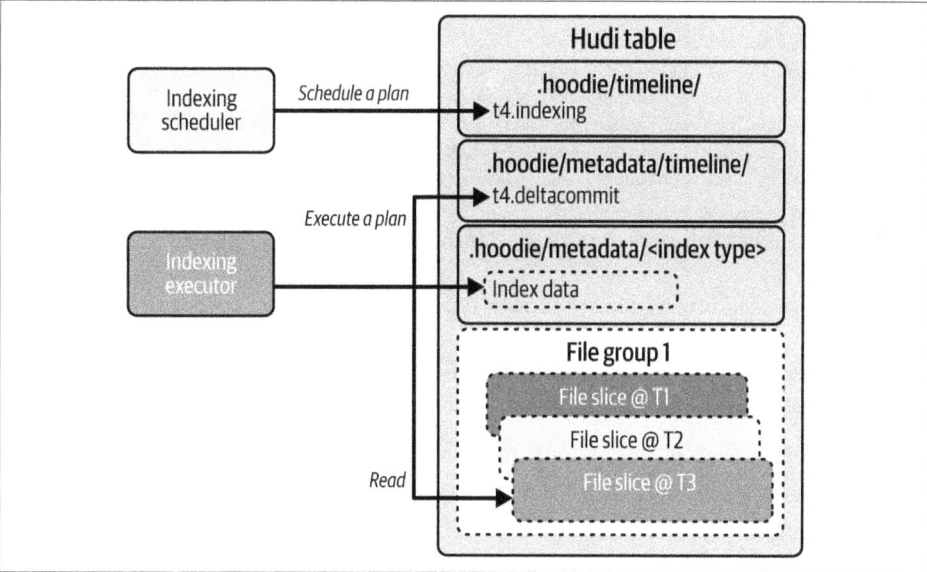

Figure 6-10. Indexing process

Thus, the primary use case for the indexing table service is to run it in the standalone mode, allowing incoming data to be written to the table while having an indexer running separately in parallel. Because ongoing writers must continue to update the partitions in the metadata table for the enabled indexes while the indexer builds the indexes for historical data, this concurrent write process must be coordinated. Therefore, running the standalone indexing service is a multiwriter scenario requiring configuration of a lock provider.

To facilitate running the standalone indexing service, Hudi provides a utility application, HoodieIndexer, that supports both scheduling and execution in Spark. A few of its important arguments include:

```
--mode <schedule or execute>
--index-types <index types to be built>
--props </path/to/indexer/properties/file>
```

Set `--mode` to `schedule` or `execute` to indicate whether to schedule indexing by making a plan, or to execute indexing based on the plan. Use `--index-types` to specify the indexes to build in the metadata table, such as `RECORD_INDEX`. Multiple index types can be provided as a comma-delimited list. The `--props` argument points to a *.properties* file containing the Hudi configurations for the HoodieIndexer. An example of this *.properties* file is as follows:

```
hoodie.metadata.index.async=true ❶
hoodie.metadata.index.record.index.enable=true ❷

hoodie.write.concurrency.mode=optimistic_concurrency_control ❸
hoodie.write.lock.provider=\
org.apache.hudi.client.transaction.lock.ZookeeperBasedLockProvider
hoodie.write.lock.zookeeper.url=<zk_url>
hoodie.write.lock.zookeeper.port=<zk_port>
hoodie.write.lock.zookeeper.lock_key=<zk_key>
hoodie.write.lock.zookeeper.base_path=<zk_base_path>
```

❶ This configuration indicates using standalone mode for indexing.

❷ The corresponding flag for the index type being built must also be set to `true`.

❸ This property and the entries below it configure the setup for the multiwriter scenario.

When running the indexer, both the indexer and the writer jobs should use the same lock provider and should enable the same indexes to be built. For more examples, please refer to the documentation page (*https://oreil.ly/SEkFM*).

Summary

In this chapter, we explored the importance of maintaining and optimizing Hudi tables to keep our data lakehouse running efficiently. Just like we should keep our home organized, we should regularly clean and reorganize our tables to ensure that they remain accessible and performant. We introduced Hudi's table services—our essential toolkit for this task—which include compaction, clustering, cleaning, and indexing.

We examined the different deployment modes available for these services—inline, async execution, and standalone—and discussed how we can balance simplicity with flexibility to meet our operational needs. Each of these table services serves a specific purpose:

- Compaction lets us improve read performance for MOR tables by merging log files and base files into optimized formats.

- Clustering enables us to reorganize and sort records to enhance query performance and reduce storage costs.

- Cleaning helps us reclaim storage by removing unnecessary file versions while retaining the historical data we need.

- Indexing builds up the index data in the metadata table.

Throughout the chapter, we reviewed strategies and configurations for scheduling and executing these services, empowering us to tailor them to our specific workloads and infrastructure. By implementing these maintenance operations, we can optimize our data lakehouse for both current and future demands, keeping it scalable, cost-efficient, and high performing.

Concurrency Control in Hudi

In the world of databases and data lakehouses, concurrency control is a critical concept that ensures data integrity and consistency in the face of multiple concurrent operations. It defines how different processes, whether they are reading or writing data, coordinate access to the shared data to prevent conflicts and maintain data integrity. Concurrency control is crucial because, without it, uncoordinated access to data can lead to various anomalies such as lost updates, dirty reads, and inconsistent data.

Imagine an ecommerce platform where two customers simultaneously attempt to purchase the last available unit of a high-demand product. If the system lacks proper concurrency control, both transactions might proceed as if the item is available, leading to one customer being charged for a product that is out of stock. This scenario can result in customer complaints, refund processing costs, and damage to brand reputation. By implementing concurrency control mechanisms, the system ensures that only one transaction succeeds, preventing overselling and maintaining accurate inventory records.

In Chapter 3, we provided an overview of Apache Hudi's write process; in this chapter, we'll dig deeper into how Hudi handles concurrent operations to protect against these kinds of problems.

Why Concurrency Control Is Harder in Data Lakehouses

Many database systems implement concurrency control mechanisms to handle multiple writers and readers. For instance, PostgreSQL uses MVCC to allow readers to access a consistent snapshot of the data while writers modify it using pessimistic row-level locking techniques.

Online transaction processing (OLTP) databases operate on individual records with transactional storage engines that provide millisecond-level latencies for reads and writes. In contrast, data lakehouses are designed for massive-scale storage, with long-running write transactions that span minutes (e.g., near-real-time ingestion) to several hours (e.g., a large-scale machine learning training pipeline) and large columnar (OLAP) scans. This makes it difficult to simply apply the same OLTP concurrency control techniques like fine-grained locking or versioning to data lakehouses, without introducing significant performance overhead or scaling bottlenecks.

Additionally, lakehouses often rely on cloud object stores (e.g., Amazon S3, GCS) for their scalable storage. While these stores have evolved to provide strong consistency guarantees for object-level operations (like read-after-write), they lack the native, multioperation transactional capabilities of traditional databases, which complicates the atomicity of complex commits. As a result, concurrency control in data lakehouses requires innovative approaches that balance consistency, scalability, and performance in a distributed environment.

Given the distributed nature of data lakehouses and the potentially limited built-in transactional guarantees in underlying storage systems, supporting multiple writers is essential for scalability and efficiency. While a single-writer approach may suffice for simple use cases, it quickly becomes a bottleneck in modern data lakehouses, where vast amounts of data flow in from multiple sources, and various operations—such as inserts, updates, deletes, and clustering—must run concurrently and safely. A sequential execution model imposed by a single writer hinders performance, limits scalability, and introduces a single point of failure, increasing operational risk.

Beyond speed, supporting multiple writers allows organizations to separate distinct workflows into independent pipelines. For example, data ingestion, backfilling, and clustering can be scheduled and executed in parallel, optimizing resource utilization. Clustering operations, such as sorting or encrypting data, can run during off-peak hours without slowing down ingestion pipelines, while regulatory compliance tasks —like GDPR-mandated deletions—can proceed without disrupting real-time data flows. Hudi addresses these challenges by enabling concurrent writes while maintaining consistency, ensuring that lakehouse workloads scale efficiently and remain adaptable to increasing data volume and complexity.

While managing concurrent writers is a primary challenge, a robust system must also guarantee that read operations are isolated from these writes to prevent exposing inconsistent or partial data to users and downstream applications. It is essential to ensure that readers are not affected by inflight writes, as this could result in inconsistent or incomplete data being exposed to downstream applications. Hudi addresses this challenge by employing snapshot isolation, which allows readers to view a consistent snapshot of the dataset, irrespective of ongoing write operations. By providing such guarantees, Hudi ensures that both writers and readers always operate on stable and reliable data without incurring the overhead of traditional locking mechanisms, addressing the problems introduced earlier.

Concurrency Control Techniques

Concurrency control in modern systems is implemented through a variety of techniques. OCC is one such method, where the system assumes that conflicts are rare and allows multiple processes to proceed concurrently. At the commit stage, the system checks for conflicts and resolves them as needed. While this minimizes locking overhead, it may require retries if conflicts are detected. In a data lakehouse, these retries can be prohibitively expensive, because writes worth several hours could be lost and would need to be reissued.

Another widely used approach is MVCC, which allows readers and writers to work on different versions of the data. Readers operate on a snapshot of the data corresponding to their transaction's start time, while writers generate new versions of the data. This method ensures isolation and avoids blocking readers. Hudi has also designed a more fitting approach for data lakehouse workloads, non-blocking concurrency control (NBCC). Processes write delta changes, and conflicts are resolved later in a deterministic order based on either commit order or an ordering field within the record. This is particularly effective for streaming workloads, where minimizing latency and zero downtime are critical.

Hudi employs these three techniques carefully to create a robust and performant concurrency model tailored to the unique requirements of data lakehouses. It employs OCC to manage conflicts between concurrent writers, ensuring consistent updates that are serialized in a consistent order. MVCC provides snapshot isolation across writers, readers, and table services, enabling table services like compaction and cleaning to run asynchronously without blocking write operations. Additionally, NBCC is a specialized approach for high-throughput lakehouse tables that allows multiple writers and concurrent table services to operate on the table without failing each other, eliminating gross compute resource wastage incurred by OCC. By combining these mechanisms, Hudi allows multiple processes to operate concurrently while maintaining consistency, isolation, and performance.

This chapter will provide a detailed explanation of how Hudi manages concurrency in distributed data lakehouses. By exploring its concurrency control mechanisms, you'll learn how Hudi enables coordinated, simultaneous operations—such as data ingestion, updates, and deletions—while preserving data consistency. This will help you design and operate scalable, high-performance data platforms that efficiently handle multiple concurrent workloads without compromising reliability.

Although Hudi's concurrency control mechanisms prevent data corruption from concurrent writes, they do not automatically resolve all logical conflicts. For instance, with OCC, duplicate records may be inserted if two writers process the same source data. Hudi guarantees that the underlying table structure always remains consistent, but users are still responsible for ensuring that their data pipelines are idempotent and partitioned to avoid logical inconsistencies.

Multiwriter Scenarios

In modern lakehouse environments, the ability to support multiple writers is not just a feature but a necessity. The demand for high throughput, operational flexibility, and efficient resource utilization makes a single-writer system insufficient for most real-world scenarios. Hudi addresses this need by allowing multiple writers to operate concurrently while ensuring that data consistency and integrity are maintained.

Why Multiwriters Are Necessary

A multiwriter system becomes indispensable for several reasons:

Handling resource limitations
> A single writer can quickly become a bottleneck, especially when dealing with large-scale data ingestion or processing workflows. Multiwriter capabilities distribute the workload across multiple processes, improving throughput and scalability.

Supporting independent pipelines
> Different types of operations—such as ingestion, ETL, backfilling, and clustering—have varying resource requirements and priorities. Running these operations in separate pipelines not only improves efficiency but also reduces operational overhead.

Minimizing operational delays
> Critical write operations must often proceed without being slowed down by other data management tasks. Multiwriter systems ensure that best-effort table services, such as cleaning or compaction, do not interfere with time-sensitive data pipelines.

Cost efficiency
> By separating high-priority and resource-intensive tasks from lower-priority ones, organizations can allocate resources more effectively. For example, backfilling operations can use low-cost resources during off-peak hours, while writes continue uninterrupted.

Scalability
> Multiple writers enable horizontal scaling of writes, allowing organizations to handle increasing data volumes without compromising performance.

Multiwriter Scenarios for OCC

Typical data lakehouse multiwriter support employs OCC and can handle scenarios where writers operate on independent portions of the data, minimizing the risk of conflicts. Following are some common scenarios where multiwriter support based on OCC works smoothly.

Backfilling data

Imagine a financial services company migrating years of transaction records from an old system into a Hudi table. A dedicated backfill writer can handle this process in parallel with the primary writer pipeline, ensuring that historical data is added without slowing down or interfering with the writing of new transactions.

Deleting older data

Organizations handling sensitive customer data must comply with regulations like GDPR, which require the deletion of certain records after a set period. For example, an insurance company may need to purge certain records older than five years. A separate writer can handle these deletions without interrupting real-time order ingestion, ensuring compliance without impacting application performance.

Post-processing data using clustering services

Large-scale analytics platforms often require periodic reorganization of data for efficiency. Consider a video streaming service storing user engagement logs in a data lakehouse. To speed up query performance, the system may cluster data by user ID or time intervals. Instead of burdening the primary ingestion process, a separate writer can run during off-peak hours to optimize file sizes and sort data, improving read performance for analytics workloads.

Scaling ingestion/ETL

In data-intensive environments, relying on a single data pipeline can become a bottleneck for high-throughput tables. For instance, a cybersecurity platform processing logs from thousands of servers might need to ingest terabytes of data per hour. By assigning multiple writers to different partitions of an Apache Kafka topic, the system can efficiently distribute the ingestion load, thereby preventing lag and improving overall throughput.

Multiwriter Scenarios for NBCC and MVCC

Scenarios involving overlapping writes to the same file groups can lead to conflicts, resulting in resource wastage or aborted operations. In particular, a multiwriter with OCC is not recommended in the following cases. Instead, a multiwriter with an NBCC or MVCC approach is required for smooth operations.

Scenarios with overlapping data modifications

Suppose two data engineers are responsible for updating customer records in a retail database, each running a job that modifies user profiles based on different sources. If both jobs attempt to update the same set of user records simultaneously, one write may be aborted, leading to wasted compute resources and inconsistencies in customer data. In such cases, using NBCC to order or merge the conflicting writes might be more effective. For example, Hudi can either pick the latest committed record (commit time ordering) or the one with the higher source timestamp (event time ordering), without failing either writer. This allows both writers to complete their writes, whereas an OCC-based approach would have failed one writer even if just one record intersected across the writes.

High-contention workloads

In some cases, writers and table services constantly contend on the same file groups or records. For example, TikTok streams 100 GB per minute into Hudi tables and cannot afford to have either process fail and retry constantly using OCC. Using the MVCC-based approach here helps by allowing both compaction and the writer to work off a single shared version of the file group.

The Simple Default: Single Writer with Table Services

While multiwriter support is essential for many scenarios, the simplest and most common use case is a single writer with no concurrent writers. Out of the box, Hudi operates under this model, eliminating the need for external lock providers to get started and simplifying the architecture. For simpler workflows, a single-writer system combined with table services can be highly effective and sufficient.

Single writer with inline table services

In the single-writer model, table services such as cleaning, compaction, and clustering can be run inline after every write. This ensures that the table is optimized and managed without the need for additional concurrency control. Inline table services are idempotent, meaning they can be retried in case of failures, and they are automatically persisted to the timeline.

Single writer with async execution table services

Alternatively, table services can be run asynchronously in the background, allowing the writer to continue ingesting data without being blocked. Table services in async execution mode are particularly useful for long-running operations, such as compaction, which can take significant time to complete. Hudi leverages MVCC to ensure that such table services can run concurrently with the writer without conflicts.

Table 7-1 highlights the guarantees provided by different concurrent control mechanisms for different types of writer workloads and concurrent readers.

Table 7-1. Guarantees in multiwriter scenarios

Scenario	UPSERT guarantee	INSERT guarantee	BULK_INSERT guarantee	INCREMENTAL QUERY guarantee
Single writer	No duplicates	No duplicates	No duplicates	No out-of-order data
Multiwriter (OCC)	No duplicates	May have duplicates (without custom conflict resolution)	May have duplicates	No out-of-order data
Multiwriter (NBCC)	No duplicates	May have duplicates (without custom conflict resolution)	May have duplicates	No out-of-order data

How Hudi Handles Concurrency Control

A good multiwriter system should possess several key features to ensure efficient and reliable concurrent operations. It should allow multiple writers to write and commit data concurrently if there are no conflicting writes to the same underlying data. It should also have mechanisms to minimize, detect, and resolve conflicts between writers that modify the same data. To handle various use cases and workflows, it should provide a pluggable interface for users to define their own conflict resolution strategies. To simplify architecture and enhance scalability, a good multiwriter system should minimize the need for additional external components and reduce the reliance on long-held locks. Additionally, it should allow table services to run concurrently with writers without blocking them, ensuring smooth and efficient data management.

Hudi's concurrency control design inherently supports all of these features.

The Foundations of Hudi's Concurrency Control

At its core, Hudi's concurrency control is built around the concept of snapshot isolation, which ensures that all processes—whether they are writers, table services, or readers—operate on a consistent snapshot of the table. This is achieved through a combination of OCC, MVCC, and NBCC. These mechanisms work in tandem to provide a robust framework for handling concurrent operations. For example, even when applying MVCC and NBCC, there is a shared understanding of the snapshot the processes are concurrently operating on, using short-lived distributed locks.

Snapshot isolation

Snapshot isolation is a critical feature that allows Hudi to maintain consistency across multiple processes. When a writer commits changes to the table, those changes are not immediately visible to readers. Instead, readers continue to access a consistent snapshot of the data as it existed before the write operation began. This ensures that readers are not exposed to partially written or inconsistent data, even while writes are in progress.

OCC

Hudi employs OCC to manage conflicts between writers. Under OCC, writers proceed with their operations optimistically, assuming that conflicts are rare. If two writers attempt to modify the same file group simultaneously, Hudi detects the conflict and resolves it by aborting one of the writes.

However, OCC is not without its challenges. In scenarios where conflicts are frequent, the cost of aborting and retrying writes can become significant. To mitigate this, Hudi introduces early conflict detection (discussed later in the chapter), which identifies potential conflicts during the data writing phase and aborts conflicting writes early in the lifecycle. This reduces the wastage of compute resources and improves overall system efficiency.

MVCC

MVCC is a foundational concept Hudi uses to provide NBCC between different types of operations. Think of it as a mechanism that keeps readers, writers, and table services from interfering with one another. MVCC allows multiple versions of the data to coexist, enabling readers to access a consistent snapshot of the table while writers and table services modify the data in the background. For example, a compaction job can safely rewrite data files in the background. While it generates new file versions, a long-running query that started before the compaction continues to read the older, consistent versions of those files. This prevents readers from seeing partial results and writers from being blocked by maintenance operations.

NBCC

Hudi's NBCC is a sophisticated mechanism designed to handle simultaneous writes to a single table without the need to abort any of those writes due to conflicts. This approach significantly improves ingestion throughput and reduces write failures, especially in high-concurrency streaming scenarios. It is a key feature that allows multiple writers to operate on the same table, and even the same file group, with conflicts being resolved automatically by the query reader and the compactor.

At its core, NBCC leverages a novel file layout strategy based on commit completion time, using TrueTime semantics, introduced in "About TrueTime Semantics" on page 28. TrueTime ensures global timestamp monotonicity across all writers. When multiple writers attempt to write to the same file group, instead of blocking or failing one of the writers, NBCC allows both to proceed. It achieves this by creating separate file slices for each concurrent write, with the conflicts resolved during read time or by the asynchronous compaction process. This is a departure from the traditional OCC model, where conflicting writes to the same file group would result in one of the writers failing and needing to retry.

The introduction of the Log-Structured Merge (LSM) Timeline in Hudi 1.0 is a foundational element for NBCC. The LSM Timeline provides a scalable and efficient way to manage table metadata, which is crucial for tracking the various concurrent writes and their states. It records both a requested time and a completion time for each action, which allows Hudi to maintain a consistent view of the table even with multiple writers operating in parallel. This detailed recordkeeping in the timeline enables the system to correctly reconstruct the state of the data for readers, ensuring data consistency and integrity without the performance bottlenecks associated with traditional locking.

Figure 7-1 shows a comparison of OCC versus NBCC when multiple writers attempt to write to the same file groups. OCC fails the second writer, but NBCC allows both writers to proceed.

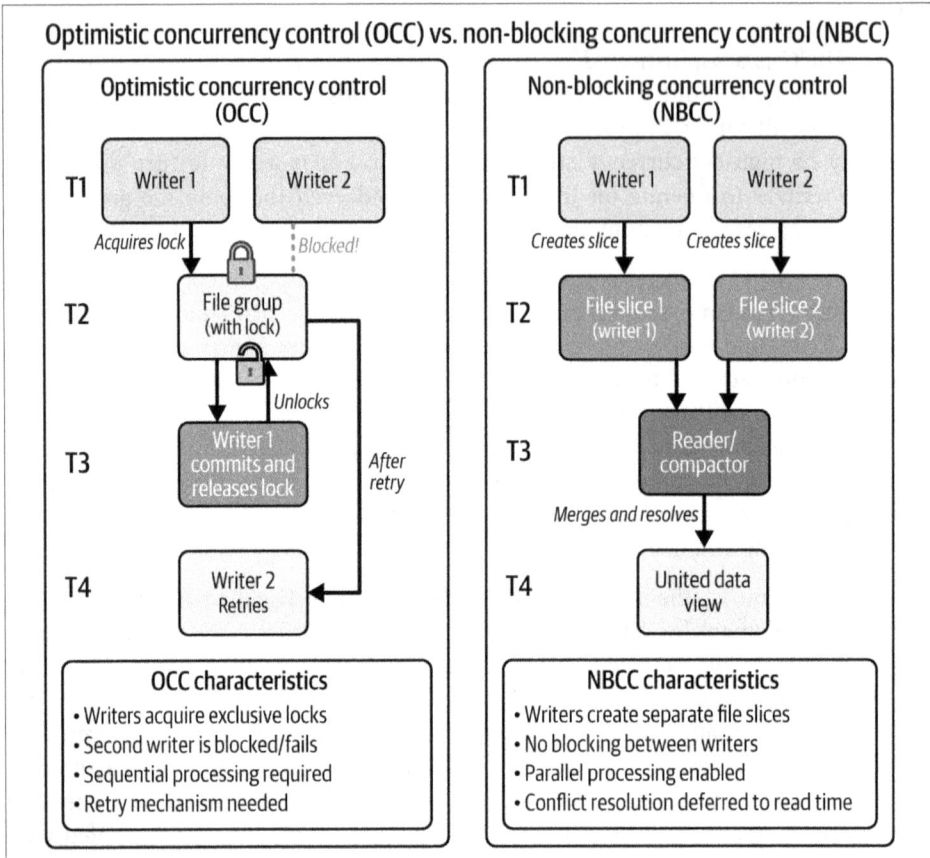

Optimistic concurrency control (OCC) vs. non-blocking concurrency control (NBCC)

Figure 7-1. Comparison between OCC and NBCC

The Three-Step Commit Process

Hudi's concurrency control is implemented through a three-step commit process (refer to Figure 7-2), which ensures that writes are atomic and consistent. This process, designed to minimize contention for locks and allow multiple writers to operate concurrently, comprises the following phases:

Phase 1: Request

In the request phase, the writer records its intent to write data in the timeline. This step generates the requested time for the transaction, which acts purely as a transaction ID for OCC and is used to sequence file slices for NBCC.

Phase 2: Inflight

In the inflight phase, the writer optionally records the plan of what changes it intends to make. This includes the file groups that will be written or modified. The inflight phase does not require locks, allowing multiple writers to proceed concurrently, writing new base files or log files. This phase can proceed in parallel with other writers, as the changes remain invisible to readers until the final commit.

Phase 3: Commit

In the commit phase, the writer updates the timeline to reflect the changes it has made. This is the atomic commit point, and it again requires a short-lived distributed lock. The lock is acquired briefly to generate a completion time to order the write, and also to ensure that no other writer can commit conflicting changes at the same time. Once the commit is complete, the lock is released, and the changes become visible to readers.

This design achieves a careful balance between concurrency and consistency, allowing maximum parallelism while maintaining strong correctness guarantees. The system maintains consistency by ensuring that readers continue to see the last successfully committed version of the data.

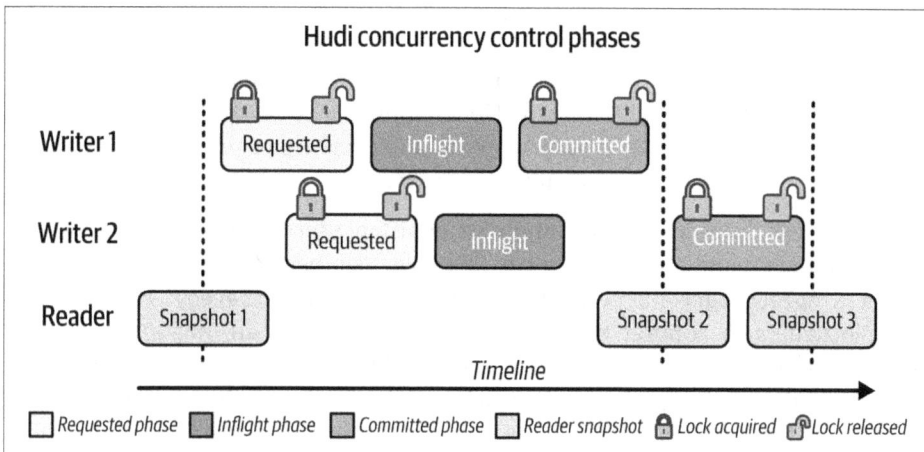

Figure 7-2. Three-step commit process with locking

Figure 7-2 depicts a timeline showing two concurrent writers. Both proceed through the requested and inflight phases in parallel. The lock is acquired during the requested phase to generate a timestamp and during the commit phase to perform the commit. Writer 1 acquires the lock first, commits, and releases the lock, creating a new table snapshot. Writer 2 then acquires the lock and attempts its commit, which will only succeed if there are no conflicts with Writer 1's changes.

While multiple writers might initiate their operations at nearly the same time, Hudi's timeline provides a strict, sequential ordering of actions. The underlying lock provider ensures that even near-simultaneous commit attempts are serialized, with one writer succeeding first and establishing the basis for any subsequent conflict checks.

The success of this protocol relies on careful management of file states and metadata. Each phase is recorded in the timeline, creating a clear audit trail of operations and enabling recovery in case of failures. This careful orchestration of concurrent operations, combined with pluggable components for locking and conflict resolution, makes Hudi a powerful platform for building scalable lakehouse solutions. The system's design reflects a deep understanding of the challenges inherent in distributed data processing, providing practical solutions that balance performance, consistency, and operational complexity.

Conflict Detection and Resolution

In concurrent systems, conflicts are inevitable when multiple writers attempt to modify the same data simultaneously. Hudi's approach to conflict handling is both pragmatic and efficient. The system allows multiple writers to proceed concurrently, maximizing throughput for nonconflicting operations.

When conflicts do occur and a winning write or table service operation needs to be picked, Hudi employs a default strategy that favors simplicity and consistency. Hudi uses a `SimpleConcurrentFileWritesConflictResolutionStrategy`, which allows multiple writers to commit their changes as long as they are not modifying the same file group. If two writers attempt to modify the same file group, the later write is aborted. This approach caters to the most common concurrent workload patterns on the data lakehouse but may be insufficient. Therefore, Hudi provides a pluggable interface for conflict resolution, allowing organizations to implement custom strategies that align with their specific requirements. For example, one can implement a strategy that actually reads out the record keys committed by conflicting writes and chooses to abort the write if duplicate keys are detected. This would come at the cost of additional I/O for every write, which lakehouse users do not typically prefer, but Hudi provides this powerful flexibility.

To illustrate this further, consider a scenario, as shown in Figure 7-3, where two writers attempt to modify records within the same file group. The first writer begins its commit process and acquires the lock. When the second writer attempts to commit, Hudi's conflict detection mechanism identifies the overlap in file groups. In the default configuration, the second writer's operation will be aborted, requiring a retry. However, a custom conflict resolution strategy might implement more sophisticated handling, such as merging the changes or applying them sequentially based on business rules.

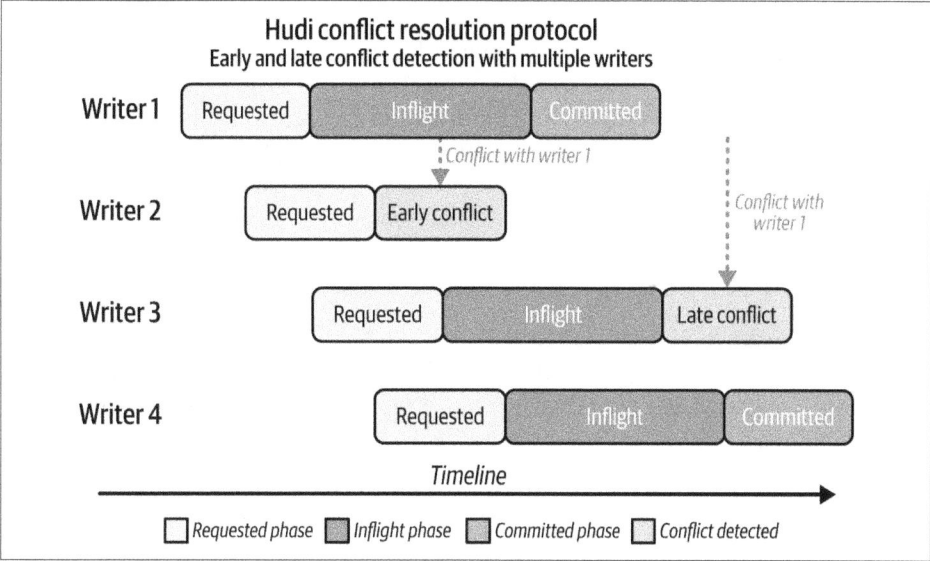

Figure 7-3. Hudi conflict resolution protocol

Locking Mechanisms

To coordinate writes in a distributed multiwriter environment, Hudi supports several distributed locking mechanisms, each with its own advantages and trade-offs. Some of the most popular locking mechanisms supported are listed here, and their features are compared in Table 7-2. The choice of locking mechanism depends on the specific requirements of the use case and the infrastructure available. Details on configuring each provider are covered in "Configuring the Locking Mechanism" on page 154.

Zookeeper-based locking

This mechanism uses Apache Zookeeper to coordinate locks between multiple writers. Zookeeper is a highly reliable distributed coordination service, providing strong consistency guarantees, but it can introduce additional operational overhead, especially in large-scale deployments. Organizations already using Zookeeper in their infrastructure may find this a natural choice, as it integrates seamlessly with existing operational practices.

For deployments on cloud providers where there is no custom locking mechanism (e.g., Google Cloud or Microsoft Azure), the most common and robust approach is to run a Zookeeper cluster on virtual machines (e.g., Google Compute Engine or Azure VMs). This provides the same strong consistency guarantees as an on-premises deployment and is a well-supported pattern for Hudi on any cloud.

Storage-based locking

This mechanism leverages conditional writes available in modern cloud storage systems to implement distributed locking through a leader election algorithm. Amazon S3 recently introduced conditional writes, and GCS and Azure storage already support them. In this approach, each process attempts an atomic conditional write to a file calculated using the table base path. The first process to succeed is elected as the leader and takes charge of exclusive operations. This method provides a straightforward, reliable locking mechanism without requiring external services, making it a cost-effective and infrastructure-light choice.

Amazon DynamoDB–based locking

This mechanism uses DynamoDB as a distributed lock provider. DynamoDB is highly scalable and easy to manage, but it may incur additional costs, especially in large-scale deployments. For cloud deployment, this option provides a cloud native solution particularly well suited to AWS deployments. The pay-per-use pricing model can be cost-effective, especially for variable workloads.

Custom locking mechanism

For advanced use cases, Hudi's pluggable lock provider interface allows for the implementation of custom providers that could leverage cloud native services like Google's Zonal Lock or Azure's Blob Lease API.

Table 7-2. Comparison of various locking mechanisms

Locking mechanism	External dependency	Scalability	Consistency	Cost	Suitability
Zookeeper	Requires dedicated ZooKeeper cluster	Highly scalable with proper configuration; can handle thousands of concurrent operations	Strong consistency guarantees with leader election and distributed consensus	Moderate infrastructure and operational costs for maintaining ZooKeeper cluster	Best for large-scale production deployments with multidatacenter requirements and where strong consistency is critical
Storage	Reuses the same distributed storage system (e.g., HDFS, Amazon S3) used for table storage	Scalability depends on underlying storage system; can handle large-scale concurrent operations	Consistency guarantees depend on storage system	Varies based on storage system used; typically cost-effective for existing infrastructure	Ideal for cloud native deployments leveraging existing distributed storage
DynamoDB	Requires AWS account and DynamoDB table	Excellent scalability with automatic scaling; handles millions of operations	Strong consistency with ACID transactions at the row level	Pay-per-use pricing; costs scale with usage	Perfect for AWS deployments, especially serverless architectures and cloud native applications

Locking mechanism	External dependency	Scalability	Consistency	Cost	Suitability
In-memory (single writer)	None	Limited to single JVM	Strong consistency within process	No additional cost	Suitable for development, testing, and simple deployments with single writer

Each of these locking mechanisms has its own advantages and trade-offs. For example, Zookeeper provides robust reliability but may introduce infrastructure complexity, while DynamoDB offers seamless cloud integration but may require careful cost management. Regardless of the mechanism chosen, Hudi's design ensures that locks are only held for a short duration during the commit phase, minimizes contention, and allows for higher concurrency so that it does not become a bottleneck.

The choice of locking mechanism should be made based on the specific requirements of the use case, taking into consideration factors such as external dependencies, scalability, consistency guarantees, and cost. Organizations should evaluate the trade-offs and select the mechanism that best aligns with their operational needs and infrastructure.

Challenges in Multiwriter Systems

One of the fundamental challenges in multiwriter systems is efficiently dividing data into independent portions that can be processed concurrently. Hudi addresses this through its file group abstraction, which provides a natural unit of parallelization. Writers can operate on different file groups simultaneously, enabling horizontal scaling of write operations. The system must also handle resource allocation effectively. When multiple writers contend for resources such as memory, CPU, and network bandwidth, the system needs to maintain fairness while preventing deadlocks or starvation. Hudi's design minimizes resource contention by limiting the scope and duration of locks, and by providing mechanisms for early conflict detection.

Early conflict detection is particularly important for resource efficiency. In earlier versions of Hudi, writers would proceed with their entire operation before detecting conflicts at commit time, potentially wasting significant computational resources. The introduction of early conflict detection allows writers to abort quickly when conflicts are detected, releasing resources that would otherwise be consumed by doomed-to-fail, wasteful operations.

Using Multiwriter Support in Hudi

Enabling multiwriter support in Hudi requires careful configuration to ensure that multiple writers can operate concurrently without conflicts. This section provides a step-by-step guide to enabling multiwriter support, including the necessary configurations, locking mechanisms, and code examples for common use cases.

Enabling Multiwriter Support

To enable multiwriter support in Hudi, you need to configure the appropriate settings in your Hudi properties file or job configuration. The key configuration parameters are:

Hoodie.write.concurrency.mode
> Set this to optimistic_concurrency_control to enable multiwriter support.

Hoodie.write.lock.provider
> Specify the locking mechanism to be used (e.g., ZookeeperBasedLockProvider, HiveMetastoreBasedLockProvider, or DynamoDBBasedLockProvider).

Hoodie.cleaner.policy.failed.writes
> Set this to EAGER to ensure that failed writes are cleaned up promptly, preventing them from blocking other writers.

Lock provider–specific settings
> Specify the required settings for the chosen lock provider. This is explained in "Storage-based locking" on page 155.

Here is an example configuration for enabling multiwriter support with Zookeeper-based locking:

```
# Enable multiwriter support
hoodie.write.concurrency.mode=optimistic_concurrency_control

# Use Zookeeper-based locking
hoodie.write.lock.provider=\
org.apache.hudi.client.transaction.lock.ZookeeperBasedLockProvider
hoodie.write.lock.zookeeper.url=<zookeeper_url>
hoodie.write.lock.zookeeper.port=<zookeeper_port>
hoodie.write.lock.zookeeper.lock_key=<lock_key>

# Clean up failed writes eagerly
hoodie.clean.failed.writes.policy=EAGER
```

This configuration specifies that Hudi will use OCC as the concurrency mode and Zookeeper as the locking mechanism. Similar configurations can be applied for other types of locking.

Configuring the Locking Mechanism

The choice of locking mechanism depends on your specific use case and infrastructure. The following sections provide a brief overview of the available options.

Zookeeper-based locking

Zookeeper-based locking is a reliable option for distributed environments. It provides strong consistency guarantees but requires additional operational overhead to manage the Zookeeper cluster:

```
hoodie.write.lock.provider=\
org.apache.hudi.client.transaction.lock.ZookeeperBasedLockProvider
hoodie.write.lock.zookeeper.url=<zookeeper_url>
hoodie.write.lock.zookeeper.port=<zookeeper_port>
hoodie.write.lock.zookeeper.lock_key=<lock_key>
```

Hive Metastore-based locking

Hive Metastore–based locking is a lightweight option for environments already using Hive Metastore. It is suitable for low to moderate concurrency scenarios:

```
hoodie.write.lock.provider=org.apache.hudi.hive.HiveMetastoreBasedLockProvider
hoodie.write.lock.hivemetastore.database=<database_name>
hoodie.write.lock.hivemetastore.table=<table_name>
```

DynamoDB-based locking

DynamoDB-based locking is a scalable option for cloud native deployments, particularly on AWS. It provides strong consistency and is easy to manage:

```
hoodie.write.lock.provider=\
org.apache.hudi.aws.transaction.lock.DynamoDBBasedLockProvider
hoodie.write.lock.dynamodb.table=<dynamodb_table_name>
hoodie.write.lock.dynamodb.region=<aws_region>
```

Storage-based locking

Storage-based locking is a cloud native solution that leverages conditional writes in cloud storage platforms (Amazon S3, GCS) to provide distributed locking without requiring additional infrastructure. This approach uses a single lock file per table stored directly in the cloud storage, making it ideal for serverless and cloud native deployments:

```
hoodie.write.lock.provider=\
org.apache.hudi.client.transaction.lock.StorageBasedLockProvider
```

Multiwriters Using Hudi Streamer

Hudi Streamer is a utility that allows you to ingest data from different sources, such as DFS or Kafka, into a Hudi table. To enable multiwriter support in Hudi Streamer, you need to add the appropriate configurations to the properties file.

Here is an example of how to configure Hudi Streamer for multiwriter support with Zookeeper-based locking:

```
# Hudi Streamer properties
hoodie.write.concurrency.mode=optimistic_concurrency_control
hoodie.write.lock.provider=\
org.apache.hudi.client.transaction.lock.ZookeeperBasedLockProvider
hoodie.write.lock.zookeeper.url=<zookeeper_url>
hoodie.write.lock.zookeeper.port=<zookeeper_port>
hoodie.write.lock.zookeeper.lock_key=<lock_key>
hoodie.cleaner.policy.failed.writes=EAGER
```

You can then trigger the Hudi Streamer job as follows:

```
spark-submit \
  --packages <dependency identifier for a Hudi utilities bundle jar> \ ❶
  --class org.apache.hudi.utilities.deltastreamer.HoodieDeltaStreamer \
  --master yarn \
  --deploy-mode cluster \
  --conf spark.serializer=org.apache.spark.serializer.KryoSerializer \
  --conf spark.sql.hive.convertMetastoreParquet=false \
  --table-type COPY_ON_WRITE \
  --source-class org.apache.hudi.utilities.sources.JsonKafkaSource \
  --source-ordering-field ts \
  --target-base-path /path/to/hudi_table \
  --target-table hudi_table \
  --props /path/to/file/with/additional/hudi.properties
```

❶ An example identifier can be `org.apache.hudi:hudi-utilities-bundle_2.13:1.1.0`.

Note that the `hudi-utilities-bundle` jar works with the latest supported version of Apache Spark for the corresponding Hudi release version. Please refer to the release notes (*https://oreil.ly/r50Uj*) for the most up-to-date information.

Multiwriters Using Spark Data Source Writer

The Hudi Spark module provides a Data Source API that allows you to write a Spark DataFrame into a Hudi table. Here is an example of how to enable multiwriter support using the Spark Data Source API:

```
import org.apache.spark.sql.SaveMode
import org.apache.spark.sql.SparkSession

val spark = SparkSession.builder()
  .appName("Hudi Multiwriter Example")
  .config("spark.serializer", "org.apache.spark.serializer.KryoSerializer")
  .getOrCreate()

// Each concurrent writer would read from its own source
val df_1 = spark.read.json("/path/to/source_data_1.json")

df_1.write.format("hudi") // "hudi" is the recommended format alias
  .option("hoodie.write.concurrency.mode", "optimistic_concurrency_control")
```

```
    .option("hoodie.write.lock.provider",
 "org.apache.hudi.client.transaction.lock.ZookeeperBasedLockProvider")
    .option("hoodie.write.lock.zookeeper.url", "<zookeeper_url>")
    .option("hoodie.write.lock.zookeeper.port", "<zookeeper_port>")
    .option("hoodie.write.lock.zookeeper.lock_key", "<lock_key>")
    .option("hoodie.clean.failed.writes.policy", "EAGER")
    .option("hoodie.table.name", "hudi_table")
    .option("hoodie.datasource.write.operation", "upsert")
    .option("hoodie.datasource.write.recordkey.field", "id")
    .option("hoodie.datasource.write.precombine.field", "ts")
    .mode(SaveMode.Append)
    .save("/path/to/hudi_table")
```

Single Writer and Multiple Table Services

In scenarios where you have a single writer and multiple table services, you can configure the table services to run in the inline, async execution, or standalone modes.

Here is an example of how to configure inline table services where the services will run in the same process as the writer:

```
# Enable inline table services
hoodie.compact.inline=true
hoodie.cluster.inline=true
hoodie.clean.inline=true
```

The modern and recommended way to run table services concurrently is to schedule them as separate jobs. For example, you would run a dedicated HoodieCompactor or HoodieClusteringJob utility job that operates on the table independently of the ingestion writer. This provides better resource isolation and control. If this option is selected, confirm that writer jobs do not have inline table services enabled.

Disabling Multiwriter Support

If you want to disable multiwriter support, you can remove the multiwriter configurations from your Hudi properties file or override them with default values:

```
# Disable multiwriter support
hoodie.write.concurrency.mode=single_writer
hoodie.cleaner.policy.failed.writes=EAGER
```

Tips and Best Practices

When working with Hudi in multiwriter environments, adhering to best practices is crucial for ensuring optimal performance, minimizing resource contention, and avoiding common pitfalls. This section provides a comprehensive guide to best practices, tips, and performance optimization techniques, drawing from real-world data lakehouse architectures and database systems.

Implement Partitioning and File Grouping

One of the most effective ways to minimize conflicts in multiwriter environments is to partition your data effectively. By dividing your data into independent partitions or file groups, you can ensure that writers operate on distinct portions of the data, reducing the likelihood of conflicts.

Example: In a time-series dataset, you would partition the data by date (e.g., `year=2023/month=10/day=01`). This allows multiple writers to operate on different partitions simultaneously without overlapping.

Use Hudi's clustering feature to optimize file sizes and grouping within partitions, ensuring that writers operate on well-organized data.

Enable Early Conflict Detection

In a standard Hudi write operation, conflict detection is a critical safeguard for data integrity that traditionally occurs during the final commit phase. After a writer has performed the computationally expensive work of processing data and writing new data files (e.g., Apache Parquet files) to storage, it attempts to atomically publish its changes to the Hudi timeline. It is only at this final stage that Hudi's concurrency control mechanism validates the transaction, checking if another writer has already committed changes to the same underlying files since the current operation began. If a conflict is found, the entire write operation must be aborted. This late-stage failure means that all the compute resources consumed during data processing and file generation are wasted, forcing a costly retry.

To mitigate this inefficiency, Hudi introduced early conflict detection. This feature fundamentally shifts the conflict check from the end of the write cycle to the beginning, integrating it directly into the initial phase of the write operation.

Here's how the enhanced write flow with early detection works:

1. *Declare intent:* Before starting the expensive data processing stage, the writer first declares which specific file groups it intends to modify. It marks these files as part of a new, pending commit on the timeline.

2. *Check timeline:* The writer then immediately checks the timeline to see if any other transaction has already successfully committed changes to the same file groups since its own transaction started.

3. *Fail fast or proceed:* If a conflict is detected, the write operation is aborted instantly, before any significant compute resources are spent on processing data. This provides immediate feedback and avoids wasting resources. If no conflict is

found, the writer proceeds with the expensive task of writing the data files, now with a high degree of confidence that the final commit will succeed.

By adopting this "fail-fast" approach, early conflict detection minimizes the cost of concurrency conflicts. It is especially beneficial in large-scale multiwriter deployments where the probability of concurrent writes is higher, and the resource cost of a failed write operation can be substantial. This proactive validation ensures that compute cycles are reserved for transactions that are likely to succeed, significantly improving the efficiency and throughput of the data lakehouse.

Example: In a large-scale deployment with multiple writers, early conflict detection can prevent a writer from processing an entire batch of data, only to abort at the commit phase due to a conflict.

Early conflict detection can be enabled with this configuration:

```
hoodie.write.concurrency.early.conflict.detection.enable=true
```

Optimize Locking Mechanisms

Choose the appropriate locking mechanism based on your infrastructure and workload. For example:

- Use Zookeeper-based locking for on-premises deployments with strong consistency requirements.
- Use DynamoDB-based locking for cloud native deployments on AWS, where scalability and ease of management are priorities.
- For cloud providers without a native locking mechanism (e.g., Google Cloud or Azure), Zookeeper-based locking can be used by running a Zookeeper cluster on virtual machines. Alternatively, you can implement custom locking strategies by extending Hudi's pluggable lock provider interface to leverage cloud-specific services like Google's Zonal Lock or Azure's Blob Lease API.

In high-concurrency environments, numerous writers competing for the same lock can cause delays and timeouts, thus decreasing throughput. To mitigate this, tune lock provider settings by configuring retries for lock acquisition, making write jobs more resilient.

Example: Configure retries for lock acquisition to handle transient failures or high contention:

```
hoodie.write.lock.wait_time_ms=10000  # Wait up to 10 seconds for a lock
hoodie.write.lock.num_retries=5       # Retry up to 5 times
```

Run Asynchronous Table Services

Run table services such as compaction, clustering, and cleaning asynchronously to avoid blocking the primary ingestion pipeline. This ensures that writers can continue ingesting data while table services optimize the table in the background. Check out Chapter 6 for more details.

Example: In a streaming pipeline, compaction in async execution mode can rewrite large files in the background without impacting the ingestion of new data:

```
hoodie.compact.inline=false
hoodie.compact.schedule.inline=true
```

Reduce Write Conflicts and Wasted Resources

In multiwriter environments, conflicts can lead to aborted jobs and wasted compute resources, especially if they are detected late in the write lifecycle.

Partitioning your workload is the most effective way to minimize conflicts, as it naturally separates writers and eliminates the chances of conflicts. Additionally, enabling early conflict detection can avoid wasting resources on writes destined to fail, as it checks for conflicts before the data writing phase and aborts the job early.

Example: To further optimize performance, enable NBCC to allow writers to proceed without waiting for locks:

```
hoodie.write.concurrency.mode=non_blocking_concurrency_control
```

Prevent Data Duplication When Using Multiple Writers

A key limitation to understand is that Hudi's multiwriter mode does not guarantee data deduplication across concurrent writers. If two writers ingest a record with the same primary key at the same time, you may end up with duplicate records in your table, as each writer only performs deduplication against the data visible at the start of its own transaction.

A best practice for Hudi is to ensure idempotent sources; for example, partition your source data by record key to prevent concurrent writes for the same data. If controlling the source isn't possible, use a staging Hudi table for raw data ingestion; run a separate, single-writer job to deduplicate; and then write to a final, clean table.

Summary

Concurrency control is a cornerstone of data systems, ensuring data consistency and operational efficiency in environments with simultaneous data reads and writes. Hudi extends this principle to distributed data lakehouses, providing mechanisms that allow multiple writers to operate concurrently while maintaining the integrity of the data. By allowing multiple writers to operate concurrently, Hudi addresses the limitations of single-writer systems and provides the flexibility needed to handle complex data ingestion, updates, and deletions.

This chapter provided a comprehensive overview of concurrency control in Hudi, exploring its importance in ensuring data consistency and enabling efficient multi-writer scenarios. We discussed how Hudi's optimistic concurrency control mechanism allows multiple writers to operate concurrently while minimizing conflicts. The different locking mechanisms available in Hudi, along with their pros and cons, were also examined, giving you the knowledge to choose the best option for your needs.

Despite its strengths, Hudi's concurrency control has limitations that warrant attention. Challenges include the potential for late conflict detection leading to resource wastage, granularity constraints in conflict detection at the file group level, and scalability bottlenecks in lock providers under extreme concurrency. Understanding these limitations and applying best practices—such as careful workload partitioning and the use of early conflict detection—can help organizations leverage Hudi effectively. By addressing the inherent complexities of distributed data lakehouses, Hudi provides a powerful framework for scalable and consistent data management.

Finally, the chapter addressed the limitations of Hudi's multiwriter implementation, such as the lack of cross-writer data deduplication and potential resource wastage due to conflicts. By understanding these limitations, you can better plan and optimize your Hudi deployments for maximum efficiency and reliability. As you venture further into the world of Hudi, remember that mastering concurrency control is crucial for building robust and scalable data lakehouse solutions.

Building a Lakehouse Using Hudi Streamer

In modern organizations, data silos create more than just fragmented data; they foster fragmented efforts. Teams across the business often find themselves independently solving the same data engineering problems, building similar ETL tools, and defining their own conventions for schemas and formats. This redundancy not only wastes valuable resources but also erects significant barriers to sharing and normalizing data. The core challenge becomes a strategic one: how can an organization move beyond this inefficiency to provide a standardized set of tools and a unified platform? How can it empower teams to collaborate on ingesting and transforming data, while sharing common datasets, catalogs, and monitoring dashboards?

The modern answer to this challenge is the data lakehouse, and Apache Hudi is a particularly strong choice for building one. If your organization is suffering from data silos and has not yet converged on a single data storage solution, Hudi offers more flexibility than the alternatives. Not only does Hudi permit different parts of an organization to maintain sovereignty over their data stacks and architectures, but it also provides a specialized ingestion tool—Hudi Streamer—that can connect to a wide array of upstream sources and streamline the construction of a data lakehouse.

In this chapter, we'll meet Alcubierre, a fictional airline company grappling with these common data silo challenges. As we imagine ourselves as part of the team spearheading Alcubierre's data unification effort, we'll explore how Hudi Streamer can be used to ingest data from the company's diverse sources. We will then walk through an end-to-end application example, sharing our favorite lakehouse ingestion tips and tricks along the way. Lastly, we'll deepen our understanding of Hudi Streamer by exploring its various options to support the different facets of building a lakehouse platform.

Alcubierre's Data Silo Woes

Established roughly 10 years ago, Alcubierre is still a relatively young airline. It quickly gained market traction by offering novel perks and loyalty programs, but it is starting to develop a reputation for poor customer experience. The company's fragmented data systems often cause maintenance-related flight delays, and the siloed data makes it difficult to estimate disruptions or implement predictive maintenance. Complaints are difficult to investigate and are often exacerbated by the data silos that have emerged from Alcubierre's various departments (Customer Service, Operations, Aircraft Maintenance, etc).

Over the past decade, each Alcubierre department has been permitted to develop mostly independently, establishing its own technology stack and architecture. This independence, which once enabled Alcubierre to rapidly bootstrap a successful global business, has gradually produced data silos that are now hindering the business from developing a holistic understanding of customer needs and organizational inefficiencies. In the following sections we'll learn a bit more about these silos, some of which will probably sound familiar!

Data Quality Assurance and Deduplication

The Customer Service department's mission is to ensure a positive travel experience for Alcubierre passengers by providing efficient assistance in a friendly, personalized manner. This department employs a multitiered help desk to triage customer issues and provide resolutions as quickly as possible. It uses specialized customer relationship management (CRM) software to store records of all calls to the help desk, together with a lot of metadata about the customer's issue and the final resolution. Records are bulk-exported from the CRM system as CSV files and are uploaded to object storage on AWS S3 nightly (Figure 8-1).

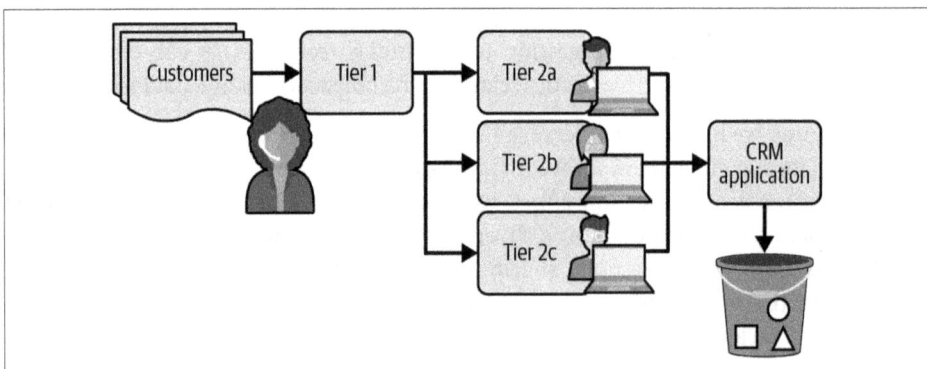

Figure 8-1. Data organization within Alcubierre's Customer Service department

Unfortunately, the multitiered structure of the help desk sometimes leads to duplicate records. This can happen in cases where the same customer contacts the help desk multiple times, or when help desk operators make data entry errors, such as entering the wrong customer ID or ticket number. Alcubierre has developed some effective deduplication techniques, but they can only be applied to the data after it has been exported to S3 and can be compared to the primary customer database, which is managed by the Finance team. Whenever the CRM export fails or is delayed, the object storage in S3 no longer reflects the most current state of customer interactions, which delays data cleaning and deduplication jobs.

Heterogeneous Data and Schema Evolution

Alcubierre's Safety and Security department ensures the highest standards of safety for passengers, crew, and aircraft by implementing safety protocols, doing risk management and emergency preparedness, maintaining regulatory compliance, and investigating incidents. The department recently adopted a microservices architecture to coordinate the multiple services using streaming data. These services manage safety auditing, risk assessment, compliance tracking, and incident reporting, and they share information via Kafka streams. Eventually, incident records are persisted to a relational database for long-term storage (e.g., for compliance audits); see Figure 8-2.

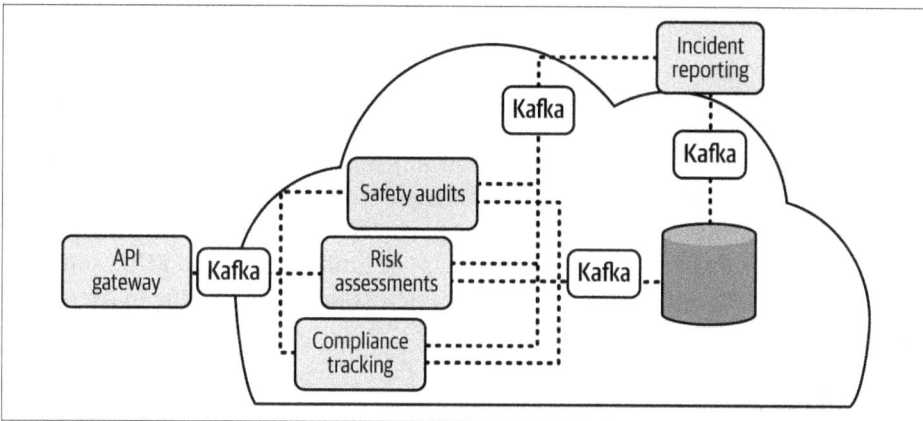

Figure 8-2. Data organization within Alcubierre's Safety and Security department

Each microservice emits data in different formats and generates different types of metadata. For instance, the incident reporting service records timestamps in UTC, while the compliance tracking service is localized (compliance varies by region) and records in local time. This can lead to confusion when correlating events or incidents across services. There have already been several incidents where API changes were not effectively socialized; the schema in the risk assessment service was updated but not synchronized with the incident reporting service, which led to a mismatch that resulted in breaking changes downstream.

Data Management, Localization, and Consistency

The Aircraft Maintenance department's crews at all 10 of Alcubierre's hubs around the world use a common software application to track maintenance, repairs, and operations (often referred to as the *MRO system*). This software enables the maintenance chief to keep track of the engineers' maintenance schedules, aircraft maintenance logs, and parts inventory. These and other engineering records are persisted to a PostgreSQL database (Figure 8-3).

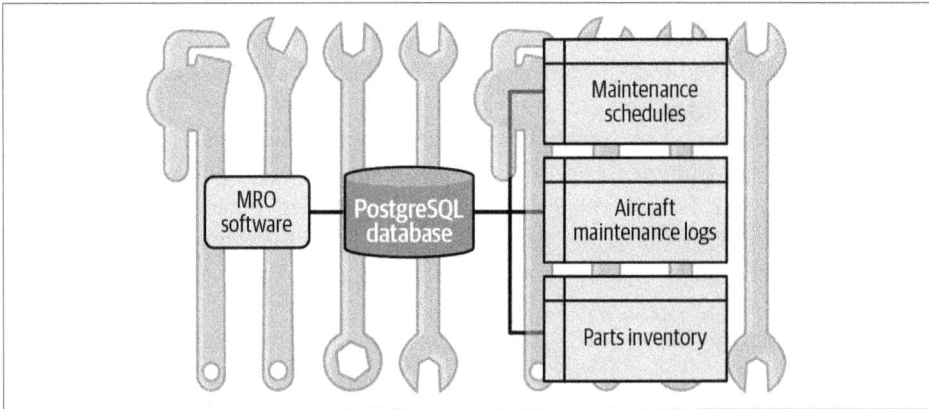

Figure 8-3. Data organization within Alcubierre's Aircraft Maintenance department

Discrepancies occur when parts are tracked differently at various Alcubierre hubs. These parts are sometimes logged with different terminologies depending on local conventions, and inconsistent localization practices lead to errors in interpreting maintenance logs or part descriptions. Because of limitations of the MRO software, inventory counts do not always sync correctly across locations, leading to overstocking and stockouts.

Problem Recap

Alcubierre must identify an architectural solution to resolve the challenges in its data silos:

- A centralized data repository is needed to host datasets and enable business analytics across multiple departments, despite varying source data storage and formats, such as CSV files in S3 buckets, messages in Kafka topics, and records in Postgres databases.

- The solution should support common data processing tasks, including deduplication and record format conversions, such as timestamp normalization.
- Additionally, the solution must enforce schema management and support schema evolution to accommodate changes from upstream data sources.

Lakehouse Architecture to the Rescue

Alcubierre has been advised to build a lakehouse to enable near real-time insights and proactive decision making. As an initial rollout, Alcubierre decides to build the lakehouse with source data from three departments: Aircraft Maintenance, Customer Service, and Safety and Security.

This "dream" lakehouse, shown in Figure 8-4, aims to enhance the flow of information between the departments, improving their individual functionality while also uncovering new initiatives across the board that could drive significant operational efficiencies and increase profitability.

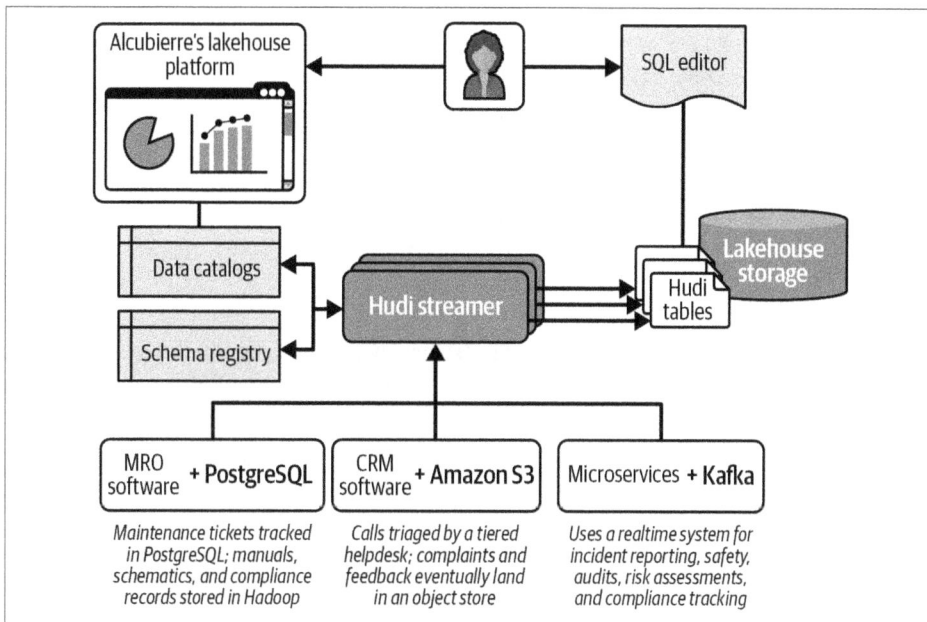

Figure 8-4. Alcubierre's planned lakehouse design

Luckily for Alcubierre, we can use Hudi to build a comprehensive lakehouse platform, leveraging Hudi Streamer as a unified framework. In the following sections, we'll learn more about what Hudi Streamer is and how we can use it to build a lakehouse tailored to Alcubierre's existing infrastructure.

What Is Hudi Streamer?

Hudi Streamer is a utility tool that runs as an Apache Spark application. It comprises a set of Java classes packaged in the Hudi bundle jars, which are publicly available for download via the Maven repository. Running Hudi Streamer is much like running any standard Spark application, with the `hudi-utilities-bundle` jar being used.

> You may use the `wget` tool to download the jar from the public Maven repository:
>
> ```
> export REPO_URL=<URL> ❶
> export HUDI_UTILITIES_JAR=<Jar path> ❷
> wget $REPO_URL/$HUDI_UTILITIES_JAR
> ```
>
> ❶ The URL for Hudi release artifacts is `https://reposi tory.apache.org/content/repositories/releases`.
>
> ❷ The jar path is like `org/apache/hudi/hudi-utilities-bundle_2.13/1.1.0/ hudi-utilities-bundle_2.13-1.1.0.jar`.
>
> In this example, you are downloading the Hudi 1.1 bundle jar that works with Spark 3.5 and Scala 2.13. Note that the `hudi-utilities-bundle` jar works with the latest supported version of Spark for the corresponding Hudi release version. Please refer to the release notes (*https://oreil.ly/r50Uj*) for the most up-to-date information.

From an API hierarchy perspective, Hudi Streamer implements the Hudi Writer interface, which internally wraps the `HoodieWriteClient` to handle write operations. As depicted in Figure 8-5, the client write layer, which includes the Hudi core models, is responsible for executing transactional writes in accordance with the Hudi table format. The Hudi Streamer layer defines and implements capabilities to interact with various lakehouse components, including ingesting diverse data source formats, plugging into schema registries, and synchronizing with data catalogs.

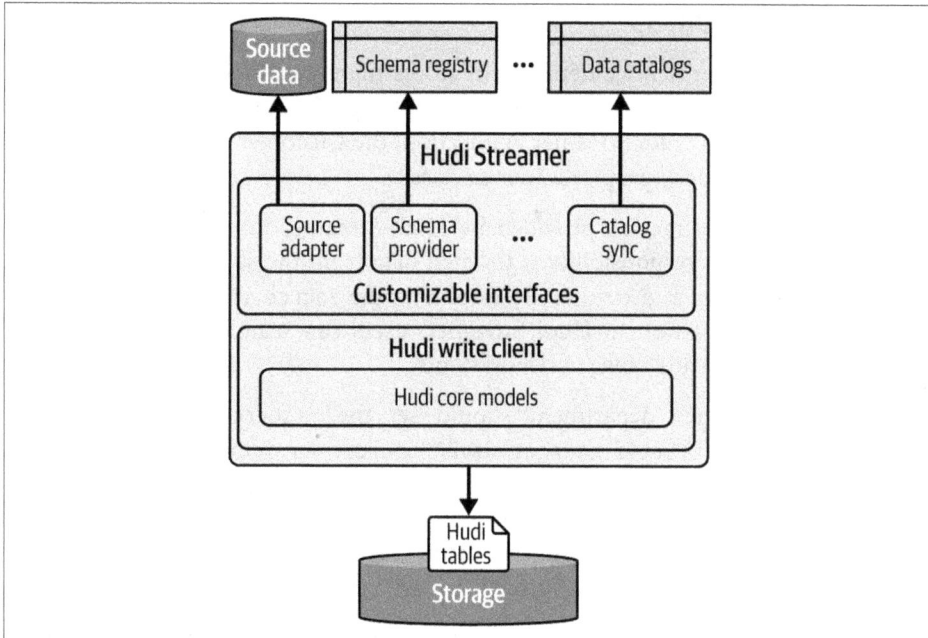

Figure 8-5. Dissecting the Hudi Streamer API hierarchy

Hudi Streamer is designed to simplify the often complex process of data ingestion into lakehouses. Acting as a bridge between upstream data sources and Hudi tables, it offers configurable and customizable interfaces for managing the various components shown in the figure.

By adjusting a few configurations, each department can tailor Hudi Streamer jobs to different data sources, while the underlying infrastructure—such as the job scheduler, monitoring service, and other components—remains use-case agnostic and highly reusable.

In the next section, we will delve into the relevant options offered by Hudi Streamer and explain how its adoption helped Alcubierre overcome the data silo challenges outlined earlier.

Getting Started with Hudi Streamer

Hudi Streamer offers a variety of customizable interfaces, as illustrated in Figure 8-5, along with a comprehensive set of configuration options. This section will explore the specific interfaces and options that are pertinent to addressing Alcubierre's previously discussed problems. By the end of this section, you will have a glimpse of Hudi Streamer's capabilities and how it can help address challenges in real-world scenarios.

Ingesting Data from S3

Alcubierre's Customer Service department stores nightly call records in S3 buckets. Daily, CSV files are deposited into an S3 path with a prefix in the format yyyy/MM/dd. When configuring its Hudi Streamer application, the Customer Service department's first step is to select the appropriate Source class.

The Source is an abstraction provided by Hudi Streamer for delivering upstream source data. Its main responsibility is to fetch data from the source system in input batches for processing and writing. By extending the Source abstract class and supplying the implementation to Hudi Streamer, users can seamlessly integrate Hudi Streamer jobs with a wide range of data systems.

The Customer Service department should set the `--source-class` option to `org.apache.hudi.utilities.sources.CsvDFSSource`, an implementation offered out of the box by the `hudi-utilities-bundle` jar. This class is specifically designed to load CSV files from a storage system path. When these daily Hudi Streamer jobs commence, the Source reads records in a distributed manner from files located at the path specified by the `--target-base-path` option.

The CSV files produced daily by the Customer Service department often contain duplicate records. To address this, the department should enable the `--filter-dupes` option, a Boolean flag in Hudi Streamer. This option removes duplicates from the loaded records, significantly enhancing the quality of downstream analysis results.

Ingesting Data from Kafka

Kafka is a widely used event streaming platform known for its high throughput and low latency. Kafka producers send data to specific topics within the Kafka platform, where the data is maintained as ordered logs, ensuring data integrity. Applications downstream, known as *Kafka consumers*, subscribe to these topics and process the data in real time.

To enable the storage of Kafka data in the lakehouse for Alcubierre's Safety and Security department, the team should configure two critical options for its Hudi Streamer applications. Each application will consume data from a Kafka topic and write it to a corresponding Hudi table:

- The `hoodie.streamer.source.kafka.topic` option was set to define the specific Kafka topic that Hudi Streamer would consume from.

- The `--source-class` option was configured as `org.apache.hudi.utilities.sources.AvroKafkaSource`, designating it as the Kafka consumer group responsible for pulling messages from the target Kafka topic.

Handling schema evolution

The Safety and Security department should also set up a schema registry, a service that centrally manages the schemas of all Kafka topics. By leveraging this, the team can enforce a backward-compatible policy for schema evolution. This policy will ensure that schema changes are limited to adding new nullable columns and widening existing column types (e.g., promoting an int column to long). This approach will help ensure that Kafka consumers don't break in the event of schema changes.

To integrate Hudi Streamer with the schema registry, the Safety and Security department should configure the following options:

- Set `hoodie.streamer.schemaprovider.registry.url` to point to the schema registry URL.
- Set `--schemaprovider-class` to `org.apache.hudi.utilities.schema.Schema RegistryProvider`, indicating that the source data adheres to the schema provided by the target registry.

Normalizing timestamps

The Safety and Security department wants to address discrepancies in timestamp formats across different Kafka topics. Some topics store timestamps as Unix timestamps in `long` format, while others use human-readable formats in various time zones. To resolve this, the team can leverage the `Transformer` interface provided by Hudi Streamer.

Upon retrieving incoming data from the `Source`, the Transformer performs lightweight transformations, such as adding or dropping specific columns or flattening the schema. The Transformer processes a Spark dataset and outputs the transformed dataset, enabling seamless data manipulation to meet the requirements of the ingestion pipeline. The `--transformer-class` option accepts one or multiple class names of Transformer implementations. When multiple transformers are given, they are applied sequentially, meaning the output of one transformer serves as the input for the next. This chained approach provides flexibility and simplifies code maintenance.

The Safety and Security department can develop a Transformer implementation to convert designated timestamp columns to ISO-8061 format in UTC. By supplying this implementation via the `--transformer-class` option, the Hudi Streamer jobs will apply common conversion logic and write normalized timestamp values to the Hudi tables. This standardization will improve data quality and reduce errors and interpretation overhead during further processing.

Ingesting Data from RDBMS

The Aircraft Maintenance department stores its application data in Postgres databases. To store this data in a lakehouse, we need to extract it first so that we can replicate it from Postgres to lakehouse storage. Because SQL queries usually retrieve only the latest record states, and performing periodic full dumps of the tables would be impractical, the change data capture (CDC) incremental extraction technique is the preferred approach for this scenario.

Postgres, like many other OLTP databases, records all transactional changes—such as inserts, updates, and deletes—in its write-ahead log (WAL). CDC is a process that reads and replays these changes, allowing the CDC application to restore the exact states of the database tables. More importantly, as new changes are continuously applied to the original tables, the CDC application can efficiently process these changes and keep the replicated data up-to-date.

Debezium is software designed to implement CDC processes for various databases, including Postgres. It operates as a Postgres plug-in that reads the database's WAL and functions as a Kafka producer, sending the extracted data to Kafka topics for flexible downstream consumption.

Hudi Streamer supports processing Debezium CDC data out of the box. The Aircraft Maintenance department can install Debezium on its Postgres database and use the Kafka platform managed by the Safety and Security department to store the Debezium output data in Kafka topics. The team should configure the `--source-class` option as `org.apache.hudi.utilities.sources.debezium.PostgresDebeziumSource`, enabling Hudi Streamer to process the Debezium data format in Kafka.

Similar to the Safety and Security department's Kafka Source setup, the Aircraft Maintenance department should specify the Kafka topics to read from and use a schema registry to govern the schemas. Additionally, the team can implement custom Transformers in some Hudi Streamer jobs to standardize naming conventions.

By properly configuring Hudi Streamer, the Aircraft Maintenance department can be successfully onboarded to Alcubierre's lakehouse platform so that it too can benefit from improved data quality, gain broader insights, and enhance its maintenance management processes.

Hudi Streamer supports a wide range of data sources to ingest data from. Table 8-1 summarizes all the sources that are supported at the time of writing.

Table 8-1. Hudi Streamer data ingestion sources

Source class	What and where is the data source?
MysqlDebeziumSource, PostgresDebeziumSource	CDC data from Debezium connector installed on MySQL and Postgres
JdbcSource	Data from RDBMS data sources
AvroDFSSource, CsvDFSSource, JsonDFSSource, ORCDFSSource, ParquetDFSSource	Apache Avro, CSV, JSON, Apache ORC, and Apache Parquet data on a DFS storage path
AvroKafkaSource, JsonKafkaSource, ProtoKafkaSource	Consume Avro, JSON, and Protobuf records from a Kafka topic
PulsarSource	Consume data from an Apache Pulsar topic
HoodieIncrSource	Hudi table; use Hudi incremental query to fetch changes
HiveIncrPullSource	Apache Hive table; use Hudi incremental query to fetch changes
SqlSource, SqlFileBasedSource	Spark table; use SQL to query and fetch records
GcsEventsSource, GcsEventsHoodieIncrSource, S3EventsSource, S3EventsHoodieIncrSource	Cloud storage events; support building a reliable pipeline to process files on GCS or AWS S3; see this blog (*https://oreil.ly/xcXBZ*) for details

Hudi Streamer in Action

Building on our exploration of Hudi Streamer's capabilities in the previous section, we now turn to a practical end-to-end example to showcase its real-world application. We'll demonstrate the process of ingesting data into a lakehouse using Hudi Streamer, focusing on a sample dataset from Alcubierre's Aircraft Maintenance department. This example will illustrate how to configure each component of the data pipeline to ensure complete and timely data ingestion.

Figure 8-6 illustrates our example application. It begins by generating sample data, which is stored in a Postgres database. We have designed a maintenance_schedule table based on Alcubierre's Aircraft Maintenance department and generated sample records for insert, update, and delete operations. Table 8-2 shows the table schema.

Table 8-2. Schema of the maintenance_schedule table

Column name	Data type	Remark
schedule_id	INT	The primary key to the table
aircraft_id	VARCHAR(255)	The aircraft for maintenance
due_date	DATE	Maintenance task due date
technician_ids	INT[]	List of assigned technicians for the maintenance task

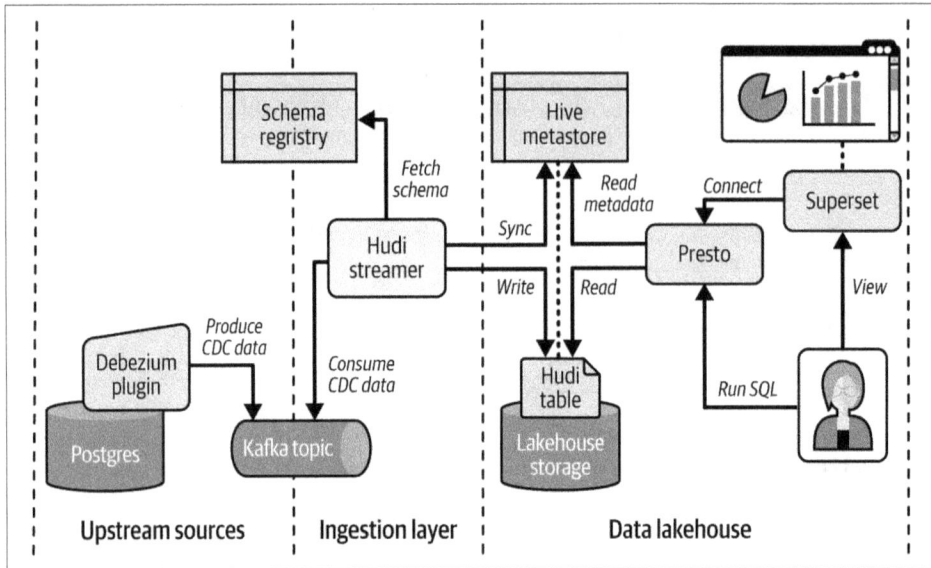

Figure 8-6. Ingesting data into a data lakehouse using Hudi Streamer (arrows indicate actions)

As explained in "Ingesting Data from RDBMS" on page 172, the Aircraft Maintenance department uses Debezium and Kafka to extract and store Postgres data via a CDC process. The lakehouse ingestion component is implemented using Hudi Streamer, which is configured to consume data from Kafka, integrate with the schema registry, and write to Hudi tables in lakehouse storage. The demo example replicates this setup to mimic the real-world configuration.

Additionally, the demo synchronizes the Hudi table with Hive Metastore, a data catalog service that integrates with Presto (*https://prestodb.io*), a popular query engine, and Apache Superset (*https://superset.apache.org/*), a data visualization platform. By reviewing the configuration details in this example shown throughout the remainder of this section, you will gain a deeper understanding of how Hudi Streamer operates and what a lakehouse platform looks like in practice.

> The following sections outline a local development setup for the end-to-end application, providing a reference for readers. Please note that when running pipelines in production, you should revisit these configurations and adjust or add more as needed, based on your specific environment and setup.

Preparing the Upstream Source

The upstream source consists of Postgres with Debezium installed, and Kafka with the schema registry connected. We use Debezium's official Docker image for Postgres (*https://oreil.ly/NDHt3*), which has the Debezium plug-in preinstalled and configured. In *docker-compose.yml*, we add this entry to run Postgres and Debezium as a service named `postgres`:

```
postgres:
  image: debezium/postgres:16-alpine
  hostname: postgres
  container_name: postgres
  ports:
    - 5432:5432
  environment:
    POSTGRES_USER: myuser
    POSTGRES_PASSWORD: mypassword
    POSTGRES_DB: postgres
```

Creating the first batch of data

Once the service is up and running, we need to prepare sample data in Postgres as the source data. Log in to Postgres to access the Postgres console by running:

```
docker compose exec -it postgres psql -U myuser -d postgres
```

From the Postgres console, we execute SQL statements to create the table and insert the first batch of records:

```
CREATE TABLE debezium_signal
(
    id   VARCHAR(100) PRIMARY KEY,
    type VARCHAR(100) NOT NULL,
    data VARCHAR(2048) NULL
);

CREATE TABLE maintenance_schedule
(
    schedule_id      INT PRIMARY KEY,
    aircraft_id      VARCHAR(255) NOT NULL,
    due_date         DATE         NOT NULL,
    maintenance_type VARCHAR(255) NOT NULL,
    technician_ids   INT[]        NOT NULL
);

INSERT INTO maintenance_schedule
    (schedule_id, aircraft_id, due_date, maintenance_type, technician_ids)
VALUES (1, 'AC001', '2024-08-15', 'corrective', ARRAY[101, 102, 103]),
       (2, 'AC002', '2024-09-01', 'routine', ARRAY[104, 105]),
       (3, 'AC003', '2024-07-30', 'routine', ARRAY[106]),
       (4, 'AC001', '2024-10-05', 'routine', ARRAY[107, 108]);
```

Setting up the Kafka stack

Now we prepare the Kafka stack, which consists of a few services including the schema registry, Kafka broker, and Kafka Connect. Kafka brokers serve as bridges between producers and consumers by routing their write and read requests to the underlying servers and storage. Kafka Connect is the pluggable, declarative data integration framework for Kafka. It supports running configurable source and sink connectors for various Kafka producers and consumers, respectively. Debezium is, in fact, implemented as a type of source connector that is executed by Kafka Connect.

In our demo example, we use Confluent-maintained Docker images (*https://oreil.ly/ gjjMu*) for the Kafka stack. We define that Kafka broker to run as a service named broker, and the connected schema registry as another service called schema-registry that handles schema fetching requests at port 8081:

```
broker:
  image: confluentinc/cp-kafka:7.6.1
  hostname: broker
  container_name: broker
  ports:
    - "9092:9092"
  environment:
    KAFKA_ADVERTISED_LISTENERS: <LISTENERS> ❶

schema-registry:
  image: confluentinc/cp-schema-registry:7.6.1
  hostname: schema-registry
  container_name: schema-registry
  depends_on:
    - broker
  ports:
    - "8081:8081"
  environment:
    SCHEMA_REGISTRY_HOST_NAME: schema-registry
    SCHEMA_REGISTRY_KAFKASTORE_BOOTSTRAP_SERVERS: 'broker:29092'
    SCHEMA_REGISTRY_LISTENERS: http://0.0.0.0:8081
```

❶ An example value can be `'PLAINTEXT://broker:29092,PLAINTEXT_HOST:// localhost:9092'`.

Then, we define Kafka Connect as a service named connect running at port 8083. Note that connect needs to depend on the Kafka broker and schema registry services. To make Debezium functional, we specify commands in the command section to install the Debezium connector in connect for the Kafka source tasks (extracting CDC data and sending it to Kafka) to be created upon request. The Debezium-extracted data is in Avro format for a high compression ratio; therefore, we set Kafka's value converter to io.confluent.connect.avro.AvroConverter for decoding the payload:

```
connect:
  image: confluentinc/cp-kafka-connect-base:7.6.1
  hostname: connect
  container_name: connect
  depends_on:
    - broker
    - schema-registry
  ports:
    - "8083:8083"
  environment:
    CONNECT_BOOTSTRAP_SERVERS: 'broker:29092'
    CONNECT_REST_ADVERTISED_HOST_NAME: connect
    CONNECT_VALUE_CONVERTER: io.confluent.connect.avro.AvroConverter
    CONNECT_VALUE_CONVERTER_SCHEMA_REGISTRY_URL: http://schema-registry:8081
    CONNECT_PLUGIN_PATH: "/usr/share/java,/usr/share/confluent-hub-components"
  command:
    - bash
    - -c
    - |
      echo "Installing Connector"
      confluent-hub install --no-prompt \
        debezium/debezium-connector-postgresql:2.5.4
      #
      echo "Launching Kafka Connect worker"
      /etc/confluent/docker/run &
      #
      sleep infinity
```

Starting the Debezium connector tasks

Now the infrastructure for running the example application is ready, but no data has been produced to Kafka yet, because the Debezium connector tasks have not been started by Kafka Connect. To start those tasks, we need to tell Kafka Connect what type of connector to run and how to set the needed configurations. The connect service offers REST API endpoints at port 8083, where we can send registration requests to supply the needed information. We define the configurations in register-postgres.json as the payload for the REST API request:

```
{
  "name": "pg-debezium-connector",
  "config": {
    "connector.class": "io.debezium.connector.postgresql.PostgresConnector",
    "tasks.max": "1",
    "database.hostname": "postgres",
    "database.port": "5432",
    "database.user": "myuser",
    "database.password": "mypassword",
    "database.dbname": "postgres",
    "topic.prefix": "hudi_tdg",
    "time.precision.mode": "connect",
    "tombstones.on.delete": false,
```

```
    "table.include.list": "public.maintenance_schedule",
    "signal.data.collection": "public.debezium_signal",
    "signal.enabled.channels": "source,kafka",
    "signal.kafka.topic": "signal-topic",
    "signal.kafka.bootstrap.servers": "broker:29092"
  }
}
```

In this example, we set `io.debezium.connector.postgresql.PostgresConnector` as the type of Kafka Connect tasks that need to connect to `postgres` via its opened port 5432 and using the database named `postgres`. The Debezium connector implements a signaling mechanism, configured by the settings prefixed with `signal`, to trigger actions on databases and manage the bookkeeping of them. This is necessary for cases like running the CDC data extraction job, which initially requires taking a snapshot action of the target table. To store the actual data in Kafka, we will end up using a topic named `hudi_tdg.public.maintenance_schedule` as specified by `topic.prefix` and `table.include.list`.

To create the Kafka Connect tasks, we send the configurations defined in the `register-postgres.json` to Kafka Connect's REST API using this command:

```
curl -i -X POST -H "Content-Type:application/json" \
  http://localhost:8083/connectors/ \
  -d @kafka-connect/register-postgres.json
```

Now the Debezium connector tasks are started, scanning the Postgres WAL and sending the CDC data to the topic `hudi_tdg.public.maintenance_schedule`. When more data is being written to the Postgres table, the connector tasks will produce the corresponding change data to the topic in real time.

Up until this step, we have completed the configuration for the upstream source that can simulate the infrastructure used by the Aircraft Maintenance department and provide sample source data for the `maintenance_schedule` table.

Setting Up Hudi Streamer

As introduced earlier, running a Hudi Streamer job is similar to running any standard Spark application. This typically involves using the `spark-submit` command, specifying the main class, and including the necessary jar files in the classpath. In this demo example, the main class is set to `org.apache.hudi.utilities.streamer.Hoodie Streamer`, and the required jar file—`hudi-utilities-bundle`—is used:

```
/opt/spark/bin/spark-submit \
  --name hudi_tdg_ch08_hudi_streamer \
  --class org.apache.hudi.utilities.streamer.HoodieStreamer\
  /opt/hudi/jars/hudi-utilities-bundle_2.13-<HUDI_VERSION>.jar \
  ...
```

```
--op UPSERT \
--continuous
```

Here are two key options in the code snippet to highlight:

`--op` *(write operation)*

Because we're processing data extracted from a Postgres database, which includes inserts, updates, and deletes, this option is set to UPSERT. This ensures that updates and deletes are correctly applied to the corresponding records, replicating the Postgres table in the lakehouse.

`--continuous`

Because we want to emulate a real-world scenario where new data continuously flows into the Postgres database, this flag is added to run Hudi Streamer as a continuous process. Without this flag, the Hudi Streamer application would run once, process a single batch of upstream data, and then exit.

To make the application fully functional, we will now configure the Source for reading from Kafka, the writer-related options, and synchronize the Hudi table with the data catalog implemented using the Hive Metastore in the example.

Configuring the source

Hudi Streamer provides many pluggable interfaces, one of which is the Source class. At the same time, Hudi offers many out-of-the-box implementations for common use cases, and extracting Debezium data is one of those. We set the `--source-class` as `org.apache.hudi.utilities.sources.debezium.PostgresDebeziumSource` to consume the Kafka topic that contains the Debezium-extracted CDC data. To connect to the Kafka broker and the schema registry, we also supply a few other options, as follows. These options primarily specify the addresses of the Kafka broker and the schema registry, enabling Hudi Streamer to connect as a Kafka consumer and continuously fetch new messages:

```
--source-class org.apache.hudi.utilities.sources.debezium.PostgresDebeziumSource
--hoodie-conf \
hoodie.streamer.source.kafka.topic=hudi_tdg.public.maintenance_schedule
--hoodie-conf hoodie.streamer.schemaprovider.registry.url=<url> ❶
--hoodie-conf schema.registry.url=http://schema-registry:8081
--hoodie-conf bootstrap.servers=broker:29092
```

❶ An example URL can be `http://schema-registry:8081/sub jects/hudi_tdg.public.maintenance_schedule-value/versions/latest`.

The extracted CDC data flowing through Kafka follows a Debezium-specific schema. For example, the original Postgres table's schema is nested under the before and/or after fields, which represent the record's state before and after a change. To replicate the original Postgres schema, PostgresDebeziumSource implements logic to flatten and extract the relevant fields from these `before` and `after` fields in the Kafka messages.

This is a key advantage of using Hudi Streamer: users don't need to implement this common transformation logic themselves. Hudi Streamer's out-of-the-box support for such scenarios reduces engineering efforts.

Configuring the Hudi writer

We set `--target-base-path` to specify where the target Hudi table should be written to in the lakehouse storage system. To properly replicate the update and delete operations, we need to set the target Hudi table's record key fields through `hoodie.datasource.write.recordkey.field` such that the fields correspond to primary key fields in the Postgres table. In addition, we configure the `hoodie.datasource.write.keygenerator.type` as nonpartitioned, and the `hoodie.datasource.write.precombine.field` to an ordering field provided by Postgres, named `_event_lsn`, for the desired nonpartitioned table layout and the correct merging behavior, respectively:

```
--target-base-path /opt/external_tables/maintenance_schedule
--hoodie-conf hoodie.datasource.write.recordkey.field=schedule_id
--hoodie-conf hoodie.datasource.write.keygenerator.type=NON_PARTITION
--hoodie-conf hoodie.datasource.write.precombine.field=_event_lsn
```

Working with data catalogs

As introduced in Chapter 4, data catalogs play a critical role in data platform architecture, serving as contact points for query engines and as centralized repositories for managing tables. Synchronizing with data catalogs is a fundamental requirement for ingestion jobs. Hudi Streamer has been designed to support this requirement from day one (see Figure 8-7). When the `--enable-sync` flag is set, Hudi Streamer will perform the "sync" operation on the target table in sequence using Hudi's sync tools specified by `--sync-tool-classes`. Typically, a sync tool will extract metadata from the target table, like table properties, schema, and partition values if applicable, and invoke the catalog service's API to upload the information.

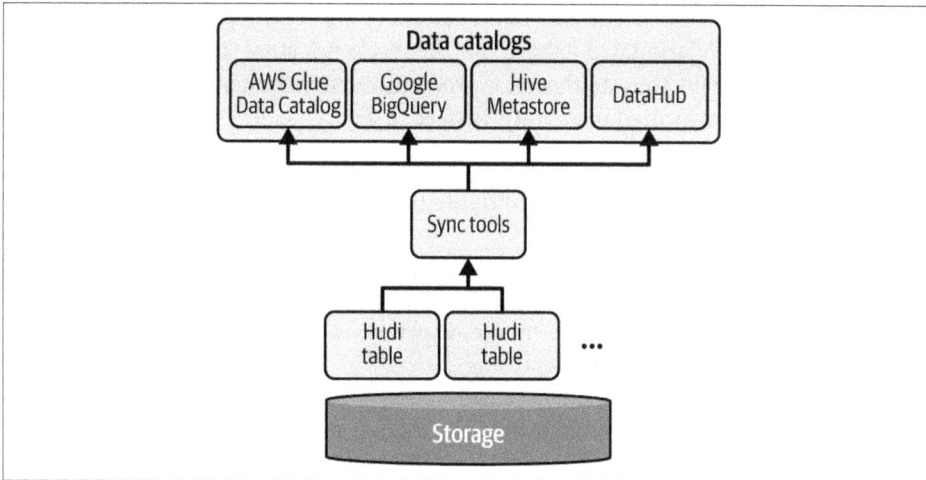

Figure 8-7. Hudi Streamer's data catalog sync flows

Multiple sync tools can be set by giving the fully qualified class name to connect with different catalogs. Hudi offers these sync tool classes out of the box as shown in Table 8-3.

Table 8-3. Supported data catalogs and their corresponding sync tool classes

Data catalog	Sync tool class
AWS Glue Data Catalog	`org.apache.hudi.aws.sync.AwsGlueCatalogSyncTool`
Google BigQuery	`org.apache.hudi.gcp.bigquery.BigQuerySyncTool`
Hive Metastore	`org.apache.hudi.hive.HiveSyncTool`
DataHub	`org.apache.hudi.sync.datahub.DataHubSyncTool`

In addition to specifying the class names, we need to configure a few additional options to ensure proper connection to the catalog service. We will discuss these options in the next section.

> You can also add a Hudi extensions jar provided by Apache XTable (*https://xtable.apache.org*) to Hudi Streamer. In addition, you can support syncing to XTable and converting to other table formats like Apache Iceberg or Delta Lake so that you can connect to more catalogs such as Apache Polaris. See more details in the documentation page (*https://oreil.ly/eZmNq*).

Configuring the data catalog sync

In this demo example, we selected Hive Metastore as the data catalog service. Hive Metastore requires a backend database to store the metadata of all the tables registered with the catalog. For this demonstration, we used Apache Derby, a lightweight, in-process relational database, as the backend store for Hive Metastore. However, it's important to note that in a production environment, Derby is not recommended due to its limited scalability. Instead, users typically deploy more-scalable databases, such as Postgres, as the backend store for Hive Metastore.

To connect with Hive Metastore, we configure the following options:

```
--enable-sync
--sync-tool-classes org.apache.hudi.hive.HiveSyncTool
--hoodie-conf hoodie.datasource.hive_sync.mode=hms
--hoodie-conf hoodie.datasource.hive_sync.metastore.uris=\
  thrift://hive-metastore:9083
--hoodie-conf hoodie.datasource.hive_sync.database=hudi_tdg
```

During the sync process, the Hudi table's metadata is extracted and passed to a Hive Metastore client, which invokes APIs to send the metadata to the server. The catalog sync step is executed synchronously after Hudi Streamer successfully commits the write; in other words, it runs "inline" with the write process, thereby adding extra latency for each write.

> Although catalog sync can usually finish within 1 minute, this could add a small delay to start the next Hudi Streamer batch. Users who prefer to minimize write latency can set up a dedicated process to run the needed sync tool classes separately.

Triggering CDC

With the Debezium connector extracting change data from Postgres and sending it to Kafka, and with Hudi Streamer running in continuous mode to consume the Kafka topic, the end-to-end CDC pipeline is now fully operational. We can run SQL commands to insert new data and update and delete existing records in the Postgres table, while Hudi Streamer performs the corresponding upsert operations to capture these changes in the lakehouse:

```
INSERT INTO maintenance_schedule
    (schedule_id, aircraft_id, due_date, maintenance_type, technician_ids)
VALUES (5, 'AC002', '2024-11-15', 'routine', ARRAY[105, 106, 109]);

UPDATE maintenance_schedule
SET due_date = '2024-08-20'
WHERE schedule_id = 1;

UPDATE maintenance_schedule
SET technician_ids = array_append(technician_ids, 109)
WHERE schedule_id = 3;

DELETE
```

```
FROM maintenance_schedule
WHERE schedule_id = 4;
```

Unlocking the Power of Analytics

Congratulations! At this point, you've successfully built a lakehouse ingestion pipeline for the Aircraft Maintenance department. With the Hudi table continuously receiving new writes and staying synchronized with its entry in the data catalog, you can now leverage powerful query engines and build analytics dashboards. This enables flexible SQL-based analysis and visual insights into the datasets, unlocking the full potential of your data.

Verifying the data using SQL

We chose Presto, a popular SQL engine, to query the Hudi table via the Hive Metastore catalog. We execute this command to first access the Presto CLI console in our Docker-based stack:

```
docker compose -f ../compose.yaml exec -i presto \
  presto-cli --catalog hudi --schema hudi_tdg
```

From the console, execute this SQL command to list all the schedules and the associated information in the table:

```
SELECT schedule_id, due_date, maintenance_type, technician_ids
FROM maintenance_schedule
ORDER BY schedule_id;
```

The SQL command returns a total of four rows. Referring to the SQL commands shown in "Creating the first batch of data" on page 175 and "Triggering CDC" on page 182, we can verify the following:

- The schedule with ID 1 has the updated due date as 2024-08-20.

- The technician with ID 109 has been added to schedule 3.

- The schedule with ID 4 was deleted.

```
 schedule_id |  due_date  | maintenance_type | technician_ids
-------------+------------+------------------+-----------------
           1 | 2024-08-20 | corrective       | [101, 102, 103]
           2 | 2024-09-01 | routine          | [104, 105]
           3 | 2024-07-30 | routine          | [106, 109]
           5 | 2024-11-15 | routine          | [105, 106, 109]
(4 rows)
```

This demonstrates that changes made to the Postgres table have successfully propagated to the end user, with all pipeline components functioning properly. By building similar pipelines for other datasets across departments, analysts can perform more complex analytical queries by joining diverse datasets, enabling deeper insights and more tailored solutions to meet business needs.

Visualizing the data using dashboards

Visualization through dashboards is a powerful way to engage stakeholders with business insights. For this demonstration, we use Superset, a data visualization platform, to build a simple chart on a dashboard. This allows us to showcase the insights derived from the data in a clear and interactive manner.

Superset supports connecting to a variety of data sources, including Presto. Once configured to connect to the Presto instance running in our example Docker stack, Superset can access the Hudi tables registered in the Hive Metastore catalog. In this case, the `maintenance_schedule` table is available as a source for creating a Superset dataset, allowing us to build charts in a Superset dashboard.

Figure 8-8 illustrates a simple example dashboard for the Aircraft Maintenance department. The pie chart, titled "Maintenance types," is configured to count the occurrences of different schedule types and display their distribution in a clear and visual format. The dashboard can be set to refresh at regular intervals, ensuring that as new data is processed by Hudi Streamer, users continue to see the most up-to-date information in the chart.

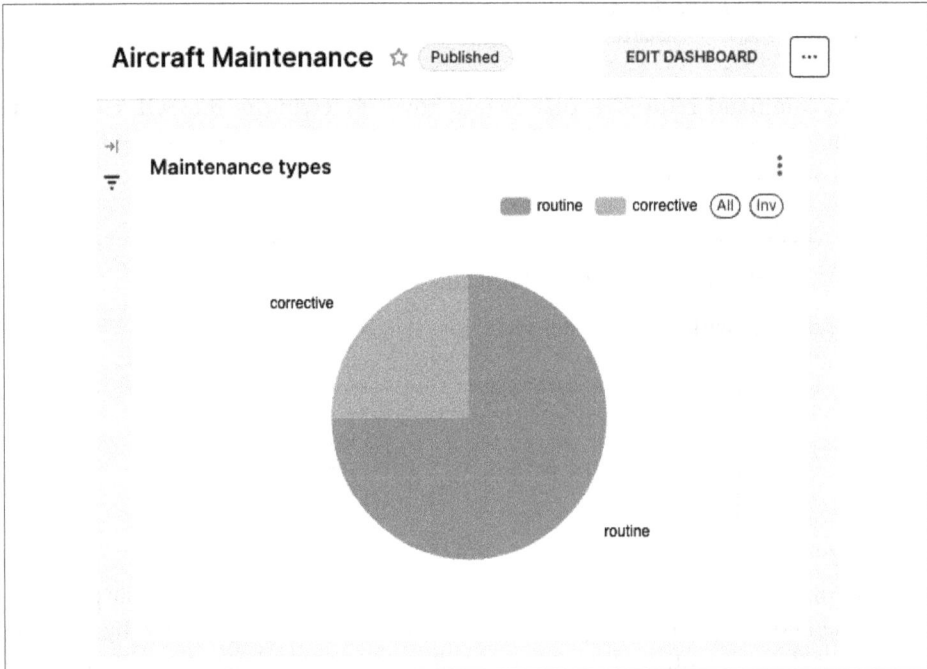

Figure 8-8. Sample analytics dashboard showing maintenance type distribution

Exploring the Hudi Streamer Options

The teams at Alcubierre quickly noticed the benefits of a simplified workflow, using Hudi Streamer as a standardized ingestion framework. Subsequently, Alcubierre decided to establish a dedicated Infra team to manage the infrastructure for running Hudi Streamer applications and overseeing the configuration sets used by various departments leveraging the lakehouse. This Infra team started serving as the tier 1 support for Hudi Streamer jobs across departments, creating templates to allow the departments to tailor their configuration sets according to specific business requirements, ensuring smooth operations, and addressing any issues as they arose. The Infra team combed through Hudi's documentation and examples and discovered many useful Hudi Streamer options, which we will explore in this section.

Hudi Streamer's wide range of features, although powerful, can present a daunting array of options for new users. To streamline understanding and utilization, we've categorized all of the options based on their functionality. Table 8-4 presents eight distinct categories and their associated options.

Table 8-4. Available options supported by Hudi Streamer

Category	Description	Options
General	Apply to general functionalities such as printing help text and passing Hudi configurations.	`--help` `--hoodie-conf` `--props`
Writer	Control the behavior of the writer used by Hudi Streamer.	`--target-base-path` `--target-table` `--table-type` `--op` `--filter-dupes` `--base-file-format` `--payload-class` `--commit-on-errors`
Bootstrap	Control the bootstrapping operation for the target Hudi table.	`--run-bootstrap` `--bootstrap-overwrite` `--bootstrap-index-class`
Source	Define the upstream data source and control the consumption behaviors.	`--source-class` `--source-ordering-field` `--source-limit` `--schemaprovider-class` `--transformer-class`
Checkpoint	Control the checkpointing behaviors.	`--checkpoint` `--initial-checkpoint-provider` `--ignore-checkpoint` `--allow-commit-on-no-checkpoint-change`

Category	Description	Options

Catalog sync	Control the synchronization behaviors with respect to data catalogs.	`--enable-sync`
		`--force-empty-sync`
		`--sync-tool-classes`

Table service	Manage the scheduling of table services such as compaction and clustering.	`--retry-last-pending-inline-clustering`
		`--retry-last-pending-inline-compaction`
		`--max-pending-compactions`
		`--max-pending-clustering`
		`--compact-scheduling-weight`
		`--compact-scheduling-minshare`
		`--cluster-scheduling-weight`
		`--cluster-scheduling-minshare`
		`--disable-compaction`

Operational	Control the runtime and operational behaviors of the Hudi Streamer job.	`--continuous`
		`--min-sync-interval-seconds`
		`--delta-sync-scheduling-weight`
		`--delta-sync-scheduling-minshare`
		`--retry-on-source-failures`
		`--retry-interval-seconds`
		`--max-retry-count`
		`--post-write-termination-strategy-class`
		`--ingestion-metrics-class`
		`--config-hot-update-strategy-class`
		`--spark-master`

In most cases, Hudi Streamer ingestion jobs will only need a small subset of available options for specific use cases. In the remainder of this section, we will explore additional details about the options categorized as general, source, and operational, providing extended knowledge beyond what was covered in the previous section. For a comprehensive introduction to all available options, please refer to Hudi's documentation page (*https://oreil.ly/h2cBQ*).

General Options

This category includes general-purpose options. A key use case involves passing arbitrary Hudi configurations or properties as key-value pairs to the Hudi Streamer job, allowing the lower-level Hudi write client to honor these settings. The repeatable `--hoodie-conf` option accepts Hudi configurations in the form of key-value pairs, delimited by an equal sign. Alternatively, users can provide a filepath to a *.properties* or *.conf* file using the `--props` option, which loads a set of key-value configuration pairs from the file.

An example usage looks like this:

```
--hoodie-conf hoodie.upsert.shuffle.parallelism=100
--hoodie-conf hoodie.delete.shuffle.parallelism=100
--props file:///etc/conf/hudi.dev.properties
```

Note that the `--hoodie-conf` option has the highest precedence among all configurations passed to Hudi Streamer, including those provided via `--props` and other overlapping command-line options. In contrast, configurations specified with `--props` have the lowest precedence.

> A *.properties* file can include configurations from other *.properties* files by adding `include=<other properties file>` on the first line. Properties defined later in the file will overwrite those from the included file if applicable. This pattern is commonly used to define base properties for most Hudi Streamer jobs on a lakehouse platform, which are then included in domain-specific properties files. This approach avoids redundant configurations and simplifies management.

Source Options

We covered the Source abstraction provided via `--source-class` in "Getting Started with Hudi Streamer" on page 169 and configured it for the demo application in "Hudi Streamer in Action" on page 173. We now have a clear understanding of the diverse support for ingesting data from various sources. To further extend this information, we will briefly introduce the additional Source implementations that are available.

The `ParquetDFSSource` is set to read plain Parquet files from file storage systems, which can be the local file system, the Hadoop file system, or cloud object stores like AWS S3, GCS, and Azure Blob Storage.

The `HoodieIncrSource` is used to read a Hudi table as the Source through incremental queries. This is particularly useful when data in tables needs further processing, such as joining with other tables. This Source implementation uses checkpointed timestamps as incremental query parameters to fetch only the changed data (new or updated) from the source Hudi table. This approach reduces redundant data processing and enhances the overall efficiency of the pipeline.

Following are some other notable Source implementations:

`MysqlDebeziumSource`
Similar to `PostgresDebeziumSource` but consumes the CDC data extracted from MySQL databases

`ProtoKafkaSource`
Consumes from Kafka topics that contain Protobuf-encoded messages

`PulsarSource`
Consumes data from Pulsar (*https://pulsar.apache.org*)

The `--schemaprovider-class` option defines how Hudi Streamer retrieves the schema of the Source data. In "Getting Started with Hudi Streamer" on page 169, we saw that Alcubierre's Safety and Security department used `SchemaRegistryProvider` to handle schema evolution scenarios. Another commonly used schema provider is `FileBasedSchemaProvider`, which points to an Avro schema file that will be read to serve the schema. Note that not all Sources require a schema provider; for example, `ParquetDFSSource` can self-provide the schema information.

The `--source-ordering-field` option indicates a field in the Source schema that determines the ordering between records. This is equivalent to `hoodie.data source.write.precombine.field`, which allows incoming records to be merged before persisting to storage to save compute costs.

The `--source-limit` option sets an upper limit on the data amount to read during each data fetch from the Source, enhancing control over the ingestion process. The limit can be in terms of data bytes or number of messages, depending on the `Source` class.

Operational Options

Hudi Streamer includes various features to ease operational efforts, offering options to specify the running mode, control retry behavior, and fine-tune scheduling priority.

Operation modes

Hudi Streamer operates in two modes:

Run once (default)
Designed for one-time batch ingestion. The Hudi Streamer job terminates automatically after processing the fetched source data. This mode is ideal for periodic batch processing, typically requiring external scheduling tools to initiate the job.

Continuous
Enabled by adding the `--continuous` option (as previously discussed in "Setting Up Hudi Streamer" on page 178). In this mode, Hudi Streamer runs in a loop, continuously fetching source data up to the specified limit (set by `--source-limit`) and writing to storage. This mode is suitable for handling unbounded streaming data or self-processing a sequence of input batches.

Minimum sync interval

The `--min-sync-interval-seconds` option functions in conjunction with the continuous mode, defining the minimum allowable interval in seconds between ingestion cycles. For example:

- If an ingestion operation takes 40 seconds and the `min-sync-interval` is set to 60 seconds, Hudi Streamer will pause for 20 seconds before starting the next cycle.
- If an ingestion takes 70 seconds, the application will immediately begin the next cycle without any pause.

This feature serves to ensure that adequate data accumulates at the upstream source for processing, thus reducing the likelihood of generating small files that can negatively impact performance.

Graceful termination

To gracefully shut down a continuously running Hudi Streamer, users can implement a custom `--post-write-termination-strategy-class` to define the conditions for job termination. An example is the `org.apache.hudi.utilities.streamer.NoNewDataTerminationStrategy`, which ends the ingestion loop after a specified number of data-pulling rounds.

This approach is particularly useful when processing large volumes of data that would typically require substantial resources. Instead, the data can be divided into batches, allowing Hudi Streamer to run continuously on a smaller-scale cluster. The cluster can then self-terminate once ingestion is complete, optimizing resource utilization.

Other operational options

The options `--retry-on-source-failures`, `--retry-interval-seconds`, and `--max-retry-count` define how the Hudi Streamer job should behave upon running into errors. The options `--delta-sync-scheduling-weight` and `--delta-sync-scheduling-minshare` inform the Spark scheduler about how much priority should be given to ingestion work compared to table service jobs running within the same application. A detailed explanation of scheduling prioritization can be found on the Spark documentation page (*https://oreil.ly/LbAge*).

Summary

In this chapter, we embarked on a detailed journey to build a data lakehouse platform. We began by reviewing the challenges faced by Alcubierre, a fictional airline grappling with data silos across its departments. Each department had adopted its own data storage system, making it difficult to gain insights across the organization and enhance overall business processes. We concluded that a lakehouse architecture could significantly address these issues.

To build a comprehensive lakehouse platform, we introduced Hudi Streamer as the core component of the ingestion layer, explaining how its versatile features and options could resolve Alcubierre's problems. We then focused on a specific department's use case, constructing an end-to-end application to demonstrate the working configurations and services necessary for the lakehouse platform, and we highlighted the benefits through a simulated real-world example.

Finally, we expanded our understanding of Hudi Streamer by exploring additional notable options and their practical applications, providing valuable insights for building lakehouses in practice.

In Chapter 9, we will delve into more aspects and use cases encountered in production environments and explore how Hudi's capabilities can address critical business challenges.

Running Hudi in Production

Moving from development to production often brings a new set of operational challenges. This chapter will equip you with the tools and best practices to manage Apache Hudi deployments smoothly in complex environments, ensuring reliable pipelines with minimal overhead.

First, we will explore tools for table management and recovery. You will learn to master the Hudi CLI, a versatile tool for performing routine maintenance, inspecting table metadata for troubleshooting, and executing various operational tasks without writing custom code. We will also cover Hudi's savepoint and restore operations, which are essential for disaster recovery.

Next, we will focus on integrating Hudi into data platforms. We will cover platform features such as post-commit callbacks, which can be used to trigger downstream processes in messaging systems like Apache Kafka or Apache Pulsar, when actions complete on Hudi tables. You will learn how to set up monitoring and export key metrics to systems like Prometheus or Amazon CloudWatch to maintain visibility into system health. We will also tackle the challenge of metadata consistency, explaining how to use Hudi's catalog sync services to keep your tables registered and accessible across multiple data catalogs like AWS Glue and DataHub, as well as data warehouses like Google BigQuery, Snowflake, and AWS Redshift.

Finally, we will delve into performance tuning, providing practical advice and proven strategies to optimize your data pipelines for throughput, latency, and cost-efficiency.

By the end of this chapter, you'll have the knowledge to efficiently operate Hudi data pipelines, tackling production challenges with ease while building integrations and maintaining high performance for your organization's data lakehouse.

Operating with Ease

In production, operational efficiency can mean the difference between a minor hiccup and a major outage. Hudi provides a comprehensive set of tools to help data engineers and administrators manage their data lakehouses effectively.

The CLI is central among these tools, enabling teams to perform routine maintenance, troubleshooting, and administrative tasks without writing custom code. Using the CLI, teams can quickly diagnose issues, apply fixes, and maintain the health of their Hudi tables at scale. Hudi's CLI empowers teams to respond rapidly to production incidents and automate routine maintenance tasks, instead of relying on ad hoc scripts or manual file inspection. This section explores how to incorporate these tools into your operational workflows, shifting from reactive firefighting to proactive management, allowing your team to truly "operate with ease" even in the most demanding data lakehouse production environments.

Getting to Know the CLI

Hudi's CLI serves as the Swiss Army knife for engineers working with Hudi tables. Through a simple terminal-based interface, engineers can quickly examine commit histories, view metadata, perform recovery operations, and execute maintenance tasks without writing custom code. Let's explore the essential CLI commands that will become part of your operational toolkit.

Understanding the setup

The Hudi CLI is usable via the *hudi-cli-with-bundle.sh* script located under the *packaging/hudi-cli-bundle/* directory of Hudi's code repository (*https://github.com/apache/hudi*). The shell script works with two bundle jars downloadable from the public Maven repository:

`hudi-cli-bundle`
Provides commands to run from the CLI

`hudi-spark-bundle`
Provides core Hudi functionalities and dependencies to work with Apache Spark applications that interact with Hudi tables

You may use the `wget` tool to download the jars from the public repository:

```
export REPO_URL=<URL> ❶
export HUDI_CLI_BUNDLE_JAR=<CLI bundle jar path> ❷
export HUDI_SPARK_BUNDLE_JAR=<Spark bundle jar path> ❸
wget $REPO_URL/$HUDI_CLI_BUNDLE_JAR
wget $REPO_URL/$HUDI_SPARK_BUNDLE_JAR
```

❶ The URL for Hudi release artifacts is `https://reposi tory.apache.org/content/repositories/releases`.

❷ The jar path is like `org/apache/hudi/hudi-cli-bundle_2.13/1.1.0/hudi-cli-bundle_2.13-1.1.0.jar`.

❸ The jar path is like `org/apache/hudi/hudi-spark3.5-bundle_2.13/1.1.0/hudi-spark3.5-bundle_2.13-1.1.0.jar`.

In this example, you are downloading the Hudi 1.1 bundle jars that work with Spark 3.5 and Scala 2.13.

Running Hudi CLI commands will submit and run Spark jobs and perform various operations with the target Hudi table (Figure 9-1). You need to have a Spark installation available when running the CLI, typically specified by `SPARK_HOME` environment variables.

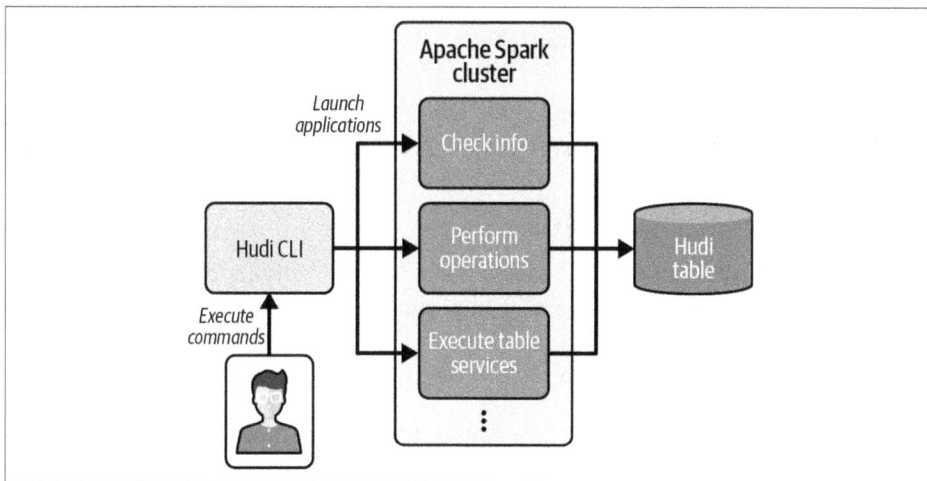

Figure 9-1. Hudi CLI flow overview

Set up the CLI as follows:

```
# Set relevant environment variables
export SPARK_HOME=</path/to/spark>
export CLI_BUNDLE_JAR=</path/to/hudi-cli-bundle/jar>
export SPARK_BUNDLE_JAR=</path/to/hudi-spark-bundle/jar>
```

Start the CLI using the script provided in the *packaging/hudi-cli-bundle/* directory:

```
# Start the CLI
./hudi-cli-with-bundle.sh
```

The script will take in the environment variables that were set before running this. Alongside the *./hudi-cli-with-bundle.sh* script, if you create a directory *conf/* and put *hudi-defaults.conf* in it, the CLI script will pick it up and you can conveniently add Hudi configurations in the *hudi-defaults.conf* to fine-tune those operations performed on Hudi tables.

> Hudi CLI functionality is also available through SQL procedures using the CALL command. This alternative provides a similar set of capabilities to the CLI, with the main difference being that commands are executed through the Spark SQL console. For detailed usage, please refer to its documentation (*https://oreil.ly/GZefk*).

Checking table info

Once the CLI is running, you can create new tables, connect to existing ones, and inspect their properties.

Let's say that you wanted to initialize a new Hudi table. The create command sets up the table structure at a specified path, defining its name and type:

```
hudi->create --path /path/to/new/table \
--tableName new_hudi_table --tableType COPY_ON_WRITE
```

If you're working with an existing Hudi table, you'll need to connect to it before running commands. Use the connect command to point the CLI to your table's base path:

```
hudi->connect --path /path/to/table/trips
```

Once connected, you can read the table's properties to verify its configurations. The desc command provides a summary of important properties, such as the table type, record keys, and schema:

```
hudi:trips->desc
```

To understand the structure of the data stored in your table, you can retrieve the table schema, especially useful when validating data or planning queries:

```
hudi:trips->fetch table schema
```

The command prompt initially shows hudi, indicating the CLI has been started and is in an idle state. Once you connect to a table, it shows the table name, such as hudi:trips, highlighting the table it's currently working on.

Inspecting commits

The commit history provides a chronological view of all write operations performed on the table. This helps track how data evolved over time and helps diagnose issues.

To get a quick sense of recent activity, you can list the latest commits along with key metrics, such as data volume. The `commits show` command helps surface high-level trends or spot anomalies in recent writes:

```
hudi:trips->commits show --sortBy "Total Bytes Written" \
--desc true --limit 5
```

For deeper inspection, you may want to break down a specific commit by partition to understand how data was distributed. The `commit showpartitions` command provides detailed statistics on each partition affected by the commit:

```
hudi:trips->commit showpartitions \
--commit 20220128160245447 \
--sortBy "Total Bytes Written" --desc true
```

When debugging a data issue, you may need to track down changes at the file level. The `commit showfiles` command lists every base file or log file updated as part of a write action, along with its partition path and other metadata:

```
hudi:trips->commit showfiles \ ,
--commit 20220128160245447 --sortBy "Partition Path"
```

Inspecting file slices and statistics

Hudi organizes data in file groups and file slices. The `show fsview` command (`fsview` is short for *file system view*) helps you examine this structure, while the `stats` command provides insights into file size distribution and write amplification.

To view all file slices for each file group:

```
hudi:trips->show fsview all
```

To view just the latest file slice for each file group:

```
hudi:trips->show fsview latest --partitionPath "2022/01/01"
```

To examine file size distribution for a specific partition:

```
hudi:trips->stats filesizes \
--partitionPath 2022/01/01 \
--sortBy "95th" --desc true
```

To check write amplification (the ratio of records written to records updated):

```
hudi:trips->stats wa
```

Managing table services

Running table services like compaction, clustering, and cleaning straight from the CLI can come in handy for various operational scenarios (indexing is not yet supported in the CLI). When you need to perform maintenance tasks outside your regular Spark or Apache Flink processing jobs, the Hudi CLI provides a convenient way to trigger these services on demand. This can be particularly beneficial during maintenance windows. For example, you can free up storage space without waiting for the next scheduled cleaning operation.

Compaction can be executed to optimize read performance after the table accumulates a series of deltacommit actions:

```
hudi:trips->compaction scheduleAndExecute --parallelism 200 --sparkMemory 4G
```

You can run clustering to optimize the table's storage layout and improve query performance:

```
hudi:trips->clustering scheduleAndExecute --parallelism 200 --sparkMemory 4G
```

You can also run a cleaning operation to reclaim storage after a large delete operation:

```
hudi:trips->clean run --commitsToClean 10 --retainCommits 24 --sparkMemory 4G
```

By using CLI commands to schedule and/or execute table services outside of data processing jobs, you will have more flexibility in maintaining and optimizing your lakehouse tables.

If you want to keep the writer job running, and run the table services from the CLI, this will effectively be the standalone deployment mode for the table services. Therefore, you should configure a lock provider and supply the concurrency control–related configurations for the writer job and the CLI program. Here is an example of using Apache Zookeeper as the lock provider:

```
hoodie.write.concurrency.mode=optimistic_concurrency_control
hoodie.write.lock.provider=\
org.apache.hudi.client.transaction.lock.ZookeeperBasedLockProvider
hoodie.write.lock.zookeeper.url=<zk_url>
hoodie.write.lock.zookeeper.port=<zk_port>
hoodie.write.lock.zookeeper.lock_key=<zk_key>
hoodie.write.lock.zookeeper.base_path=<zk_base_path>
```

You can add the configurations to the *hudi-defaults.conf* as instructed in "Understanding the setup" on page 192, along with other Hudi configurations.

Performing Table Operations

Production data systems require operational flexibility to handle both routine maintenance and unexpected issues. The Hudi CLI provides commands to manage Hudi tables in various scenarios, from creating recovery points and rolling back problematic changes to modifying fundamental table properties and maintaining data quality. This section introduces four key scenarios: creating and restoring savepoints for data reprocessing, repairing data (e.g., deduplication) to maintain integrity, changing table types to adapt to evolving workloads, and upgrading and downgrading table versions to manage compatibility. With these tools, administrators can confidently evolve Hudi tables to meet changing requirements while maintaining reliability and performance.

Using savepoint and restore

Managing and recovering from data issues is a critical aspect of production operations. Whether caused by corrupted writes, bad source data, or application logic errors, the need to roll back to a known good state is a common requirement. Hudi's savepoint and restore feature addresses this challenge by creating recoverable snapshots of table state.

Understanding savepoints. As the name suggests, a savepoint saves the table as of a specific commit action time, allowing you to restore the table to this savepoint at a later point if needed (Figure 9-2). When a savepoint is created, Hudi ensures that the cleaning table service will not remove any files that are part of the savepoint, preserving them for potential future restoration. Importantly, you cannot create a savepoint for a commit that has already been cleaned up. Usually, you would want to create a savepoint at one of the most recent commit actions, which are very unlikely to be covered by the cleaning process.

Conceptually, creating a savepoint is similar to taking a backup, but with an important distinction: Hudi doesn't make a new copy of the table data. Instead, it saves the state of the table at a particular commit point so that you can return to it if necessary.

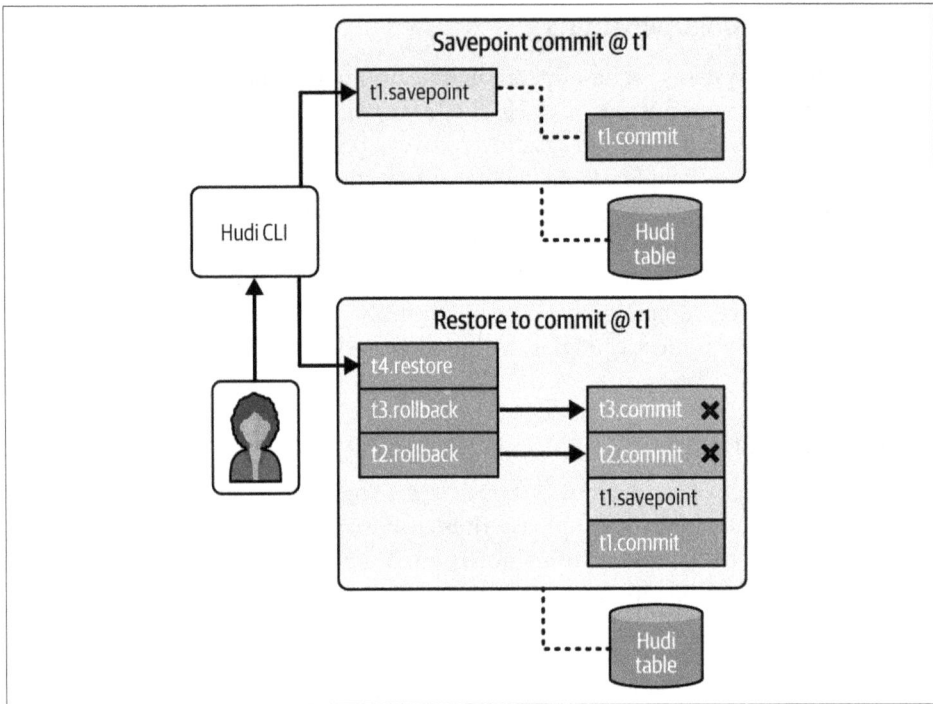

Figure 9-2. Hudi CLI savepoint and restore

Using the restore process.   The restore operation allows you to revert your table to a previously created savepoint commit. This is a powerful but irreversible operation that should be approached with caution. When you initiate a restore, Hudi will delete all data files and commit files (timeline files) created after the savepoint commit to which you're restoring.

During a restore operation, it's critical to pause all write operations to the table, because they are likely to fail while the restore is in progress. Similarly, read operations might also fail because snapshot queries would be accessing files that could be deleted during the restore process.

Using savepoint and restore via the Hudi CLI.   To create a savepoint, start the CLI command as instructed earlier, and then connect to your Hudi table:

```
connect --path </path/to/your/hudi_table/>
commits show
savepoint create --commit <COMMIT_TIMESTAMP> --sparkMaster local[2]
```

Before performing a restore, it's crucial to shut down all writer processes to avoid data conflicts or corruption. Then, using the Hudi CLI, issue these commands:

```
connect --path </path/to/your/hudi_table/>
commits show
savepoints show
savepoint rollback --savepoint <SAVEPOINT_TIMESTAMP> --sparkMaster local[2]
```

Replace *<SAVEPOINT_TIMESTAMP>* with the actual savepoint timestamp that you want to restore to. This can be found using the `savepoints show` command. The code example sets the Spark job to run using the local mode for illustration purposes. You may need to configure the relevant Spark options to choose a right setup for the job.

After a successful restore operation, the table will be reset to the exact state it was in at the time of the savepoint. Both file slices and timeline entries created after the savepoint will be deleted from the file system. The table will contain only the records that were present at the time the savepoint was created.

> It's recommended to create savepoints at regular intervals, especially before significant operations. However, it's also important to manage your savepoints by deleting older ones when newer ones are created. The Hudi CLI provides a `savepoint delete` command for this purpose.

> Remember that the cleaner process won't remove files that are part of active savepoints. If you don't delete unnecessary savepoints, this can prevent storage reclamation and lead to increased storage costs over time.

Repairing data with deduplication

Data pipelines occasionally produce duplicate records due to processing retries, source system issues, or application logic errors. The Hudi CLI provides deduplication functionality to identify and remove duplicates based on record keys (Figure 9-3).

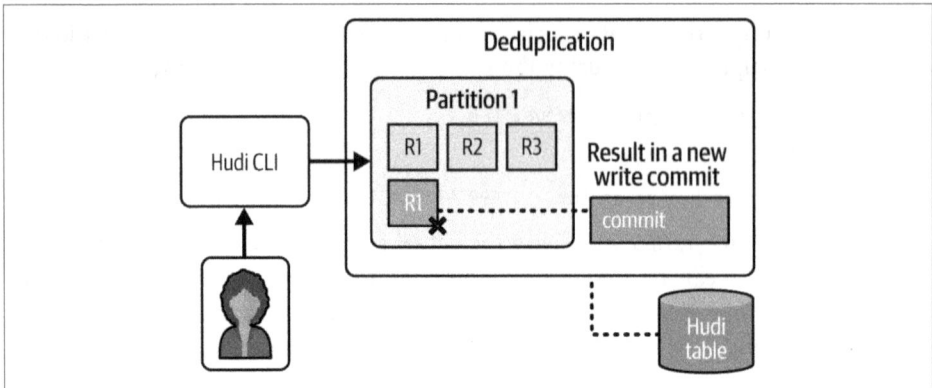

Figure 9-3. Hudi CLI deduplication

The deduplication repair command allows you to identify duplicate records within a partition and generate repaired files that can be used to replace the corrupted partition data, helping you maintain data integrity without having to reprocess entire datasets:

```
connect --path </path/to/your/hudi_table/>

# Run deduplication repair for a specific partition
repair deduplicate --duplicatedPartitionPath "2022/01/15"
```

> When performing deduplication, the process can be resource intensive, due to a full read of the table partition and the inner-join operation. You can use the --sparkProperties argument of the deduplication repair command to specify Spark-related configurations to tune operation performance.

Changing table types

Hudi's flexibility allows you to change table types between Copy-on-Write (COW) and Merge-on-Read (MOR) based on evolving workload patterns (Figure 9-4). As your application requirements evolve, you may need to switch between these table types to optimize for different access patterns.

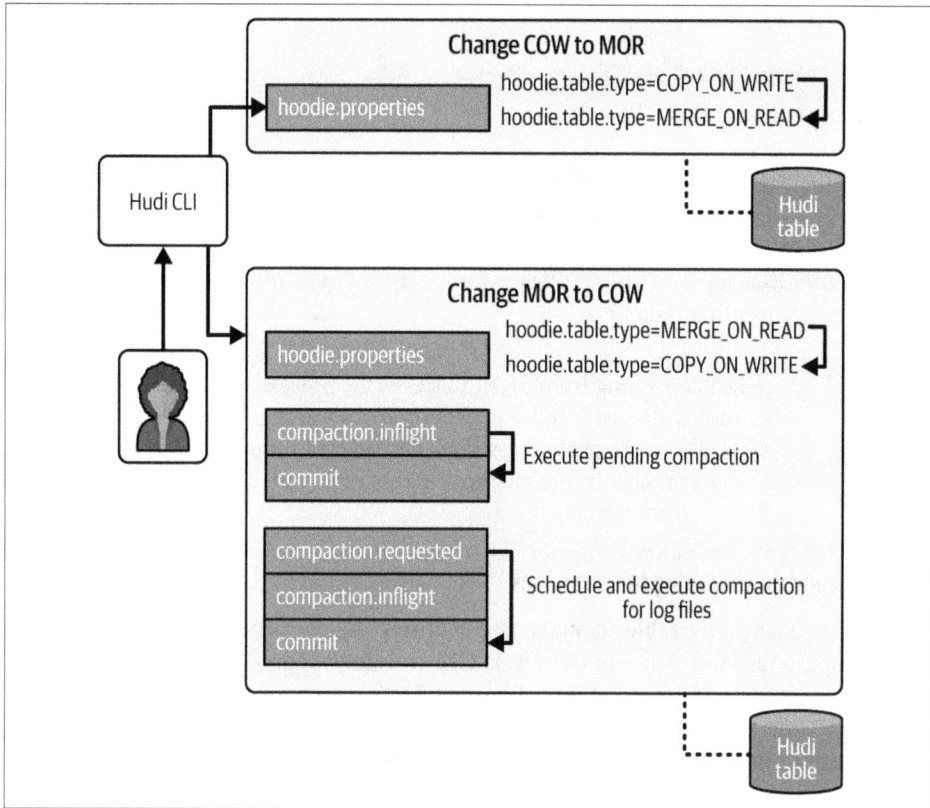

Figure 9-4. Hudi CLI change table type

Changing from COW to MOR. When your application requires more efficient writes, you might want to convert a COW table to an MOR table. This change is straightforward and can be accomplished with a simple command:

```
connect --path </path/to/your/hudi_table/>
```

```
table change-table-type MOR
```

This command modifies the `hoodie.table.type` property in the table's *hoodie.properties* file to `MERGE_ON_READ`.

Changing from MOR to COW. When read performance and compatibility with downstream engines become more important than write efficiency, you may want to convert an MOR table to a COW table. This conversion requires special attention because MOR tables have log files that need to be compacted:

```
connect --path </path/to/your/hudi_table/>

table change-table-type COW
```

By default, changing to COW will:

- Execute all pending compactions.
- Perform a full compaction if any log files remain.

This ensures that all data in log files is properly merged into base files before the conversion, preventing data loss.

> When converting from MOR to COW, the process can be resource intensive, due to a full compaction to be running on the whole table. There are parameters available, such as --parallelism and --sparkMemory, in the change-table-type command to tune the Spark job accordingly.

Upgrading and downgrading table versions

As Hudi evolves, new table formats and features are introduced that may require version upgrades. You can use the Hudi CLI to safely upgrade table versions while maintaining backward compatibility (Figure 9-5).

Understanding table versions. Hudi maintains a versioning system for tables, where each table's version is stored in the hoodie.table.version property in the *.hoodie/hoodie.properties* file. Different Hudi release versions support different table versions, and tables may need to be upgraded or downgraded when switching between Hudi library versions.

Table 9-1 shows the correspondence between Hudi table versions and Hudi release versions.

Table 9-1. Hudi table versions and their corresponding release versions

Hudi table version	Hudi release version(s)
9	1.1
8	1.0
6	0.14–0.15
5	0.12–0.13
4	0.11
3	0.10
2	0.9
1	0.6–0.8
0	0.5 and below

Upgrading a table version. The Hudi CLI provides the ability to manually upgrade a Hudi table version. This process modifies the *hoodie.properties* file with the required configuration values and adds properties that are required by the target version.

To upgrade a Hudi table through the CLI:

```
connect --path <table_path>
upgrade table --toVersion <target_version>
```

If you don't specify a target version, the command `upgrade table` will use the latest table version corresponding to the library release version.

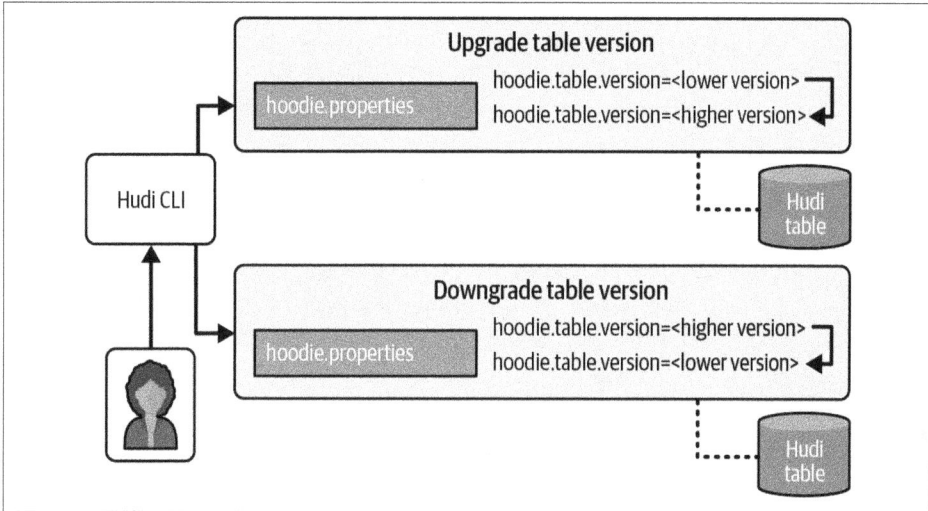

Figure 9-5. Hudi CLI upgrade and downgrade

Downgrading a table version. When you need to use an older version of the Hudi library, you must first downgrade the table version using the newer version of the Hudi CLI before switching libraries. This process modifies the *hoodie.properties* file with the required configuration values and removes properties that aren't compatible with the target version.

To downgrade a Hudi table through the CLI, specify the target Hudi table version as follows:

```
connect --path <table_path>
downgrade table --toVersion <target_version>
```

For example, to downgrade a table from version 6 to 2, you would run:

```
downgrade table --toVersion 2 --sparkMaster local[2]
```

It's important to note that table upgrades are automatically handled by the Hudi write client in different deployment modes, such as Hudi Streamer, after upgrading the Hudi library. This automatic upgrade is the *recommended* approach in general, rather than using the manual upgrade CLI command, because a table version upgrade may require writer configurations as input to derive corresponding table properties. You can only manually downgrade a table using the CLI.

Smooth Upgrade to Hudi 1.0

Hudi 1.0 is a milestone release that significantly advances the platform's feature set and architectural robustness. A key change in this release is an update to the table format. For users currently running Hudi 0.*x* versions, a smooth migration path is essential to ensure that production pipelines continue to operate without major interruptions.

To facilitate this, Hudi 1.0 provides a backward-compatible write mechanism, enabling a phased upgrade. The process involves several steps to update the Hudi artifacts used by table services, writers, and readers. For detailed, step-by-step instructions, please refer to the official migration guide in the 1.0 release notes (*https://oreil.ly/jPn7B*).

Integrating into the Platform

Hudi provides strong standalone value, but its true power comes when it's fully integrated with your broader data platform. Connecting Hudi with complementary tools enables workflows like triggering downstream processing via post-commit callbacks, implementing monitoring for pipeline health, and synchronizing metadata across catalogs. These integrations elevate Hudi from a data management tool to a core component of your lakehouse architecture. A well-integrated deployment ensures data consistency across query engines, offers a unified view of data assets, and supports seamless data flow throughout your organization. This section explores key integration patterns to help you maximize Hudi's value while keeping operations simple and reliable.

Triggering Post-Commit Callbacks

When a data pipeline updates a Hudi table, it rarely exists in isolation. Consider a common scenario where a data engineering team ingests customer transaction data into a Hudi table. Once that data is committed, several downstream systems need to be notified: a search index must be updated to make the new transactions searchable; a real-time dashboard needs refreshing to reflect the latest business metrics, such as merchant performance, transaction volume, and revenue attribution; and an event-driven workflow must be triggered to process high-value transactions. Without a proper notification mechanism, teams often resort to scheduled polling or complex orchestration tools that create tight coupling between systems.

Hudi's post-commit callback feature enables real-time event notifications for write operations, forming the foundation for event-driven data architectures. This powerful capability allows your data pipeline to trigger downstream processes immediately after a successful write commit without relying on scheduled jobs or polling mechanisms.

As shown in Figure 9-6, callback will be invoked by a Hudi writer that completes a write commit. By configuring callbacks to HTTP endpoints or message brokers like Kafka or Pulsar, you can build loosely coupled, event-driven architectures that react to data changes instantly, ensuring that downstream consumers always have access to the freshest data available.

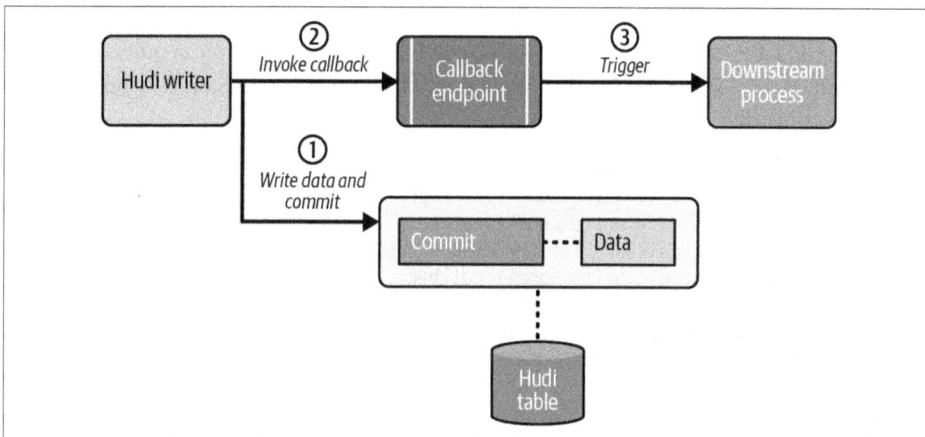

Figure 9-6. Hudi writer invoking post-commit callback

HTTP endpoints

You can send commit notifications to REST APIs or webhook receivers to trigger serverless functions, workflow orchestrators, or custom microservices. This approach makes it easy to integrate Hudi with modern cloud native architectures by informing other systems as soon as data becomes available.

The following example demonstrates how to configure an HTTP callback using Hudi's Spark writer. This setup notifies a downstream service whenever a commit is completed, which is ideal for workflows that need to kick off jobs after fresh data is ingested.

Start by initializing your Spark session and preparing the data you plan to write to the Hudi table:

```java
// Spark Writer Example (Java)
SparkSession spark = SparkSession.builder()
  .appName("Hudi HTTP Callback Example").getOrCreate();

Dataset<Row> dataFrame = spark.read().json("/path/to/input/data");
```

Next, define the writer configurations, including the table name, record key, and partition path:

```java
// Configure Hudi options for the writer
Map<String, String> hudiOptions = new HashMap<>();

// Table configuration
hudiOptions.put("hoodie.table.name", "customer_orders");
hudiOptions.put("hoodie.datasource.write.recordkey.field", "order_id");
hudiOptions.put("hoodie.datasource.write.partitionpath.field", "order_date");
hudiOptions.put("hoodie.datasource.write.operation", "upsert");
```

Enable the HTTP callback and set the target URL along with any required headers or authentication. This ensures that your downstream service receives a notification after each commit:

```java
// HTTP Callback configuration
hudiOptions.put("hoodie.write.commit.callback.on", "true");
hudiOptions.put("hoodie.write.commit.callback.class.name",
  "org.apache.hudi.callback.impl.HoodieWriteCommitHttpCallback");
hudiOptions.put("hoodie.write.commit.callback.http.url",
  "https://order-processing.example.com/api/data-ready");
hudiOptions.put("hoodie.write.commit.callback.http.timeout.seconds", "5");
hudiOptions.put("hoodie.write.commit.callback.http.api.key",
  "secret_api_key_123");
hudiOptions.put("hoodie.write.commit.callback.http.custom.headers",
  "X-Source:hudi-lakehouse;X-Table:customer_orders");
```

Finally, run the write operation with your configured options. Once the commit completes, the HTTP callback will automatically fire:

```java
// Apply configuration to your Hudi write
dataFrame.write()
  .format("org.apache.hudi")
  .options(hudiOptions)
  .mode("append")
  .save("/path/to/hudi/customer_orders");
```

Kafka endpoints

You can push commit events to Kafka topics to create an event stream that can be consumed by multiple downstream systems. This enables parallel processing workflows and decoupled architectures where different applications can react to new data independently.

Start by initializing your Spark session and preparing the data you plan to write to the Hudi table:

```java
// Spark Writer Example (Java) with Kafka Callback
SparkSession spark = SparkSession.builder()
    .appName("Hudi Kafka Callback Example").getOrCreate();

Dataset<Row> dataFrame = spark.read().parquet("/path/to/input/data");
```

Next, define the writer configurations, including the table name, record key, and partition path:

```java
// Configure Hudi options for the writer
Map<String, String> hudiOptions = new HashMap<>();

// Table configuration
hudiOptions.put("hoodie.table.name", "product_inventory");
hudiOptions.put("hoodie.datasource.write.recordkey.field", "product_id");
hudiOptions.put("hoodie.datasource.write.partitionpath.field", "category");
hudiOptions.put("hoodie.datasource.write.operation", "bulk_insert");
```

Enable the HTTP callback and set the relevant Kafka-related properties:

```java
// Enable callback with Kafka implementation
hudiOptions.put("hoodie.write.commit.callback.on", "true");
hudiOptions.put("hoodie.write.commit.callback.class.name",
    "org.apache.hudi.callback.impl.HoodieWriteCommitKafkaCallback");

// Kafka specific configuration
hudiOptions.put("hoodie.write.commit.callback.kafka.bootstrap.servers",
    "kafka1:9092,kafka2:9092");
hudiOptions.put("hoodie.write.commit.callback.kafka.topic",
    "inventory-updates");
// Using single partition ensures strict ordering
hudiOptions.put("hoodie.write.commit.callback.kafka.partition", "0");
// Ensure durability
hudiOptions.put("hoodie.write.commit.callback.kafka.acks", "all");
// Retry configuration
hudiOptions.put("hoodie.write.commit.callback.kafka.retries", "3");
```

Finally, run the write operation with your configured options. Once the commit completes, the HTTP callback will automatically fire:

```java
// Apply configuration to your Hudi write
dataFrame.write()
    .format("org.apache.hudi")
    .options(hudiOptions)
    .mode(SaveMode.Append)
    .save("/path/to/hudi/product_inventory");
```

Pulsar endpoints

Similar to the Kafka integration, you can invoke Pulsar endpoints through post-commit callbacks by simply configuring the appropriate Pulsar-specific parameters for your Hudi writer.

Begin by initializing the Spark session and loading the data you want to ingest into Hudi:

```
// Spark Writer Example (Java) with Pulsar Callback
SparkSession spark = SparkSession.builder()
  .appName("Hudi Pulsar Callback Example").getOrCreate();

Dataset<Row> dataFrame = spark.read().json("/path/to/input/data");
```

Set the relevant writer configurations, including the table name, record key, partition path, and precombine field (used for upserts):

```
// Configure Hudi options for the writer
Map<String, String> hudiOptions = new HashMap<>();

// Table configuration
hudiOptions.put("hoodie.table.name", "financial_transactions");
hudiOptions.put("hoodie.datasource.write.recordkey.field", "txn_id");
hudiOptions.put("hoodie.datasource.write.partitionpath.field", "txn_date");
hudiOptions.put("hoodie.datasource.write.precombine.field", "txn_ts");
hudiOptions.put("hoodie.datasource.write.operation", "upsert");
```

To activate the callback, set the `callback.on` flag to `true` and specify the Pulsar callback implementation class:

```
// Enable Pulsar callback
hudiOptions.put("hoodie.write.commit.callback.on", "true");
hudiOptions.put("hoodie.write.commit.callback.class.name",
  "org.apache.hudi.callback.impl.HoodieWriteCommitPulsarCallback");
```

Now configure the Pulsar broker URL, topic, and other producer settings. These options control how the callback publishes commit messages to Pulsar:

```
// Pulsar specific configuration
hudiOptions.put("hoodie.write.commit.callback.pulsar.broker.service.url",
  "pulsar://pulsar-broker:6650");
hudiOptions.put("hoodie.write.commit.callback.pulsar.topic",
  "persistent://finance/transactions/hudi-commits");
hudiOptions.put("hoodie.write.commit.callback.pulsar.producer.route-mode",
  "RoundRobinPartition");
hudiOptions.put(
    "hoodie.write.commit.callback.pulsar.producer.pending-queue-size", "2000");
hudiOptions.put("hoodie.write.commit.callback.pulsar.operation-timeout", "45s");
hudiOptions.put("hoodie.write.commit.callback.pulsar.connection-timeout", "15s");
```

Finally, run the write operation with all options applied. The Pulsar callback will automatically publish a message to the specified topic when the commit completes:

```
// Apply configuration to your Hudi write
dataFrame.write()
  .format("org.apache.hudi")
  .options(hudiOptions)
  .mode(SaveMode.Append)
  .save("/path/to/hudi/financial_transactions");
```

> While HTTP, Kafka, and Pulsar are supported out of the box, you can extend the org.apache.hudi.callback.HoodieWriteCommit Callback interface to create your own implementation, offering unlimited flexibility in how commit events are processed and distributed.

Wiring Up Monitoring Systems

Running a data pipeline without monitoring metrics is like driving at night without headlights; you might get where you're going, but you'll miss warning signs along the way. Monitoring provides real-time visibility into table health, performance bottlenecks, and anomalies before they escalate into failures. For Hudi deployments, proper monitoring becomes the difference between proactive management and reactive troubleshooting. When write commits slow down, storage grows unexpectedly, or query performance degrades, metrics are the early warning system, helping teams diagnose and resolve issues before users are affected. By integrating Hudi with systems like Prometheus, AWS CloudWatch, or Datadog, you gain clear insight into the state of your data lakehouse, making operations and server status transparent and observable so that data pipelines can be continuously optimized and reliably maintained (Figure 9-7).

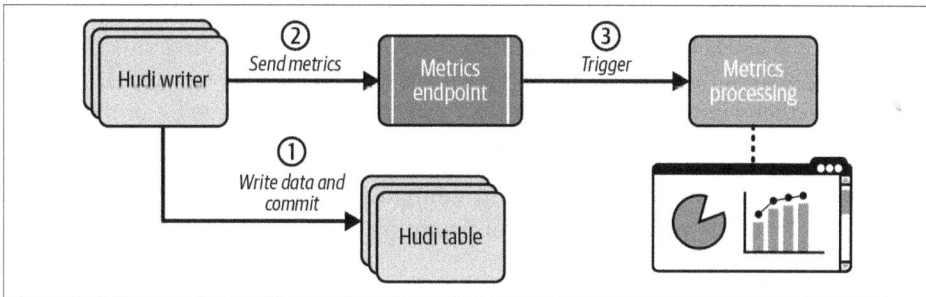

Figure 9-7. Hudi writer sending metrics to the monitoring dashboard

Enabling metrics in Hudi

Hudi provides a flexible metrics framework that can integrate with various monitoring backends. To enable metrics collection in Hudi, you need to set the following basic configuration:

```
hoodie.metrics.on=true
hoodie.metrics.reporter.type=<REPORTER_TYPE>
```

where `<REPORTER_TYPE>` can be one of the supported reporters: JMX, GRAPHITE, DATA DOG, PROMETHEUS_PUSHGATEWAY, CLOUDWATCH, or a custom implementation.

Available metrics

Hudi exposes comprehensive metrics that provide insights into various operations:

Commit performance
    Duration of commits, rollbacks, and other timeline operations

Data management
    Statistics on files created, updated, or deleted

Record processing
    Counts of records inserted, updated, or deleted

Resource utilization
    Time taken for scanning, merging, and other operations

These metrics can help you track the health and performance of your Hudi tables and identify potential issues before they become critical problems.

Integration examples

Let's review some examples for integrating with monitoring systems.

Prometheus and Grafana.   Prometheus (*https://prometheus.io*) is a popular open source monitoring system that collects and stores metrics from various services. Hudi supports Prometheus integration through the Pushgateway, which acts as an intermediary between Hudi jobs and the Prometheus server.

To enable this integration, you'll start by configuring Hudi to push metrics to the Prometheus Pushgateway. In your job configuration, set the following options:

```
hoodie.metrics.on=true
hoodie.metrics.reporter.type=PROMETHEUS_PUSHGATEWAY
hoodie.metrics.pushgateway.host=prometheus-pushgateway
hoodie.metrics.pushgateway.port=9091
# Optional: Configure job name
hoodie.metrics.pushgateway.job.name=hudi-metrics
# Optional: Keep metrics after job completion
hoodie.metrics.pushgateway.delete.on.shutdown=false
```

Next, update your Prometheus configuration to scrape metrics from the Pushgateway. In your *prometheus.yml*, add a scrape job similar to this:

```
scrape_configs:
  - job_name: 'pushgateway'
    honor_labels: true
    static_configs:
      - targets: ['prometheus-pushgateway:9091']
```

Once Prometheus is collecting metrics, you can visualize them using Grafana, a popular open source companion to Prometheus. Grafana lets you build real-time dashboards to track metrics such as commit duration trends, record processing rates, and file I/O activity.

Although we won't cover dashboard creation in detail here, Grafana's documentation (*https://oreil.ly/gIm3x*) provides guidance on connecting to Prometheus and setting up your first dashboard.

Datadog. Datadog is a popular cloud-based monitoring and analytics platform that helps teams track infrastructure, application performance, and logs in one place. Hudi offers native integration with Datadog, allowing you to send operational metrics directly to your Datadog account for visualization and alerting.

To enable Datadog integration, add the following configuration to your Hudi job:

```
hoodie.metrics.on=true
hoodie.metrics.reporter.type=DATADOG
# api.site can be either US or EU based on your Datadog instance
hoodie.metrics.datadog.api.site=US
hoodie.metrics.datadog.api.key=<YOUR_DATADOG_API_KEY>
hoodie.metrics.datadog.metric.prefix=hudi
```

Once configured, metrics will appear in your Datadog account, where you can create dashboards, set up alerts, and integrate Hudi insights with the rest of your infrastructure monitoring. For details on dashboard creation, refer to Datadog's documentation (*https://docs.datadoghq.com*).

AWS CloudWatch. AWS CloudWatch is Amazon's native monitoring and observability service, offering real-time insights into resource utilization, application performance, and operational health. Hudi supports CloudWatch integration out of the box, making it easy to monitor Hudi jobs alongside your other AWS services.

To enable CloudWatch integration, use the following configuration:

```
hoodie.metrics.on=true
hoodie.metrics.reporter.type=CLOUDWATCH
# Optional: Configure AWS credentials if not using instance profiles
hoodie.aws.access.key=<YOUR_ACCESS_KEY>
hoodie.aws.secret.key=<YOUR_SECRET_KEY>
```

Building custom metrics dashboards

When building dashboards for Hudi monitoring, consider including these key metrics:

- Write performance
  - *<table_name>*.`commit.duration`: Time taken for commits
  - *<table_name>*.`totalRecordsWritten`: Number of records processed
  - *<table_name>*.`totalFilesInsert` and *<table_name>*.`totalFilesUpdate`: File operations
- Data freshness
  - *<table_name>*.`commitFreshnessInMs`: Latency between data event time and commit time
  - *<table_name>*.`commitLatencyInMs`: End-to-end processing latency
- Storage efficiency
  - *<table_name>*.`totalBytesWritten`: Data volume written
  - File counts by partition
  - Compaction metrics

Best practices for monitoring

To fully make use of the monitoring system, consider the following best practices:

- Set meaningful thresholds for alerts based on your workload patterns.
- Monitor trends over time rather than absolute values.
- Correlate Hudi metrics with infrastructure metrics (CPU, memory, disk I/O).
- Create dedicated dashboards for different personas (operators, developers, data engineers).
- Include business context by relating technical metrics to data SLAs.

> For metrics monitoring, please consult the documentation page (*https://oreil.ly/FcjnQ*) outlining Hudi's supported metrics systems. If your preferred metrics system isn't listed among the supported options, you can create a custom metrics integration by extending the `org.apache.hudi.metrics.custom.CustomizableMetrics Reporter` class.

By properly integrating Hudi with your monitoring systems, you gain visibility into the health and performance of your data lakehouse, enabling proactive management and optimization of your data pipelines.

Syncing with Catalogs

In the world of data management, a lakehouse without a catalog is like a library without an index—vast and valuable, but difficult to navigate efficiently. Data catalogs bridge the gap between raw data storage and usability, providing the metadata layer that allows users to discover, understand, and query data assets without needing to know their physical location or structure. While traditional data warehouses include this by default, data lakehouses require explicit integration with catalog services. Hudi's ability to sync table metadata with popular catalogs such as Apache Hive Metastore, AWS Glue, and Google BigQuery ensures that tables remain visible and accessible across the analytics ecosystem. This synchronization enables seamless querying through familiar SQL engines like Presto, Trino, Spark SQL, and Athena, combining the governance and structure of a data warehouse with the flexibility and cost-efficiency of a data lakehouse. By automating metadata management, organizations maintain a single source of truth, empowering users to access and analyze data independently, without relying on engineering teams.

Catalog synchronization

Catalog synchronization is the process by which Hudi keeps external metadata repositories (data catalogs) updated with the latest information about tables stored in the data lakehouse. This synchronization creates a bridge between physical data storage and the metadata required for discovery and querying.

A data catalog entry for a Hudi table typically contains:

- Table schema information (column names, data types)
- Partition structure information and list of available partitions
- Table properties and statistics
- Table location information
- Table format and version metadata

Catalog synchronization in Hudi is implemented as a separate process to be executed after successful write commits happen (Figure 9-8). Here's how the process works:

1. A write operation (insert, upsert, delete, etc.) is performed on a Hudi table.
2. After the operation successfully commits, Hudi examines the commit metadata.
3. If sync is enabled, Hudi triggers the configured sync tool(s).

4. The sync tool extracts the latest metadata from the Hudi table, including:

   • Current schema

   • Partition information

   • Table properties

5. The sync tool connects to the target data catalog and updates the corresponding table entry.

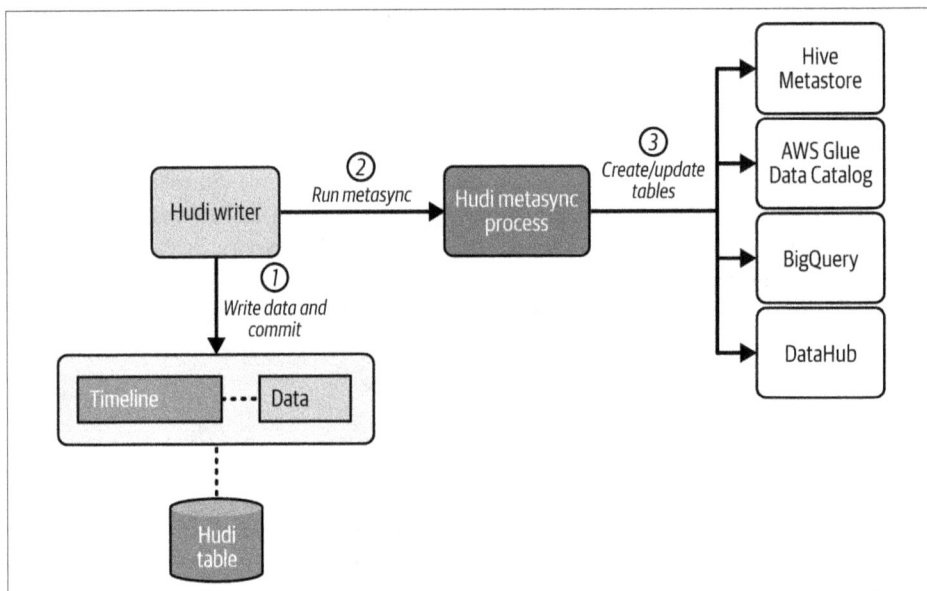

Figure 9-8. Hudi writer running metasync process with catalogs

This process ensures that the metadata in the catalog remains consistent with the actual data in the Hudi table.

Metadata versioning

Each time a commit occurs with meaningful metadata changes, a new version of the table entry may be created in the catalog, depending on how the catalog handles updates. These changes can include:

   • Schema evolution (added, removed, or modified columns)

   • Newly added or deleted partitions

   • Changes to table properties or statistics

Some catalogs, like AWS Glue, maintain versioned table entries. To avoid creating excessive versions, Hudi provides conditional sync options that only trigger synchronization when there are actual metadata changes (schema or partition changes), rather than after every commit.

For efficiency, especially with catalogs that track versions (like AWS Glue), Hudi provides a conditional sync feature. When enabled with:

```
hoodie.datasource.meta_sync.condition.sync=true
```

Hudi will only sync to the catalog when there are actual metadata changes, such as:

- Schema evolution (new or modified columns)
- New partitions added
- Partitions deleted
- Other significant metadata changes

This prevents unnecessary catalog updates and reduces the proliferation of catalog versions.

Supported catalog integrations

Hudi supports synchronization with several popular catalog services:

Hive Metastore
The most widely used catalog for data lakehouse implementations, Hive Metastore stores metadata about tables and partitions. Hudi's integration with Hive Metastore makes tables queryable through Hive, Presto, Trino, and other SQL engines that can connect to the Hive Metastore. For detailed configuration options, refer to the Syncing with Hive Metastore documentation (*https://oreil.ly/_fwPo*).

AWS Glue Data Catalog
AWS Glue Data Catalog is AWS's managed metadata repository, compatible with the Hive Metastore interface. Hudi provides a dedicated sync tool that can directly update the Glue Data Catalog, making Hudi tables available for querying through AWS Athena, Amazon EMR, and other AWS analytics services. For AWS Glue–specific configurations, see the Syncing with AWS Glue documentation (*https://oreil.ly/0OKGB*).

Google BigQuery
Hudi tables can be synced to Google BigQuery as external tables. This integration enables you to query Hudi data using BigQuery's powerful SQL engine without moving the data from its original storage location. For BigQuery sync details, refer to the BigQuery integration documentation (*https://oreil.ly/X2fyH*).

DataHub

DataHub is an open source metadata platform for data discovery and governance. Hudi can sync table metadata to DataHub, enhancing discoverability and providing rich metadata context for Hudi tables. For DataHub sync options, see the Syncing with DataHub documentation (*https://oreil.ly/1G4jz*).

Apache XTable

Apache XTable (*https://xtable.apache.org*) provides cross-table omnidirectional interoperation between lakehouse table formats. Let's say you have a Hudi table. You can use XTable to translate its metadata to Apache Iceberg's metadata format such that the same table can be read as an Iceberg table while keeping the original Hudi table as is. This conversion can be done in all directions between the supported formats (Hudi, Iceberg, and Delta Lake). This would allow you to integrate with more catalogs, such as Snowflake Polaris, for example, after converting Hudi to Iceberg. For XTable sync options, see the XTable sync documentation (*https://oreil.ly/LeQSN*).

Example: Hive Metastore sync with HMS mode

One of the most common catalog integrations is with the Hive Metastore, which serves as a central metadata repository for many SQL engines. Hudi supports syncing to Hive in multiple modes; here, we use HMS mode (Hive Metastore Service), which connects directly to the metastore service via Thrift.

The following Spark writer example (Scala) demonstrates how to enable Hive sync when writing a Hudi table using the Spark DataSource API. In addition to standard Hudi write options, notice the Hive-specific configurations that control the sync behavior:

```
// Write to Hudi with Hive sync enabled
dataFrame.write.format("hudi")
  // Essential Hudi configs
  .option("hoodie.datasource.write.recordkey.field", "recordKey")
  .option("hoodie.datasource.write.partitionpath.field", "partitionPath")

  // Hive sync configurations
  .option("hoodie.datasource.meta.sync.enable", "true")
  .option("hoodie.datasource.hive_sync.mode", "hms")
  .option("hoodie.datasource.hive_sync.metastore.uris",
    "thrift://hive-metastore:9083")
  .option("hoodie.datasource.hive_sync.database", "my_database")
  .option("hoodie.datasource.hive_sync.table", "my_table")
  .option("hoodie.datasource.hive_sync.partition_fields", "partition_field")
  .save("/path/to/hudi/table")
```

Let's break down a few of the key options:

`hoodie.datasource.meta.sync.enable`
> This flag must be set to true to activate metadata syncing after each write.

`hoodie.datasource.hive_sync.mode`
> By specifying `hms`, you're telling Hudi to sync directly with the Hive Metastore service. This is useful when you have a metastore running independently of HiveServer2.

`hoodie.datasource.hive_sync.metastore.uris`
> This points to your Hive Metastore's Thrift URI. This allows the sync client to communicate directly with the metastore.

`hoodie.datasource.hive_sync.database` *and* `hoodie.data`
`source.hive_sync.table`
> These define where the Hudi table appears in Hive, which is essential for ensuring that your data is queryable via engines like Hive, Presto, or Trino.

`hoodie.datasource.hive_sync.partition_fields`
> This lists the partition keys so that the sync process correctly registers partitioned data in Hive.

This minimal configuration is often sufficient to get started, but additional options (e.g., handling of schema evolution or case sensitivity) may be needed depending on your production setup. For the full range of available configs and deeper examples, refer to the Hive Sync documentation (*https://oreil.ly/_fwPo*).

Using multiple catalog syncs

In many enterprise environments, the data platforms are heterogeneous. Different teams or applications rely on different catalog services to query the same datasets. For example, one team might use the Hive Metastore for on-premises analytics with Hive or Trino, while another uses AWS Glue Data Catalog to access the same data via Athena. In these cases, it's critical to keep metadata consistent across catalogs to ensure that everyone sees the same version of the table, regardless of which tool they're using.

Hudi supports synchronizing a table with multiple catalogs simultaneously by specifying multiple sync tool classes. This ensures that after each write, all connected catalog systems stay up-to-date automatically.

Here's a simple configuration example that syncs a Hudi table with both the Hive Metastore and AWS Glue Data Catalog after each commit:

```
hoodie.meta.sync.client.tool.class=\
org.apache.hudi.hive.HiveSyncTool,\
org.apache.hudi.aws.sync.AwsGlueCatalogSyncTool
```

With this setup, Hudi will first sync with Hive Metastore, and then with Glue, maintaining consistent table definitions across both systems.

Performance Tuning

Even a well-designed data lakehouse can encounter performance bottlenecks. In Hudi, performance tuning is the key to transforming a data platform from merely functional to truly high performing. By optimizing key configurations, you can significantly reduce processing times, ensure predictable SLAs, and handle larger data volumes more efficiently.

Optimal performance requires careful tuning because every production environment is unique. The ideal configuration depends on your specific use case, data characteristics (volume, velocity, update frequency), and the trade-offs between conflicting goals, such as write speed versus query latency.

This section serves as a compendium of the most impactful tuning strategies discussed throughout this book. We will recap fundamental principles and specific configurations for write, read, and table service operations, and provide cross-references to the chapters where these concepts are explained in greater detail.

Storage Layout Tuning

Before diving into specific operations, it's crucial to understand the foundational tuning options on Hudi table's storage layout that have the broadest impact on the table performance.

Table type selection

The choice between COW and MOR is the most fundamental performance decision you will make. As detailed in Chapter 2, these table types offer different trade-offs between write and read performance.

The COW table format is optimized for read performance. Updates require rewriting entire base files, which can lead to higher write amplification. This type is ideal for read-heavy workloads with infrequent updates. On the other hand, the MOR table format is optimized for write performance. Updates are appended to lightweight log files, resulting in minimal write amplification and faster writes. However, snapshot queries need to merge base files and log files on the fly, which increases query latency. This type is best for write-intensive or streaming workloads with frequent updates.

The table format can be configured by setting the following config during table creation:

```
hoodie.table.type=COPY_ON_WRITE // or MERGE_ON_READ
```

It's a best practice to choose your table type based on your primary workload pattern. In case your business requirements or workload patterns change, you can use Hudi CLI to change the table type as shown in "Changing table types" on page 200.

File sizing

Hudi performs best when data is stored in optimally sized files (typically 128 MB to 1 GB). A large number of small files—the small-file problem—can severely degrade the overall read and write performance because of the overhead in opening, closing, and reading metadata for each file.

As discussed in Chapter 3, Hudi provides a file-sizing mechanism to automatically manage file sizes during writes. Important configs include:

`hoodie.parquet.max.file.size`
Sets the upper limit for base file sizes

`hoodie.parquet.small.file.limit`
Defines a threshold below which Hudi will pad new inserts into existing small files instead of creating new ones

While these inline controls are effective, you can also leverage the Clustering table service (see Chapter 6) for more robust, asynchronous optimization of file sizes over the long term.

Partitioning

Physical partitioning is a traditional and effective way of improving table performance. By dividing a table into partitions based on column values (e.g., date, region), you enable query engines to perform partition pruning, skipping irrelevant data and drastically reducing scan times.

As introduced in Chapter 2, the key is to choose partition columns that align with the most common WHERE clause predicates in your queries. You should balance the number of partitions to avoid creating too many small, sparsely populated ones, which can lead back to the small-file problem.

When partitioning is unsuitable for some tables or doesn't match common access patterns, you can build expression indexes, as introduced in Chapter 5, for the Hudi table to flexibly optimize for a diverse range of query predicates.

Write Performance Tuning

Optimizing write performance is crucial for meeting ingestion SLAs and efficiently handling data updates. The key areas to focus on are parallelism, indexing, and bulk insert optimizations.

Tuning parallelism

Parallelism is a major lever for balancing throughput, resource use, and output file sizes. Too little parallelism can bottleneck your job; too much can overwhelm your cluster or produce too many small files. In Spark, Hudi write operations include shuffle stages, so tuning shuffle parallelism is critical. Important configs include:

- `hoodie.insert.shuffle.parallelism`
- `hoodie.upsert.shuffle.parallelism`
- `hoodie.bulkinsert.shuffle.parallelism`

A good starting point is to set parallelism based on data size; for example, around `input_data_size / 500MB`. Understanding how your Spark tasks, executor cores, and parallelism settings interact is key to efficient execution.

For Flink, parallelism tuning involves adjusting task slots (`taskmanager.numberOf TaskSlots`) and setting parallelism for different stages of the Hudi pipeline, such as:

- `write.tasks` (main write)
- `compaction.tasks` (background compaction)
- `read.tasks` (index bootstrapping, if used)

Getting parallelism right means faster jobs, better resource usage, and well-sized output files.

Tuning indexes

Choosing a suitable Hudi writer index type is critical for update and delete operations. A writer index maps incoming record keys to their physical file location, avoiding costly full table scans. As detailed in Chapter 5, Hudi offers several writer index types, each with different characteristics:

Record
> General purpose, high-performance indexing that works well for tables at all sizes and all workload patterns

Bucket
> Fastest option for update-heavy write workloads, suitable for tables of all sizes

Simple
> Applicable for random update/delete patterns, not suitable for large-scale tables

Bloom
> Suitable for skewed update/delete patterns, not suitable for random update/delete patterns

Bulk insert optimizations

For initial data loading or append-only pipelines, the `bulk_insert` operation offers the best performance. As explained in Chapter 3, it bypasses the indexing and auto file sizing steps, writing data at speeds close to that of plain Apache Parquet.

Bulk insert and sort mode can be configured as follows:

```
hoodie.datasource.write.operation=bulk_insert
hoodie.bulkinsert.sort.mode=PARTITION_PATH_REPARTITION
```

To further boost performance, use a lightweight compression codec (e.g., Snappy): `hoodie.parquet.compression.codec=snappy`.

Read Performance Tuning

Minimizing query latency is the primary goal for read-heavy workloads. Hudi provides powerful features to accelerate queries.

Data skipping with the metadata table

One of the most effective ways to speed up queries is data skipping. As explained in Chapter 5, Hudi's metadata table can store column-level statistics (min/max values, null counts) aggregated at file and partition level (column stats and partition stats indexes). When a query with relevant predicates is executed, Hudi uses these statistics to skip reading partitions and files that could not possibly contain matching data.

Important configs on the read side include:

- `hoodie.enable.data.skipping=true`
- `hoodie.metadata.enable=true`

By default, since Hudi 1.0, metadata table is enabled and the column stats and partition stats indexes are also enabled. This can lead to order-of-magnitude performance improvements for selective queries on large tables.

Query types for MOR tables

For MOR tables, you can choose between two query types to balance data freshness and performance, as discussed in Chapter 4:

Snapshot query (default)
    Provides the most up-to-date view of the data by merging base files and log files on the fly. This ensures data freshness but incurs read-time overhead.

Read-optimized query

> Provides maximum query speed by reading only the columnar base files and ignoring the log files, hence no merging on the fly. The returned records may be stale, but the query can achieve faster performance.

Query type can be set using the following config:

```
hoodie.datasource.query.type=snapshot // or read_optimized
```

> The read optimized query type is not applicable to COW tables because COW tables don't have log files to merge with base files; the snapshot queries on a COW table is already optimized.

Table Services Tuning

As detailed in Chapter 6, Hudi supports running *table services* to maintain the long-term health and performance of your tables.

Compaction

Compaction is a critical service for MOR tables. It merges row-based log files with columnar base files, preventing read performance from degrading over time. It is a best practice to run compaction asynchronously, as this separates the resource-intensive compaction work from your primary ingestion pipeline, reducing write latency. You should also tune the trigger strategy (e.g., `hoodie.compaction.trigger.strategy=NUM_COMMITS`) and planning strategy (`hoodie.compaction.strategy`) to match your workload.

Clustering

Clustering rewrites data to optimize the physical layout, typically by sorting records based on frequently filtered columns and consolidating small files. Like compaction, it is best to run clustering asynchronously to avoid impacting write performance. You should also use a planning strategy (`hoodie.clustering.plan.strategy.class`) to target specific file groups for optimization, such as those with many small files.

Cleaning

The cleaning service reclaims storage space by removing old, unused file versions created by updates and table services. You should configure a cleaner policy (`hoodie.cleaner.policy`) that aligns with your organization's data retention and time travel requirements. The `KEEP_LATEST_COMMITS` policy is a common choice, ensuring that long-running queries do not fail while old file versions are being cleaned.

Summary

In this chapter, we explored the core components needed to run Hudi in production. We looked at how the CLI simplifies administrative tasks, how savepoint and restore safeguard your data, and how integration tools like post-commit callbacks and catalog synchronization help Hudi fit smoothly into your broader data platform. We also recapped performance tuning tips from previous chapters to help you get the most out of your setup.

These foundational practices are essential for any production Hudi deployment. But in real-world scenarios, success often comes from combining these building blocks into tailored solutions that meet specific business needs. In Chapter 10, we'll take things a step further with end-to-end examples that show Hudi in action across different industries. You'll see how organizations have solved unique data challenges by weaving Hudi into their data architectures, and you'll get some practical blueprints you can adapt to your own production environment.

Building an End-to-End Lakehouse Solution

Having established the operational foundations to run a production lakehouse, the stage is set for us to build a comprehensive, integrated solution atop Hudi. This chapter will demonstrate how to construct an end-to-end production data lakehouse architecture with Apache Hudi as its foundation. Rather than examining isolated components, we'll follow a single dataset through its entire lifecycle, from initial ingestion to analytical insights and AI-driven applications.

Modern data architectures require seamless data integration from upstream sources, unified support for both streaming and batch processing, reliable handling of diverse data types, and the ability to serve multiple downstream consumers with varying requirements. The magic isn't about having perfect data, but about nimbly stitching together key features to deliver novel insights despite real-world problems like data silos and operational challenges. You have to "make data easy" for your organization and empower your teams to build on top of it.

This chapter will explain how to tackle these challenges in style by combining multiple processing frameworks on top of a unified data lakehouse. Hudi's versatility supports this level of integration while making it easy to do things "the right way," with respect to data consistency, performance, and governance.

In this chapter, we'll construct a complete data platform that progressively transforms raw data into business value. You'll learn how to do the following:

- Process streaming changes with Apache Flink and Hudi Streamer, handling complex update patterns while maintaining transactional guarantees.

- Ingest high-volume log data through the Hudi Kafka Connect sink, efficiently capturing append-only event streams.

- Transform and extract business insights with SQL capabilities, from incremental processing to interactive analytics.

- Leverage data for AI applications, creating contextual knowledge bases for large language models (LLMs) to provide business insights.

> The Hudi Streamer tool, which we discussed in Chapter 8, can also be used for the ingestion functionality across all layers in the architecture. This chapter additionally showcases Flink and Kafka Connect to illustrate the rich diversity of tools in Hudi's toolchain.

You'll see how Hudi's streaming ingestion, table storage formats, incremental processing, and query optimization enable a clean data architecture that efficiently serves multiple stakeholders while minimizing data sprawl and processing overhead.

Architecture Overview

In this chapter, we embark on a practical journey with a fictional company, RetailMax Corp., demonstrating how to build a data platform, from ingestion to applied AI for deriving business insights. By working through this scenario, we'll see how Hudi's features address the real-world problems that led you to open this book.

Figure 10-1 depicts our architecture, which is based on the Medallion architecture. By the end of this chapter, you'll have a blueprint for implementing your own end-to-end data lakehouse with Hudi. The patterns and techniques demonstrated here can be adapted to diverse use cases across industries, providing a flexible foundation for your organization's data strategy.

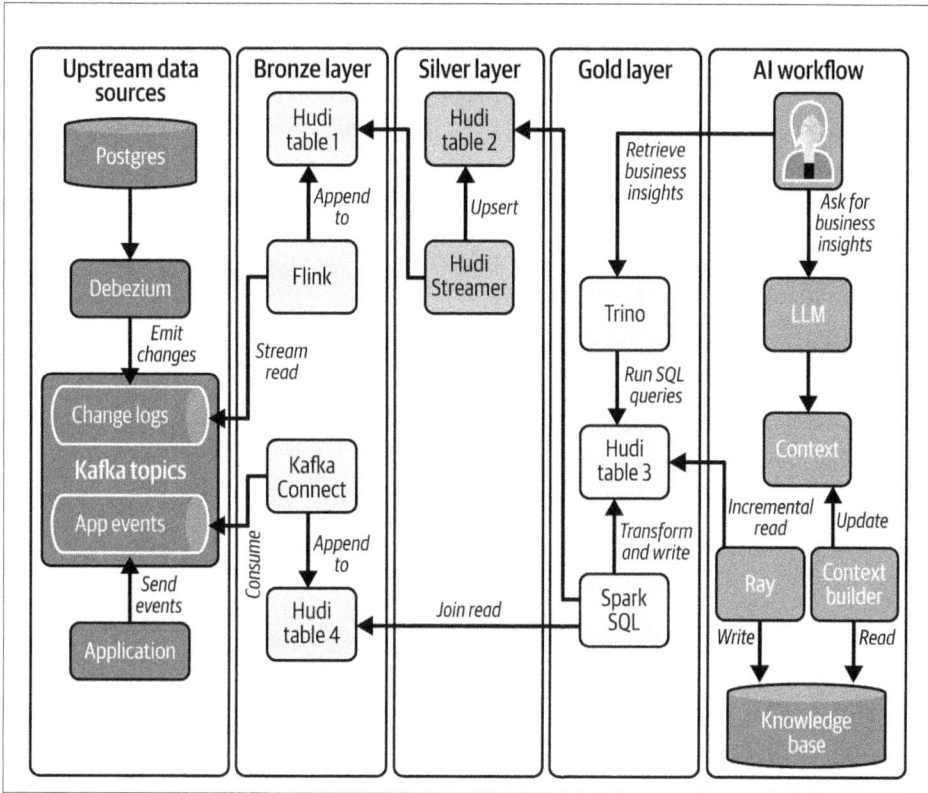

Figure 10-1. Medallion-based architecture using Hudi tools, components, and integrations

RetailMax Corp: A Real-World Lakehouse Scenario

RetailMax Corp. manages a thriving business with a significant online presence—both an ecommerce site and a mobile app. Current strategic objectives are centered on enhancing customer experience, optimizing operations, and driving revenue growth. Some of the key initiatives in progress include:

360-degree customer view
> Consolidating customer data from all touchpoints (online interactions, purchases, loyalty programs, and in-store transactions) to understand customer behavior and preferences comprehensively.

Real-time personalization
> Delivering personalized product recommendations, offers, and content to users on the RetailMax website and mobile app.

Inventory and supply chain optimization

Maintaining accurate, real-time visibility into inventory levels across all channels to prevent stockouts, reduce overstocking, and improve fulfillment efficiency.

Fraud detection

Identifying and preventing fraudulent transactions in real time.

Self-service analytics

Empowering business users (marketing, sales, operations) with the ability to perform ad hoc analysis and generate reports without heavy reliance on IT.

RetailMax has a ton of data and it's all over the place.

Similar to the airline company we met in Chapter 8, RetailMax has a data silo problem. It has several important relational tables that are stored in its "good 'ol" PostgreSQL database. These include:

`customer_master`

Contains customer profiles, demographic information, and contact details.

`product_catalog`

Stores detailed information about products, including SKUs, descriptions, categories, and pricing.

`sales_transactions`

Records historical sales data from both online orders and in-store point-of-sale (POS) systems.

The company also has two Kafka topics that each represent updates to objects that change frequently and in near real time:

`web_clickstreams`

A high-volume, append-only stream of real-time user interactions from the ecommerce website and mobile application. This includes page views, product detail views, clicks on recommendations, add-to-cart events, and search queries.

`inventory_updates`

Real-time events indicating changes in stock levels originating from warehouse and in-store POS systems. These are crucial for timely inventory management and can involve frequent updates to specific product SKUs.

Table 10-1 provides a summary of RetailMax's data sources and its planned ingestion into the Hudi-based lakehouse.

Table 10-1. RetailMax data sources and characteristics

Data source name	System of record	Data type/ data model	Ingestion method	Target Hudi table	Velocity/ volume
customer_mas ter	PostgreSQL	Structured/ mutable	Change data capture (CDC) via Debezium/Flink	hudi_customer_mas ter_bronze	Medium/ moderate
product_cata log	PostgreSQL	Structured/ mutable	CDC via Debezium/Flink	hudi_product_cata log_bronze	Low/ moderate
sales_transac tions	PostgreSQL	Structured/ mutable	CDC via Debezium/Flink	hudi_sales_transac tions_bronze	Medium/ high
web_click streams	Apache Kafka	Semi- structured/ append-only	Kafka Connect	hudi_web_click streams_bronze	Very high/ very high
inven tory_updates	Kafka	Semi- structured/ mutable	Kafka Connect or Flink	hudi_inven tory_updates_bronze	High/high

Implementing Medallion Architecture with Hudi

The Medallion architecture is a popular data design pattern for organizing data in a lakehouse. Data is organized into layers, often referred to as *Bronze*, *Silver*, and *Gold*, to provide structured and progressive refinement. The Bronze layer stores raw, immutable data from source systems for auditing and reprocessing. The Silver layer then cleanses, standardizes, and transforms this data, aiming for a unified and consistent view with schema enforcement and basic quality checks. Finally, the Gold layer contains highly refined, aggregated, and denormalized data optimized for business intelligence, analytics, and machine learning applications. This layered approach promotes data governance, reusability, and scalability, addressing the common issue of data lakes devolving into "data swamps."

Configuring RetailMax's Hudi Tables

RetailMax will make critical business decisions based on this lakehouse, so the lakehouse must be highly reliable, which is not an easy goal to achieve. Event streams and relational databases are two very different kinds of systems that introduce all kinds of complexity around scale and consistency. To make sure we start off on the right foot, we need to make some configuration decisions to ensure that we can make those kinds of guarantees and feel good about making them.

Record Keys

Every Hudi table needs a reliable way to identify records uniquely. This is what powers its efficient update and delete capabilities. Think of the record key (introduced in Chapter 2) as the table's anchor in all future updates.

Finding the anchor is sometimes straightforward; for instance, in RetailMax's Bronze customer table (hudi_customer_master_bronze), the record key is simply customer_id. Sometimes it requires more work; for the Bronze sales table (hudi_sales_transactions_bronze), we could combine order_id and line_item_id to form a composite record key, which will give us the granularity to track every transaction. For the Bronze clickstream table (hudi_web_click streams_bronze), we could use a generated event_id or create a composite of session_id and event_timestamp, depending on how event tracking is implemented upstream. If the use case does not inherently provide a suitable unique record key, users can leave the record key unconfigured and Hudi can assign an auto-generated key for each record that is highly compressible.

Ordering Field

Sometimes multiple versions of the same record show up, especially in streaming systems with out-of-order delivery. That's where the ordering field (introduced in Chapter 3) comes in. It decides which version "wins."

An updated_at timestamp is a common choice. It's straightforward and makes it easy to reason about deduplication and data freshness. It helps guard against challenges like stale change records from a different region/zone making the table state go backward in time or become incorrect.

Partitioning

Partitioning (introduced in Chapter 2) helps downstream query engines skip irrelevant data and also makes data easier to manage at scale. But it's a balancing act; you want to improve performance without creating too many small files by accidentally over-partitioning the table. As a general rule of thumb, you should only employ partitioning for tables that are larger than 250 GB or so.

Choosing the right partitioning strategy involves balancing query patterns, data distribution, and partition management overhead, but we can start by partitioning the Bronze sales table (hudi_sales_transactions_bronze) by order_date (e.g., year/month/day) and partitioning the Bronze clickstream table (hudi_web_click streams_bronze) by event_date. This strategy is a good starting point because it aligns with typical time-series queries (e.g., analyzing sales by day or web activity over a period) and helps manage data growth by segmenting it into manageable chronological units.

Table Types

Finally, there's the question of table type. As we discussed in Chapter 2, choosing the right table type will have a major impact on RetailMax's lakehouse performance. Because we'll be creating several Hudi tables, we should carefully think through which table type makes sense for each.

Merge-on-Read (MOR) is great for high-frequency update scenarios. Writes are fast, updates are cheap, and compaction can be executed asynchronously. This will be helpful for streaming-heavy Bronze tables like hudi_web_clickstreams_bronze and hudi_inventory_updates_bronze.

Copy-on-Write (COW) is better for read-heavy use cases. Writes can be more expensive, but reads are fast and convenient. COW is perfect for Gold tables like hudi_daily_sales_gold where data is already clean and doesn't change often, or for Silver tables with infrequent updates.

Table 10-2 outlines the proposed Hudi table designs for RetailMax's lakehouse, connecting the conceptual Medallion architecture layers to concrete Hudi configurations. This blueprint provides a practical reference for understanding how Hudi is applied across the different stages of data refinement.

Table 10-2. RetailMax's lakehouse blueprint

Hudi table name	Source	Record key(s)	Ordering field	Partitioning strategy
hudi_customer_mas ter_bronze	customer_master (Postgres)	customer_id	updated_ts	country
hudi_sales_transac tions_bronze	sales_transactions (Postgres)	order_id, line_item_id	transaction_ts	dt (YYYY-MM-DD)
hudi_web_click streams_bronze	web_clickstreams (Kafka)	event_id	event_ts	dt (YYYY-MM-DD)
hudi_inven tory_updates_bronze	inventory_updates (Kafka)	sku, loca tion_id	update_ts	dt (YYYY-MM-DD)
hudi_unified_cus tomer_orders_silver	hudi_sales_transac tions_bronze, hudi_customer_mas ter_bronze	order_id, line_item_id	last_updated_ts	order_dt
hudi_session ized_clickstreams_sil ver	hudi_web_click streams_bronze	session_id	session_end_ts	ses sion_dt

Hudi table name	Source	Record key(s)	Ordering field	Partitioning strategy
hudi_prod uct_daily_inven tory_silver	hudi_inven tory_updates_bronze, hudi_product_cata log_bronze	sku, date	last_checked_ts	date
hudi_daily_sales_gold	hudi_unified_cus tomer_orders_silver	date, prod uct_cate gory, region	aggregation_ts	year, month
hudi_customer_seg ments_gold	hudi_unified_cus tomer_orders_silver, hudi_customer_mas ter_bronze	customer_id	segmentation_ts	seg ment_name

Bronze Layer: Ingesting Upstream Data

The Bronze layer will serve as the initial ingestion point for all raw data into RetailMax's Hudi-based lakehouse. The primary objective here is to capture data from diverse upstream sources with high fidelity, preserving the original structure as much as possible, but also making it easier to do efficient incremental processing downstream in the Silver and Gold layers. The primary goals are to capture data accurately from source systems, maintain historical archives, and enable reprocessing if needed.

In the Bronze layer, Hudi acts as an efficient landing zone for raw data. You have the option to leverage schema-on-read flexibility, or to ask Hudi to enforce schemas upon write (Hudi supports schema evolution, which helps strike a good balance). For streaming sources like Kafka events or CDC streams, we recommend the MOR table type due to its lower write amplification and latency, with record index and async compaction ensuring smooth operations for even the toughest workload patterns. Conversely, for batch sources with infrequent updates, COW may be a simpler, more cost-effective choice. Additionally, Hudi can be configured to store enough version history for the table, to aid with rollback process in case of bad data errors like an upstream write producing bad record values.

Setting Up Upstream Data Sources

RetailMax's data ecosystem comprises both transactions that happen inside a PostgreSQL database and events that live in Kafka topics. Key relational tables that change frequently and drive business functions (like customer_master, product_catalog, and sales_transactions) are the sources of structured operational data. Changes in these systems need to be captured and propagated to the lakehouse in near real time. Topics such as web_clickstreams and inventory_updates carry high-velocity, semi-structured event data reflecting real-time business activities.

Many companies rely on both event streams and relational databases to power mission-critical parts of the business. As you might imagine, these sources require different ingestion mechanisms to efficiently land data into the Bronze layer.

Let's start with the transactional data.

Streaming Mutable, Transactional Data with Debezium, Flink, and Hudi

The challenge is that transactional databases don't naturally emit event streams, so we have to reconstruct a timeline of these changes to bring them onto the same playing field as our Kafka topics. For RetailMax's PostgreSQL database, capturing and streaming CDC events is essential for keeping the lakehouse synchronized with operational systems.

Capturing CDC from PostgreSQL

Debezium is an open source distributed platform for CDC. For RetailMax, Debezium connectors will be configured to monitor the `sales_transactions`, `customer_mas ter`, and `product_catalog` tables in their PostgreSQL database. Debezium basically just sits next to the database and records everything that changes. It reads the database's transaction logs (write-ahead logs or WALs), captures row-level changes (inserts, updates, deletes) as they happen, and produces corresponding event streams.

These events can then be published to Kafka topics, transforming database changes into a stream of structured messages that can be consumed by downstream processing engines. This approach ensures that every modification in the source database is captured, enabling the lakehouse to maintain a consistent and up-to-date view of the operational data.

Processing CDC events with Flink

Flink, a powerful stream processing framework, is well suited for consuming and processing the CDC event streams generated by Debezium. Flink offers low-latency processing, stateful computations, and robust connectors. RetailMax will use Flink jobs to do the following:

1. Consume CDC events from the Kafka topics populated by Debezium.
2. Perform light transformations or cleansing if necessary. This might include mapping Debezium's event structure to the desired schema for Hudi, handling different message formats (e.g., before/after images for updates), or basic data type conversions.
3. Write the processed data into Bronze Hudi tables.

The Flink Hudi sink provides options to define record keys, specify write operations, and manage how records are merged, which are critical for CDC workloads. Example integrations often show Flink processing Debezium data and sinking it to Hudi.

Writing to Bronze Hudi tables

The processed CDC events will be written into Hudi tables in the Bronze layer, such as `hudi_sales_transactions_bronze` and `hudi_customer_master_bronze`.

We recommend using MOR for streaming CDC ingestion. MOR tables handle frequent small updates efficiently by writing changes to log files, deferring the merge with base files to an asynchronous compaction process. This results in lower write amplification and latency compared to COW tables.

Figure 10-2 shows the CDC pipeline to configure a Flink sink for writing to a Hudi table. You will need to specify a few key settings. The Hudi table type is typically set to `MERGE_ON_READ`, enabling efficient streaming writes with asynchronous compaction. The table base path indicates the target location of the Hudi table, like a URL of an Amazon S3 path. Set the record key(s), such as `order_id` for a sales dataset, so that Hudi can identify individual records. To determine record merging order, set the ordering field to a timestamp field like `update_timestamp`, allowing Hudi to determine which record version is the most recent. Partitioning is handled by setting the partition fields, often based on the transaction or event date to support efficient querying. Finally, the Hudi write operation (discussed in Chapter 3) is typically set to `upsert`, ensuring that new data either inserts or updates records appropriately based on the primary key.

A critical aspect of reliable data ingestion is ensuring exactly-once processing semantics. Flink achieves this through its robust checkpointing mechanism, which periodically snapshots the state of the application and the position in input streams. When combined with Hudi's transactional commit protocol, where each batch of writes is committed atomically to the Hudi timeline, end-to-end exactly-once semantics can be achieved. This guarantees that each CDC event affects the Hudi table exactly once, even in the presence of failures.

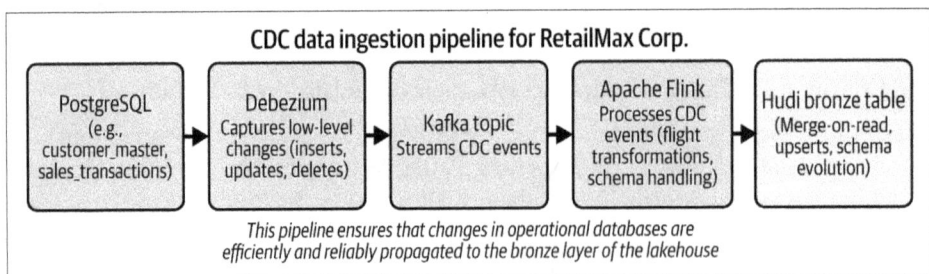

Figure 10-2. Flink-based CDC ingestion pipeline

Handling schema evolution

Source database schemas rarely stay the same because business needs evolve, new columns get added, and data types shift. A reliable CDC pipeline needs to handle these changes without breaking the flow of data. Flink CDC connectors, including those built on Debezium, are built for this: they detect schema changes upstream and propagate them downstream.

Hudi recommends backward-compatible schema evolution. By setting the table schema in the processing engine (like Spark or Flink) and enabling schema evolution on write (discussed in Chapter 3), Hudi can automatically accommodate new fields from incoming data, preventing pipeline failures. This kind of adaptability is essential for keeping ingestion pipelines resilient and ensuring that they continue to work as source systems grow and change, without introducing brittleness or manual rework.

Ingesting Application Event Streams with Hudi Kafka Connect Sink

In the preceding section, we hooked up the transactional tables. Now it's time to connect Hudi to RetailMax's high-volume, real-time data.

For these application event streams, like `web_clickstreams` and `inventory_updates`, originating from Kafka, the Hudi Sink Connector for Kafka Connect provides an efficient and scalable ingestion path. These Kafka topics carry events that are often append-only (like clickstream events) or may involve updates based on a specific key (e.g., an inventory update for a product SKU). The Hudi Kafka Connect sink is designed to stream these records from Kafka into Hudi tables.

Using the Hudi Sink Connector for Kafka Connect

The Hudi Sink Connector for Kafka Connect offers a straightforward way to ingest data from Kafka topics directly into Hudi tables, without a separate processing engine like Spark or Flink, when you just want simple pass-through ingestion. This architecture is shown in Figure 10-3.

To get this connector working, we'll need to configure a few key settings. Start by specifying `connector.class='org.apache.hudi.connect.HudiSinkConnector'` and set `tasks.max` to define how many parallel tasks Kafka Connect should use. Use `topics` or `topics.regex` to identify the source Kafka topics you're pulling from. Then, set `target.base.path` to point to your destination storage location, and `target.table.name` to name the target Hudi table (for RetailMax, this can be `hudi_web_clickstreams_bronze`, for example).

Most streaming workloads benefit from using MOR as the table type. You'll also need to define the record key field(s), choose a field like `event_timestamp` for record ordering and merging logic, and set up your partitioning strategy.

A couple of Kafka-specific settings are worth noting too. The `hoodie.kafka.con` `trol.topic` helps coordinate transactions across tasks, and `hoodie.kafka.com` `mit.interval.secs` controls how frequently the connector commits data to the Hudi table (60 seconds by default).

With these settings in place, the connector can write cleanly into your Bronze Hudi tables, such as `hudi_web_clickstreams_bronze` and `hudi_inven` `tory_updates_bronze`, without adding unnecessary pipeline complexity.

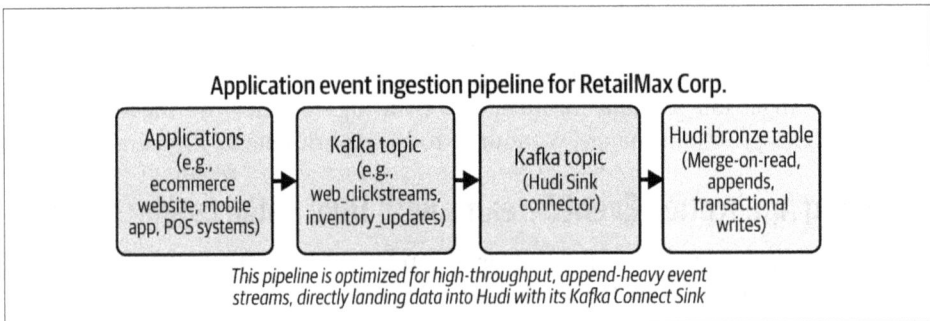

Figure 10-3. Kafka Connect–based ingestion pipeline architecture

Transaction coordination and performance

A significant feature of the Hudi Kafka Connect sink is its distributed transaction coordination mechanism. The task owning partition 0 of the source topic acts as a coordinator. It uses the `hoodie.kafka.control.topic` to manage a two-phase commit protocol across all worker tasks. This design achieves high throughput and low latency while limiting the number of write actions (commits) on the Hudi timeline to just one per commit interval. This is crucial for scaling table metadata, especially with high-volume writes, compared to approaches where each worker commits independently, potentially leading to a very large number of small commits on the timeline.

By default, the sink uses the MOR table type. This means incoming Kafka records are typically appended directly to Hudi log files, which is a low-latency operation. An asynchronous compaction/clustering table service can then merge these log files into columnar base files. This approach reduces memory pressure often associated with writing columnar files directly in a streaming fashion.

For performance tuning, standard Kafka Connect worker configurations and Kafka producer override configurations (e.g., `batch.size`, `linger.ms`, `compression.type`) can be adjusted to optimize throughput. While these are general Kafka Connect settings, they influence how data is delivered to the Hudi sink, thereby impacting overall ingestion performance.

Silver Layer: Creating Derived Datasets

The Silver layer serves as the primary source for business intelligence, reporting, and ad hoc analytics, providing users with clean, conformed, and enriched data.

Data from the Bronze layer is transformed, cleansed, validated, and conformed in the Silver layer. This process, shown in Figure 10-4, involves operations like filtering out bad records, handling nulls, standardizing data types and formats, resolving data discrepancies, and joining datasets from different sources to create an integrated view. Silver tables are often modeled to resemble enterprise data warehouse dimensions and facts and are suitable for business intelligence reporting and ad hoc analytics.

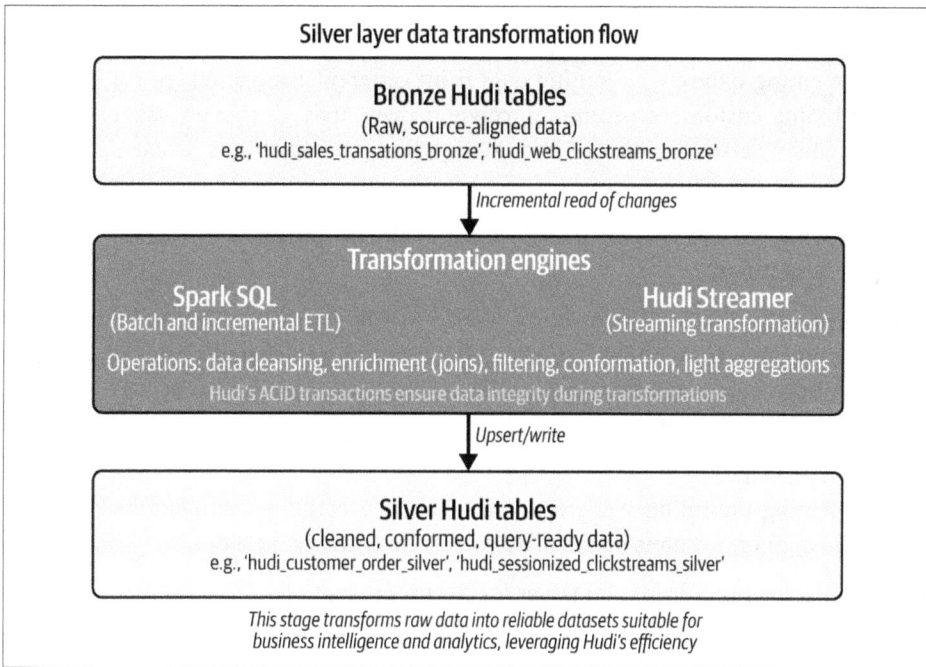

Silver layer data transformation flow

Bronze Hudi tables
(Raw, source-aligned data)
e.g., 'hudi_sales_transations_bronze', 'hudi_web_clickstreams_bronze'

Incremental read of changes

Transformation engines

Spark SQL
(Batch and incremental ETL)

Hudi Streamer
(Streaming transformation)

Operations: data cleansing, enrichment (joins), filtering, conformation, light aggregations
Hudi's ACID transactions ensure data integrity during transformations

Upsert/write

Silver Hudi tables
(cleaned, conformed, query-ready data)
e.g., 'hudi_customer_order_silver', 'hudi_sessionized_clickstreams_silver'

This stage transforms raw data into reliable datasets suitable for business intelligence and analytics, leveraging Hudi's efficiency

Figure 10-4. Data transformation flow in the Silver Layer

This layer involves significant data processing, such as joins, aggregations, and data quality enforcement, making Hudi's incremental processing capabilities key to efficiently updating these tables. The choice between MOR and COW depends on the specific table's characteristics; if a Silver table is frequently updated by streaming ETL jobs and needs to support near-real-time queries, MOR might be suitable, whereas if it's updated less frequently (e.g., a daily batch ETL) and primarily serves read-heavy analytical queries, COW can offer better read performance. Hudi's ACID transactions ensure that transformations are applied atomically, maintaining data consistency while seamlessly unifying the two processing models, batch and streaming, on the same table in storage.

Goals of the Silver Layer for RetailMax

The Silver layer aims to bridge the gap between raw, often messy source data and the structured, reliable information needed for decision making. For RetailMax, key objectives for the Silver layer include:

Data cleansing
> Addressing inconsistencies, handling missing values (nulls), correcting erroneous data, and standardizing formats (e.g., date formats, categorical values).

Enrichment
> Augmenting datasets by joining data from different Bronze tables; for example, combining customers' profile information from `hudi_customer_master_bronze` with their transaction history from `hudi_sales_transactions_bronze`.

Filtering
> Removing records that are irrelevant for analytical purposes or that do not meet quality standards.

Harmonization
> Aligning data from different sources to a common schema or set of business definitions (e.g., ensuring that product categories are consistent across online and in-store sales data).

Light aggregations
> Performing preliminary aggregations, such as creating session summaries from raw `web_clickstreams` or calculating daily inventory snapshots.

Specific examples of Silver Hudi tables for RetailMax include:

`hudi_unified_customer_orders_silver`
> A table that integrates online and in-store sales data, joined with customer and product details, providing a comprehensive view of each order.

`hudi_sessionized_clickstreams_silver`
> Raw clickstream events from the Bronze layer, which are processed to identify user sessions and aggregate key metrics per session (e.g., pages viewed, session duration, conversion events).

`hudi_product_daily_inventory_silver`
> A table providing a daily snapshot of inventory levels for each product across different locations, derived from the real-time `hudi_inventory_updates_bronze`.

`hudi_customer_profiles_silver`
> An enriched view of customer data, potentially including calculated attributes like lifetime value (LTV) or purchase frequency.

Streaming-Based Transformations with Hudi Streamer

Given that its use cases require real-time or near-real-time data processing in the Bronze layer, RetailMax can choose either Hudi Streamer (which is Spark based) or Flink for Silver layer ingestion, both offering native streaming ingest support. Retail-Max decides on Hudi Streamer due to its simplicity and native streaming ingest capabilities (see Chapter 8 for setup and usage). Because Bronze tables are Hudi tables, Hudi Streamer can be configured with `HoodieIncrSource`, which queries the source table's timeline and reads only commits since the last checkpoint. This allows continuous incremental reads from MOR tables such as `hudi_web_clickstreams_bronze` and `hudi_inventory_updates_bronze`.

With Hudi Streamer, RetailMax can apply transformers for multitable joins and enrichment—for example, sessionizing clickstreams or joining inventory updates with product metadata or other dimension tables—before the output flows into Silver Hudi tables such as `hudi_sessionized_clickstreams_silver` and `hudi_prod uct_realtime_stock_silver`. Thanks to Hudi Streamer checkpointing and Hudi's transactional commits, these pipelines can guarantee consistency.

When transformation logic becomes too complex or use-case specific, RetailMax can add custom transformers to give engineers precise control over the pipeline and sophisticated business rules. These transformers can be chained as well, for multiple transformations. For instance, RetailMax could derive near-real-time customer engagement features from page views, dwell time, and cart activity, and write them into Silver Hudi tables such as `hudi_customer_engagement_silver`.

In this layer, Hudi's upsert semantics are essential. As new data flows into the Bronze layer and existing records are updated, the Hudi Streamer job processes those changes incrementally and updates the Silver tables accordingly, keeping downstream datasets fresh and accurate in real time.

Batch and Incremental Transformations with Spark SQL

Not every transformation needs to happen in real time. For batch-oriented workflows and processing data from batch sources, RetailMax decides to use Spark SQL as the preferred engine.

Spark SQL handles a range of batch ETL use cases. For example, RetailMax could run nightly jobs that enrich customer profiles by joining `hudi_customer_master_ bronze` with aggregated purchase data from `hudi_sales_transactions_bronze`, and occasionally with third-party demographic datasets that update less frequently.

Other common workloads include performing daily aggregations to generate summary tables like `hudi_daily_regional_sales_silver` or joining transactional sales records with slower-moving reference data from the product catalog.

These Spark SQL jobs typically read from Bronze Hudi tables, apply business logic, and write the results into Silver Hudi tables. For read-heavy Silver tables that are updated less frequently (e.g., once a day), RetailMax should opt for the COW table type, which offers strong read performance and simpler storage layouts.

Hudi's incremental processing capabilities add another layer of efficiency. Rather than scanning full tables or partitions on every batch run, Spark can issue incremental queries that pull only the new or updated records since the last checkpoint. This is done by using the table-valued function `hudi_table_changes` and specifying a starting commit timestamp.

For RetailMax, that means a nightly job building `hudi_daily_sales_silver` only needs to process the last 24 hours' worth of changes from `hudi_sales_transactions_bronze` (there is no need to reprocess the entire sales history!). This dramatically reduces the volume of data scanned, cuts compute costs, and shortens ETL runtime. It turns batch processing from a brute-force operation into a much more surgical, delta-based workflow.

Let's step through an illustrative example of a Spark SQL script performing an incremental ETL to populate a Silver table, `hudi_daily_sales_summary_silver`, from two Bronze predecessors.

First, we establish the start commit time for the incremental processing process. This would typically be fetched from a control table or the last successful run's end commit time (say, 20250608000000). We'll also tell Hudi to read incremental changes from our first Bronze source, `hudi_sales_transactions_bronze`, which holds transactions:

```
CREATE OR REPLACE TEMPORARY VIEW incremental_sales_view AS
SELECT
    order_id,
    customer_id,
    product_id,
    quantity,
    price,
    transaction_ts,
    dt AS order_date
FROM
    hudi_table_changes(
        'hudi_sales_transactions_bronze', 'latest_state', '20250608000000');
```

Next, we'll read in the customer data so that we can join it with the transactions:

```
CREATE OR REPLACE TEMPORARY VIEW customer_view AS
SELECT
```

```
    customer_id,
    customer_name,
    city,
FROM
    hudi_customer_master_bronze;
```

Then, we'll go ahead and do the necessary transformations and aggregations:

```
CREATE OR REPLACE TEMPORARY VIEW daily_sales_aggregated_view AS
SELECT
    s.order_date,
    c.city,
    p.category,
    SUM(s.quantity * s.price) as total_sales_amount,
    COUNT(DISTINCT s.order_id) as total_orders,
    MAX(s.transaction_ts) as last_transaction_ts_in_batch
FROM
    incremental_sales_view s
JOIN
    customer_view c ON s.customer_id = c.customer_id
JOIN
    hudi_product_catalog_bronze p
ON s.product_id = p.product_id
GROUP BY
    s.order_date,
    c.city,
    p.category;
```

And finally, we'll write the aggregated data into a Silver Hudi table:

```
INSERT INTO hudi_daily_sales_summary_silver
-- Use INSERT OVERWRITE for full partition replacement if logic dictates,
SELECT
    order_date,
    city,
    category,
    total_sales_amount,
    total_orders,
FROM
    daily_sales_aggregated_view;
```

Maintaining Data Quality and Consistency in the Silver Layer

Whether you're using Flink or Spark for transformations, maintaining a high standard of data quality and consistency in the Silver layer is critical. RetailMax can ensure this through a combination of Hudi's built-in guarantees and disciplined pipeline practices.

First, Hudi's support for ACID transactions means every transformation, whether batch or streaming, is applied atomically. If a job fails partway through, Hudi prevents partial writes from being committed, ensuring that Silver tables remain in a consistent and query-safe state.

To further protect data quality, each transformation job includes validation checks. These checks verify data types, confirm referential integrity (where applicable), and ensure that values fall within expected ranges. Any records that fail these checks can be flagged or quarantined for follow-up, keeping bad data from polluting trusted downstream assets.

Finally, Hudi handles failed writes gracefully. If a commit doesn't complete successfully, Hudi rolls it back automatically. Incomplete data is never exposed to readers and is typically cleaned up during the next successful write or by a background cleaning process. This self-healing mechanism is essential for keeping the Silver layer healthy and trustworthy over time.

By building on these capabilities, RetailMax ensures that the Silver layer remains a dependable foundation for analytics: clean, consistent, and always ready.

Gold Layer: Querying the Lakehouse for Insights

RetailMax's users—business analysts, data scientists, and reporting tools—need efficient ways to query the data curated in the Silver layer.

The Gold layer contains highly refined, aggregated, and business-centric data for exactly this purpose. Golden datasets are typically project specific or tailored for consumption by specific downstream applications, such as AI/machine learning models, advanced analytics, or executive dashboards. Gold tables often represent key business entities or metrics and are optimized for performance and ease of use by end users.

Hudi tables in the Gold layer store highly refined, aggregated data ready for consumption and are often optimized for specific read patterns of business intelligence tools or machine learning model training. COW tables are commonly used in the Gold layer, especially for datasets that are read heavy and updated less frequently, such as daily or weekly aggregations, because COW tables provide better read performance due to data being stored in columnar base files without on-the-fly log file merging. Additionally, data models in the Gold layer are usually denormalized and focused on specific business use cases.

The RetailMax Hudi lakehouse supports multiple query engines for different analytical needs (see Figure 10-5). Business analysts use Trino for interactive SQL and ad hoc analysis, while data scientists leverage Spark SQL for batch analytics and complex transformations. Automated applications access data through scheduled reports and APIs. The lakehouse supports snapshot, read-optimized, incremental, and time travel queries to serve diverse use cases across the organization.

Interactive Analytics with Trino

Trino is a high-performance, distributed SQL query engine designed for fast analytic queries against various data sources, including data lakes. For RetailMax, Trino will be the engine of choice for business analysts who need to perform ad hoc exploration of customer behavior from `hudi_customer_profiles_silver`, analyze sales trends using `hudi_daily_sales_silver`, or check current inventory levels from `hudi_product_daily_inventory_silver`. Setting this up will involve configuring a catalog properties file (e.g., *etc/catalog/hudi.properties*) on both the Trino coordinator and worker nodes.

The configuration starts with `connector.name=hudi` to activate the Hudi connector. Next, `hive.metastore.uri` must be set to point to the Hive Metastore Service, which Hudi uses to manage table schemas and partition metadata. Depending on your storage backend, you'll also need to include the appropriate file system settings (i.e., `s3.region` and `s3.endpoint` for Amazon S3–based storage).

With this setup in place, Trino can efficiently query Hudi tables across the Bronze, Silver, and Gold layers, making it easy for analysts and downstream systems to access up-to-date data without additional pipeline complexity. The Hudi-Trino connector also supports using the multimodal index to accelerate queries on the tables, providing one of the fastest choices for interactive analytics.

Once the connection is set up, Trino users can query Hudi tables using familiar SQL syntax. For COW tables, Trino runs snapshot queries directly against the latest Apache Parquet (or Apache ORC) base files, always reflecting the most recent committed data. For MOR tables, Trino can perform an efficient merge of base files and log files in a vectorized manner, still offering great query performance.

In some environments, time travel queries are also available. If both your Trino Hudi connector and your Hudi table version support it, you can query the table as it existed at a specific commit timestamp, which is useful for auditing, debugging, or reproducing historical results.

Batch Analytics and Reporting with Spark SQL

While Trino can power RetailMax's interactive querying needs, Apache Spark SQL will be the company's go-to tool for complex transformations that feed into Gold tables, support scheduled reports and dashboards, and enable data scientists to run intensive exploratory analyses and feature engineering workflows.

Spark SQL provides robust support for querying Hudi tables across both COW and MOR formats. A basic `SELECT * FROM hudi_table` runs a snapshot query, returning the most up-to-date view of the data. For MOR tables, Spark merges the base files and log files on the fly to construct this real-time snapshot. Alternatively, when freshness is less critical, users can query the read-optimized view of MOR tables to access only the compacted base files, improving performance.

To keep Spark queries fast and efficient, RetailMax can lean on several key optimization strategies. Data skipping provides a major performance boost. With column stats and partition stats (discussed in Chapter 5), Spark can prune irrelevant files based on min/max values in query predicates, reducing I/O significantly. File sizing also matters; keeping base files large and well aligned with storage block sizes (typically between 128 MB and 1 GB) helps Spark avoid the overhead that comes with processing lots of small files. Hudi's write-time sizing and background clustering services help maintain that balance.

Spark tuning basics still apply. Configurations like `spark.sql.shuffle.partitions`, executor memory, and core counts make a difference, and Hudi-specific settings around metadata caching or read parallelism can unlock further gains. Finally, appropriate partitioning strategy and building relevant expression indexes can dramatically reduce the data scanned during query execution.

Together, these practices will ensure that Spark SQL delivers scalable, reliable performance across RetailMax's analytical workloads.

Advanced Querying: Time Travel and Point-in-Time Analysis

At RetailMax, time travel queries will play a critical role in day-to-day data reliability and long-term analytical workflows. For example, when investigating anomalies in `hudi_inventory_updates_bronze`, teams will be able to query the table at a specific historical timestamp to audit exactly what changed and when. The same principle will help them debug ETL pipelines. By comparing snapshots of a Silver table such as `hudi_unified_customer_orders_silver` before and after a failed job, teams can pinpoint where a transformation went wrong or where data corruption occurred.

Time travel also supports machine learning operations. When a model is trained on feature data from a Gold table (such as `hudi_customer_segmentation_fea tures_gold`), RetailMax can query that table at the exact commit used during training. This ensures that experiments are fully reproducible, even months later.

Finally, analysts can use point-in-time queries to understand seasonal trends by pulling consistent snapshots of sales data across different years, directly from the sales tables. This level of historical precision is a strategic asset in RetailMax's data platform.

Hudi's timeline architecture will make these queries practical and precise. In Spark SQL, time travel is as simple as using the `TIMESTAMP AS OF` clause. For example:

```
SELECT * FROM
hudi_unified_customer_orders_silver
TIMESTAMP AS OF '2023-01-15 10:30:00.000';
```

This query retrieves the exact state of the `hudi_unified_customer_orders_silver` table as it existed at 10:30 a.m. on January 15, 2023. Spark also supports shorter formats such as YYYY-MM-DD or raw commit timestamps for flexibility.

In Flink SQL, time travel works slightly differently. It's typically treated as a bounded (batch) query using commit markers. You specify the historical view by setting the `read.end-commit` option:

```
SELECT * FROM hudi_inventory_updates_bronze
/** OPTIONS('read.end-commit'='20230210120000000') */;
```

You can also define `read.start-commit` to scope a specific range of changes. This approach lets Flink reconstruct the table's state based on precise commit metadata.

Underlying all of this is Hudi's timeline, which records every action with associated instant times. This detailed history provides the foundation for data observability and reproducibility that's difficult to achieve in traditional lakehouse systems. For RetailMax, that means better audits, clearer rollback paths, and the ability to answer critical "what happened when" questions with confidence (Figure 10-5).

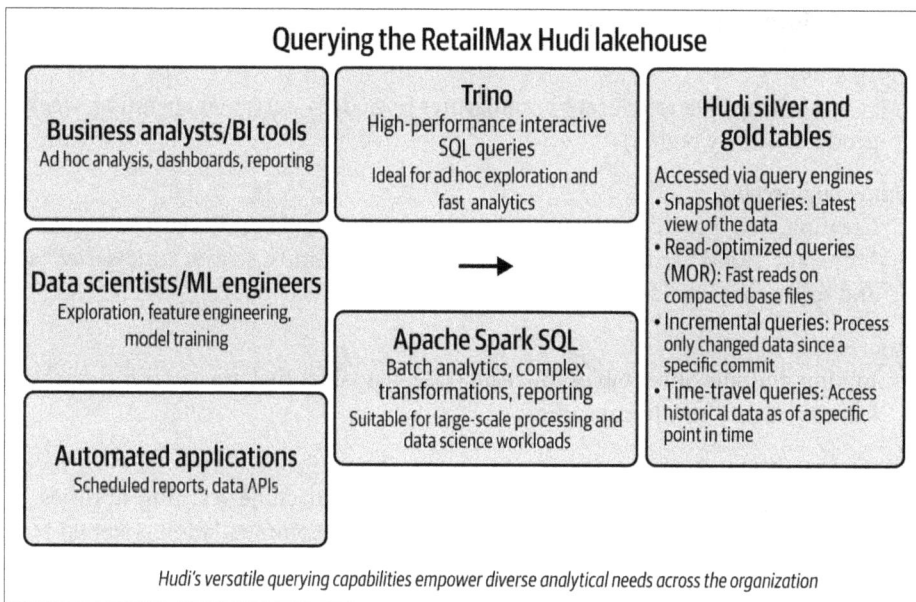

Figure 10-5. Querying the Lakehouse in the Gold Layer

Business Layer: AI-Driven Insights for RetailMax

While not officially in the Medallion architecture, there's one more layer that we need to talk about, and it's the layer that delivers the most visible value to business stakeholders.

The business layer directly drives business value, such as AI-driven recommendations, personalized marketing campaigns, and executive dashboards providing real-time performance insights.

You can think of the business layer as a virtualization layer on top of the Gold layer. The Gold table contains data that has already been transformed into highly specific, business-oriented datasets. While these datasets are primarily designed for consumption by advanced analytics, AI and machine learning applications, and executive dashboards, in our experience, each new application of the data usually requires additional data engineering work. It's much better for these kinds of experimental aggregations and transformations to happen via Hudi than in some data scientist's one-off Jupyter notebook, especially if there's a chance the experiment could go to production.

Preparing Data for AI/Machine Learning in the Gold Layer

The primary purpose of the Gold layer is to create datasets that are optimized for AI/machine learning model training, inference, and other specialized analytical tasks. This often involves:

Aggregations
Summarizing data to relevant granularities (e.g., daily customer spending, weekly product sales by region)

Feature engineering
Creating new predictive features from existing data (e.g., Recency, Frequency, Monetary [RFM] scores for customers; product affinity scores; time-series lags and rolling averages for demand forecasting)

Denormalization
Joining multiple Silver tables to create wide, flat tables that are easier for machine learning algorithms to consume

Specific formatting
Structuring data in formats required by specific machine learning libraries or platforms (e.g., user-item interaction matrices for recommendation systems)

Examples of Gold Hudi tables for RetailMax include:

`hudi_customer_segmentation_features_gold`
Contains features like RFM scores, average purchase value, preferred product categories, and demographic information, used for training customer segmentation models

`hudi_product_recommendation_user_item_gold`
> Stores user-item interaction data (e.g., views, purchases, ratings) or precomputed embeddings, serving as input for collaborative filtering or content-based recommendation engines

`hudi_demand_forecasting_ts_gold`
> Aggregated time-series data of product sales at the SKU/store level, used for training demand forecasting models

`hudi_marketing_campaign_roi_gold`
> A dataset that combines campaign spend, customer engagement, and sales uplift attributed to specific marketing campaigns, used to calculate ROI

These Gold tables are typically created using Spark SQL or Flink SQL, performing final transformations on Silver layer data. For optimal read performance by machine learning frameworks, these tables are often configured as COW tables, as they are usually updated less frequently (e.g., daily or weekly) and are read intensively during model training or batch inference.

Building a Knowledge Base for LLM-Powered Applications with Ray and Hudi

The Marketing department is gearing up to roll out an LLM-based AI assistant for internal teams. This assistant allows users to ask natural language questions about customer trends, product performance, or campaign effectiveness (e.g., "What were the top-selling product categories for customers aged 25 to 35 in California last quarter?"). This requires building a specialized knowledge base from RetailMax's data.

To do this at scale, RetailMax might use Ray, an open source distributed compute framework built for scaling AI and Python applications. With `ray.data.read_hudi()`, the team can load large volumes of data from Gold Hudi tables (such as `hudi_customer_segments_gold` and `hudi_product_summaries_gold`) into Ray datasets. Ray's parallel execution then handles preprocessing, feature extraction, and any necessary text processing to prepare the data for the next stage.

At the heart of RetailMax's internal AI assistant is a Retrieval-Augmented Generation (RAG) architecture: a system that combines the reasoning capabilities of LLMs with real-time access to curated company data. This architecture enables nontechnical users, like marketing analysts, to ask complex data questions in plain language and receive grounded, data-backed answers without touching SQL or business intelligence dashboards.

Building this kind of system involves a series of deliberate steps:

1. *Data selection:* RetailMax pulls the most relevant structured and unstructured content from Gold Hudi tables, aggregated customer behavior, product descriptions, sales summaries, and even customer reviews.

2. *Preprocessing with Ray:* Ray cleans and chunks this data, especially text-heavy content, into segments that can be embedded.

3. *Embedding generation:* Each chunk is passed through a high-quality embedding model, such as a sentence transformer or OpenAI's embeddings API, converting it into a dense vector representation.

4. *Vector database population:* These embeddings, along with metadata such as the source Hudi table and primary keys, are stored in a vector database such as FAISS, Milvus, or Pinecone. The architecture includes a "context builder" that reads from a Gold Hudi table and populates the "knowledge base" used during inference.

The reliability and accuracy of this AI assistant depend entirely on the quality of the data feeding it. Hudi provides the foundation here, ensuring that the Gold layer offers not just fresh and consistent data, but also auditability via time travel and incremental processing. This will give RetailMax a major edge: a trustworthy, dynamic knowledge base rooted in governed, production-grade data (unlike many ad hoc RAG pipelines that rely on brittle, stale sources).

Here's how the AI/RAG workflow would play out behind the scenes. A team member might ask, "Compare the average spending of loyalty program members versus non-members in the last month." The system takes that question and generates a query embedding using the same model that was originally used to build the knowledge base. This embedding acts as a fingerprint of the query's meaning.

This embedding fingerprint is then used to search RetailMax's vector database for the most semantically similar data chunks. These will be small, meaningful segments of context previously extracted from Gold Hudi tables and might include recent sales summaries, loyalty program metrics, or customer segmentation statistics.

The retrieved content is then combined with the original query during the augmentation step. This combined prompt is carefully formatted, often using a template that guides the LLM on how to interpret and use the retrieved data effectively.

Finally, in the generation phase, the augmented prompt is sent to an LLM, such as GPT-5 or Llama. The LLM responds with a fluent, grounded answer that reflects both the user's intent and the data pulled from RetailMax's knowledge base.

This RAG-powered pipeline, illustrated in Figure 10-6, gives RetailMax a fast, intuitive layer of insight that removes friction from decision making. It bridges the gap between structured data and natural language, democratizing access to analytics and empowering teams to ask better questions and get better answers on demand.

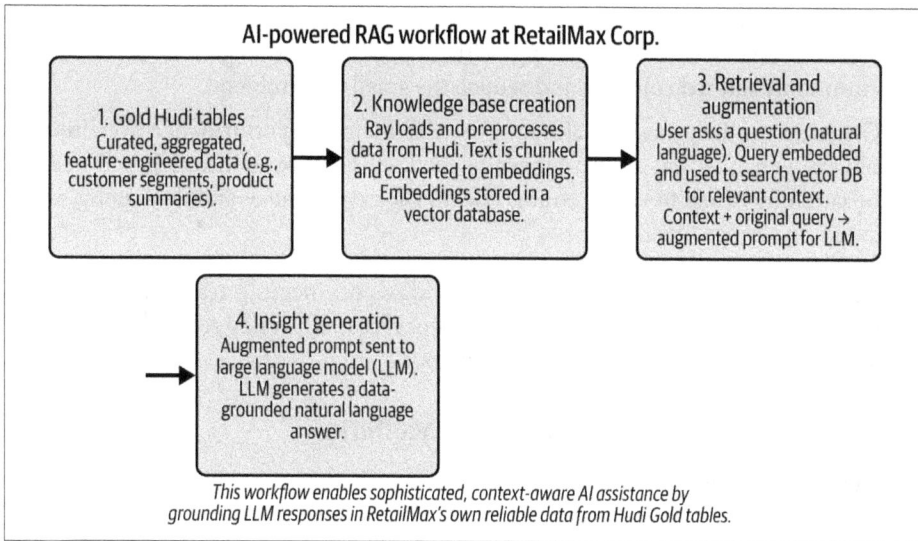

AI-powered RAG workflow at RetailMax Corp.

1. Gold Hudi tables
Curated, aggregated, feature-engineered data (e.g., customer segments, product summaries).

2. Knowledge base creation
Ray loads and preprocesses data from Hudi. Text is chunked and converted to embeddings. Embeddings stored in a vector database.

3. Retrieval and augmentation
User asks a question (natural language). Query embedded and used to search vector DB for relevant context. Context + original query → augmented prompt for LLM.

4. Insight generation
Augmented prompt sent to large language model (LLM). LLM generates a data-grounded natural language answer.

This workflow enables sophisticated, context-aware AI assistance by grounding LLM responses in RetailMax's own reliable data from Hudi Gold tables.

Figure 10-6. AI-powered workflow in the Business layer

Operationalizing and Optimizing the Hudi Lakehouse

Building out the initial ingestion pipelines, transformation jobs, and AI applications is only the beginning of the lakehouse adventure. Keeping RetailMax's lakehouse reliable, performant, and cost-effective over the long term will be a different kind of journey: one of continuous optimization. This means going beyond data engineering to manage performance, cost, and table health over time.

At the center of this work are Hudi's background table services, covered in depth in Chapter 6, which must be tuned and scheduled for the evolving workload. These services can also be deployed in different modes (inline, async execution, and standalone), which will be critical to adapting to shifting latency and throughput requirements.

RetailMax will use compaction, clustering, and cleaning to keep things running smoothly across different layers of its lakehouse. For example:

- Compaction will help ensure fast reads from write-intensive MOR tables like `hudi_sales_transactions_bronze` and `hudi_web_clickstreams_bronze`. By compacting delta logs into Parquet base files, RetailMax can deliver fresh data without overwhelming its query engines. It can use asynchronous scheduling (e.g., triggered by the number of new commits) to balance ingestion throughput with read performance.

- Clustering will improve its query performance on Silver and Gold tables like `hudi_unified_customer_orders_silver` or `hudi_customer_segments_gold`, which will power product analytics and machine learning workflows. RetailMax can use asynchronous clustering with Spark-based strategies to sort data on commonly filtered columns and reduce the small-file problem.

- Cleaning can help manage storage cost and metadata performance by removing old file versions that are no longer needed. At RetailMax, cleaning will need to be carefully tuned to retain enough history for compliance and debugging, while avoiding storage bloat.

Each service is highly configurable, so RetailMax's engineering team can tune them to match their unique data freshness/read latency/cost-efficiency requirements across ingestion, transformation, and reporting layers.

Concurrency Control and Multiwriter Scenarios

As RetailMax's lakehouse matures, scenarios may arise where multiple processes need to write to the same Hudi table concurrently. For example:

- A Hudi Streamer job performs real-time updates to a Silver table, while a nightly Spark batch job appends corrections or enrichments to the same table.

- An ingestion writer runs concurrently with an asynchronous table service (like compaction or clustering) on the same table.

As we learned in Chapter 7, Hudi provides concurrency control mechanisms to manage such scenarios.

Monitoring the Lakehouse

Effective monitoring is crucial for maintaining the health and performance of Retail-Max's Hudi lakehouse.

As introduced in Chapter 9, Hudi integrates with a number of monitoring systems such as AWS CloudWatch, Datadog, and Prometheus, covering important metrics like commit latency and duration; the number of records inserted, updated, and deleted; compaction and clustering backlog, duration, and efficiency; file sizes and counts; index lookup performance; and timeline activity. These metrics should be ingested into a centralized monitoring system like Prometheus and visualized using dashboards in Grafana, which provides visibility into the operational status of Hudi tables and ingestion/transformation pipelines. RetailMax should also configure alerts for critical conditions, such as failed Hudi commits, excessive compaction or clustering lag, a rapid increase in small files, low disk space on storage systems, and high error rates in ingestion jobs.

Data Resilience

Ensuring business continuity in the event of data corruption, accidental deletions, or system failures is critical for RetailMax. Hudi provides features that aid in commit rollback processes and enhance data resilience (discussed in Chapter 9):

Savepoint

A savepoint marks a specific commit on the Hudi timeline as preserved. The Hudi cleaner service will not delete any data files associated with a savepointed commit or any commits leading up to it. This effectively creates a restorable backup of the table's state at that point in time. RetailMax should regularly create savepoints for critical Hudi tables, such as `hudi_unified_customer_orders_silver` and key Gold tables, based on its recovery point objective (RPO). Savepoints can be created using Spark SQL with the command `CALL create_savepoint('table_name', 'commit_timestamp')` or through the Hudi CLI/utilities.

Restore

The restore operation allows reverting a Hudi table to a previously created savepoint. This operation is destructive in that it effectively rolls back all changes made after the savepoint commit. All writes to the table should be paused during a restore operation. This is a powerful tool for recovering from logical data corruption or major errors.

By diligently implementing these operational practices, RetailMax can ensure that its Hudi lakehouse remains a high-performing, reliable, secure, and resilient platform for all its data-driven initiatives.

Performance Benchmarks and Considerations

While this chapter has focused on building an end-to-end solution, it's important to acknowledge that the performance of any data lakehouse is a critical concern. Hudi's performance has been evaluated in various contexts, including comparisons with other open source table formats like Apache Iceberg and Delta Lake using industry-standard benchmarks such as TPC-DS.

These benchmarks typically measure data loading times, query execution speeds across a range of analytical queries, and the performance of operations like merges (updates/deletes). The results often show that performance is highly dependent on the specific workload (read heavy versus write heavy, batch versus streaming), the chosen table type (COW versus MOR), the configurations applied, and the maturity of query engine integrations. For example, TPC-DS results have shown varying performance characteristics: Hudi's MOR tables can offer faster merges compared to its COW tables, but potentially at the cost of slower query performance if compaction is not aggressively managed. Data loading performance can also differ; Hudi's focus on keyed upserts and preprocessing during ingestion can sometimes lead to longer initial load times compared to formats optimized purely for bulk append-only ingestion, but this provides benefits for incremental updates later.

Rather than pinning any single set of benchmark numbers, RetailMax should focus on the architectural features and tuning strategies that most directly impact performance:

Indexing for writes

Indexing is fundamental to keeping read and write operations performant at scale. Hudi supports several indexing types (discussed in detail in Chapter 5), including record, bucket, simple, and bloom, which speed up upserts by identifying which file groups need updating without scanning the entire table.

Indexing for reads

With column stats and partition stats maintained in the metadata table, query engines can prune entire files or partitions that don't match query predicates, dramatically reducing I/O. Enabling the record index, secondary index, and expression index in the metadata table further improves read performance for equality-matching queries and flexible predicate handling, unlocking the true power of Hudi's multimodal indexing.

File sizing

Tuning settings like `hoodie.parquet.small.file.limit` and `hoodie.parquet.max.file.size`, and using Hudi's built-in clustering, helps avoid the small-file problem.

Table services

Asynchronous compaction and clustering keep MOR and COW tables physically optimized over time, reducing small files and ensuring that queries don't slow down as data grows.

Incremental queries

Hudi supports delta-based querying. Instead of reprocessing entire datasets, downstream jobs can efficiently process just the changes since the last run.

Table 10-3 summarizes the Hudi features that influence performance and their key use cases for RetailMax.

Table 10-3. Hudi feature impact on lakehouse performance for RetailMax

Hudi feature	Write latency	Update/delete speed	Snapshot query speed (e.g., Trino, Spark)	Incremental query speed (ETL)	Key use case for RetailMax
MOR table type	Lower (appends to log files)	High (efficiently handles frequent small updates)	Moderate (requires merge of base + log or reads _ro view)	High (changelog can be derived from logs)	Ingesting streaming CDC (`hudi_sales_transac tions_bronze`) and Kafka events (`hudi_web_click streams_bronze`)
COW table type	Higher (rewrites files on update)	Lower (higher write amplification)	High (reads directly from columnar base files)	Moderate (requires diffing snapshots)	Gold layer tables for business intelligence/machine learning (`hudi_daily_sales_gold`), Silver tables with infrequent updates
Writer-side indexes (bloom, bucket, etc.)	Improves by speeding up record location for upserts	Critical for efficient upserts/deletes on large tables	Indirectly (by enabling efficient writes)	N/A	All tables requiring upserts/deletes, especially `hudi_customer_mas ter_bronze` and `hudi_inven tory_updates_bronze`
Metadata table and data skipping	Minor impact on writes (metadata update overhead)	Minor impact on writes	Very high (reduces planning time, skips files)	Moderate (can help identify changed partitions)	All frequently queried Silver and Gold tables to accelerate Trino and Spark SQL queries
Multimodal index acceleration	High	High (fast record-level update with record index)	High (drastically reduces amount of data scanned)	N/A	Fast writes for Bronze and Silver layers and fast queries for Gold layer
Asynchronous compaction (MOR)	Decouples compaction from ingest, maintaining low latency	N/A (compaction is post-write)	Improves _ro query view freshness and performance	N/A	All MOR tables to maintain query performance and prevent log file buildup
Asynchronous clustering (COW/MOR)	Decouples clustering from ingest	N/A (clustering is post-write)	High (optimizes file sizes and layout, enables sorting)	N/A	Query-heavy Silver/Gold tables to improve scan efficiency and leverage data skipping (e.g., `hudi_unified_cus tomer_orders_silver`)
Incremental queries	N/A	N/A	N/A	Very high (processes only changed data)	All ETL jobs that are transforming data from the Bronze to the Silver layer and from the Silver to the Gold layer, reducing processing load significantly

Hudi feature	Write latency	Update/delete speed	Snapshot query speed (e.g., Trino, Spark)	Incremental query speed (ETL)	Key use case for RetailMax
Optimized file sizing	Can slightly increase latency if merging small files	Can improve by reducing metadata operations over many files	High (reduces scan overhead, fewer tasks)	Moderate (fewer files to check for changes)	All tables, to avoid the small-file problem and ensure efficient scans by query engines

Summary

This chapter walked through the full lifecycle of building a modern data lakehouse for RetailMax Corp., a fictional company that mirrors real-world complexity. Hudi served as the backbone for managing ingestion, transformation, querying, and AI-driven insight generation across the Bronze, Silver, and Gold layers.

We began by showing how Hudi supports a wide range of ingestion needs, from streaming CDC using Flink and Debezium to high-throughput event processing with Kafka Connect. Features like schema evolution, transactional integrity, and exactly-once semantics helped ensure that these pipelines were both reliable and future-proof.

In the transformation layer, we explored how Flink and Spark SQL each play complementary roles, with Flink powering real-time data reshaping and Spark enabling batch and incremental ETL. Here, Hudi's support for incremental queries proved critical to efficiency, especially as data volumes scaled.

We then turned to the querying layer, where users at RetailMax can rely on Trino for fast, interactive analytics and Spark SQL for deeper, batch-driven exploration. Features like Hudi's metadata table, pluggable indexing, and time travel queries elevated the performance and observability of the entire platform.

Finally, we arrived at the Gold layer, where curated Hudi datasets fuel AI and machine learning. We walked through how RetailMax uses Ray to build an LLM-ready knowledge base from Hudi data, ultimately powering a RAG system that delivers grounded, high-quality answers to natural language questions.

Many of Hudi's core capabilities surfaced in this chapter:

ACID transactions
　　Ensuring data consistency and reliability across all layers

Record-level updates and deletes
　　Allowing for efficient updates to data, crucial for CDC and maintaining current views

Schema evolution
Adapting to changes in source data schemas without disrupting pipelines

Table services
Essential for maintaining long-term table health, performance, and storage efficiency

Query engine integration
Providing broad access to data via popular engines like Spark, Flink, and Trino

Incremental processing
Revolutionizing ETL by allowing jobs to process only changed data

For readers embarking on their own Hudi lakehouse journey, the experience of RetailMax Corp. offers several key takeaways:

Understand your data
Thoroughly analyze data sources, access patterns, and update frequencies to make informed decisions about Hudi table types (COW versus MOR), record key, ordering field, and partitioning.

Embrace the Medallion architecture
Use the Bronze, Silver, and Gold layers to progressively refine data quality and tailor datasets for specific use cases.

Operationalize table services
Automate compaction, clustering, and cleaning. These are not afterthoughts but critical components for a healthy, performant Hudi deployment.

Leverage Hudi's ecosystem
Utilize Hudi's strong integrations with ingestion tools (Flink, Kafka Connect, Spark), processing engines, and query engines to build a cohesive data platform.

Prioritize performance from the start
Implement file sizing best practices, utilize Hudi's metadata table and indexing features, and design for incremental processing to ensure that your lakehouse scales efficiently.

The data lakehouse paradigm, powered by technologies like Hudi, represents the future of data platforms. It offers a unified approach to managing diverse data types and workloads, breaking down silos and enabling organizations to unlock the full potential of their data assets. As Hudi continues to innovate in areas of performance, scalability, and ease of use, its role as a cornerstone of modern data architectures will only continue to grow. The patterns and techniques demonstrated in this chapter provide a solid blueprint for building your own powerful and flexible end-to-end solutions with Hudi.

Index

C

callbacks, triggering post-commit, 204-209
catalog synchronization
    Hive Metastore example, 216
    metadata versioning, 214
    process of, 213
    purpose of, 213
    supported catalog integrations, 215
    using multiple catalog syncs, 217
change data capture (CDC), 47, 84-87, 172, 182
change tracking, record-level, 82
chapter overviews, xiv-xvi
cleaning (table service), 132-134, 222
CLI (see Hudi CLI)
clustering (table service), 128-132, 158, 222
code level integration, 16
command line interface (see Hudi CLI)
comments and questions, xviii
commit changes (write flow), 49
commit showfiles command, 195
commit showpartitions command, 195
commit-based retention, 133
commits
    commit process, 148-150
    inspecting commit history, 195
    triggering post-commit callbacks, 204-209
commits show command, 195
COMMIT_TIME_ORDERING, 66
compaction (table service)
    versus clustering, 132
    executing, 127
    in MOR versus COW tables, 124
    process of, 124
    scheduling, 125
    tuning, 125, 222
compression, 128
concurrency control
    difficulties of, 139
    Hudi's approach to, 145-153, 250
    multiwriter scenarios, 142-145
    purpose of, 139
    techniques for, 13, 141
    tips and best practices, 157-160
    using multiwriter support in Hudi, 153-157
conflict detection and resolution, 150, 158, 160
connect command, 194
consistent hashing bucket index, 100
Copy-on-Write (COW) tables
    creating, 22

file slices in, 33
layout after writes, 27
versus MOR tables, 35-39, 218
reading file slices, 79
create command, 194
CREATE TABLE AS SELECT (CTAS) statement, 39
curve-drawing methods, 131
custom locking mechanisms, 152
custom merging logic, 53, 67

D

DAGs (directed acyclic graphs), 75
dashboards, visualizing data using, 184
data
    accessing historical versions of, 42
    data quality, 164
    derived datasets, 237-242
    heterogeneous data, 165
    ingesting from Kafka, 170
    ingesting from RDBMS, 172
    ingesting from S3, 170
    ingesting upstream data, 232-236
    maintaining quality and consistency of, 241
    management, localization, and consistency of, 166
    optimized for machine learning, 246
    preventing data duplication, 160, 165, 199
    retrieving incremental changes to, 42
    verifying data using SQL, 183
    visualizing data using dashboards, 184
data catalogs, 75, 180-182, 213-218
data lake architecture, 2, 5 (see also lakehouse architecture)
data platforms
    building end-to-end lakehouse solutions, 225 (see also RetailMax Corp. lakehouse example)
    challenges of building, 1
    integrating Hudi into, 204-218
        benefits of, 204
        syncing with catalogs, 213
        triggering post-commit callbacks, 204
        wiring up monitoring systems, 209
    potential problems with, 2
data resilience, 251
data silos
    Alcubierre airline example, 164-167
    challenges of, 163

About the Authors

Shiyan Xu is a founding engineer at Onehouse and currently working as an open source engineer. He has been an active contributor to Apache Hudi since 2019 and is serving as a PMC member of the project since 2021. Prior to joining Onehouse, Shiyan worked as a tech lead manager at Zendesk, leading the development of a large-scale data lake platform using Apache Hudi. He is passionate about open source development and engaging with community users.

Prashant Wason is a staff software engineer at Uber Technologies and a PMC member of the Apache Hudi project. He has been an active contributor to the Hudi project since 2019 with features like Metadata Table and Record Index. Prashant has been working in the storage and data infrastructure space for over 15 years.

Sudha Saktheeswaran is a software engineer at Onehouse and a PMC member of the Apache Hudi project. She comes with vast experience in real-time and distributed data systems through her work at Moveworks, Uber, and LinkedIn's data infra teams. Sudha is also a key contributor to the early Presto integrations of Hudi. She is passionate about engaging with and driving the Hudi community.

Dr. Rebecca Bilbro is a data scientist, Python programmer, and author in Washington, DC. She specializes in data visualization for machine learning, from feature analysis to model selection and hyperparameter tuning. Rebecca is an active contributor to the open source community and has conducted research on natural language processing, semantic network extraction, entity resolution, and high dimensional information visualization. She earned her doctorate from the University of Illinois, Urbana-Champaign, where her research centered on communication and visualization practices in engineering. Rebecca is cofounder and CTO of Rotational Labs.

Colophon

The animal on the cover of *Apache Hudi: The Definitive Guide* is an armed bullhead (*Agonus cataphractus*), also known as the hooknose or pogge. It lives in coastal waters of the northeastern Atlantic and parts of the Arctic Ocean, from the English Channel to the Baltic Sea in the south and from Iceland to northwestern Russia in the north.

The armed bullhead has a wide, triangular head and is grayish-brown with darker patches on the back and a pale belly. It can reach up to 20 cm in length, though 10 to 15 cm is more typical. Instead of scales, it is covered in bony plates that form rows of spines, and it has numerous whisker-like barbels on the underside of its head that it uses to find food. The armed bullhead's diet consists of small bottom-dwelling invertebrates like worms, crustaceans, brittle stars, and mollusks.

Due to its plentiful numbers, the armed bullhead is considered a species of least concern. Many of the animals on O'Reilly covers are endangered; all of them are important to the world.

The cover illustration is by José Marzan Jr., based on an antique line engraving from Lydekker's *Royal Natural History*. The series design is by Edie Freedman, Ellie Volckhausen, and Karen Montgomery. The cover fonts are Gilroy Semibold and Guardian Sans. The text font is Adobe Minion Pro; the heading font is Adobe Myriad Condensed; and the code font is Dalton Maag's Ubuntu Mono.

O'REILLY®

Learn from experts.
Become one yourself.

60,000+ titles | Live events with experts | Role-based courses
Interactive learning | Certification preparation

**Try the O'Reilly learning platform
free for 10 days.**